MEMORIAL RIDE

RED
PLANET
BOOKS

LEE FRANCIS 4 SERIES EDITOR

Red Planet Books features
Native American graphic novels
and illustrated histories by important and emerging
Native writers and artists. Copublished by the
University of New Mexico Press and Red Planet
Books & Comics, the volumes in the series explore
a wide range of Indigenous experience through
Native storytelling. With rich prose and vivid artwork,
each book showcases contemporary Native voices
across literature, history, current events, and more.
Designed for all ages, the cutting-edge creative works
in Red Planet Books will be a valuable addition
to every collection.

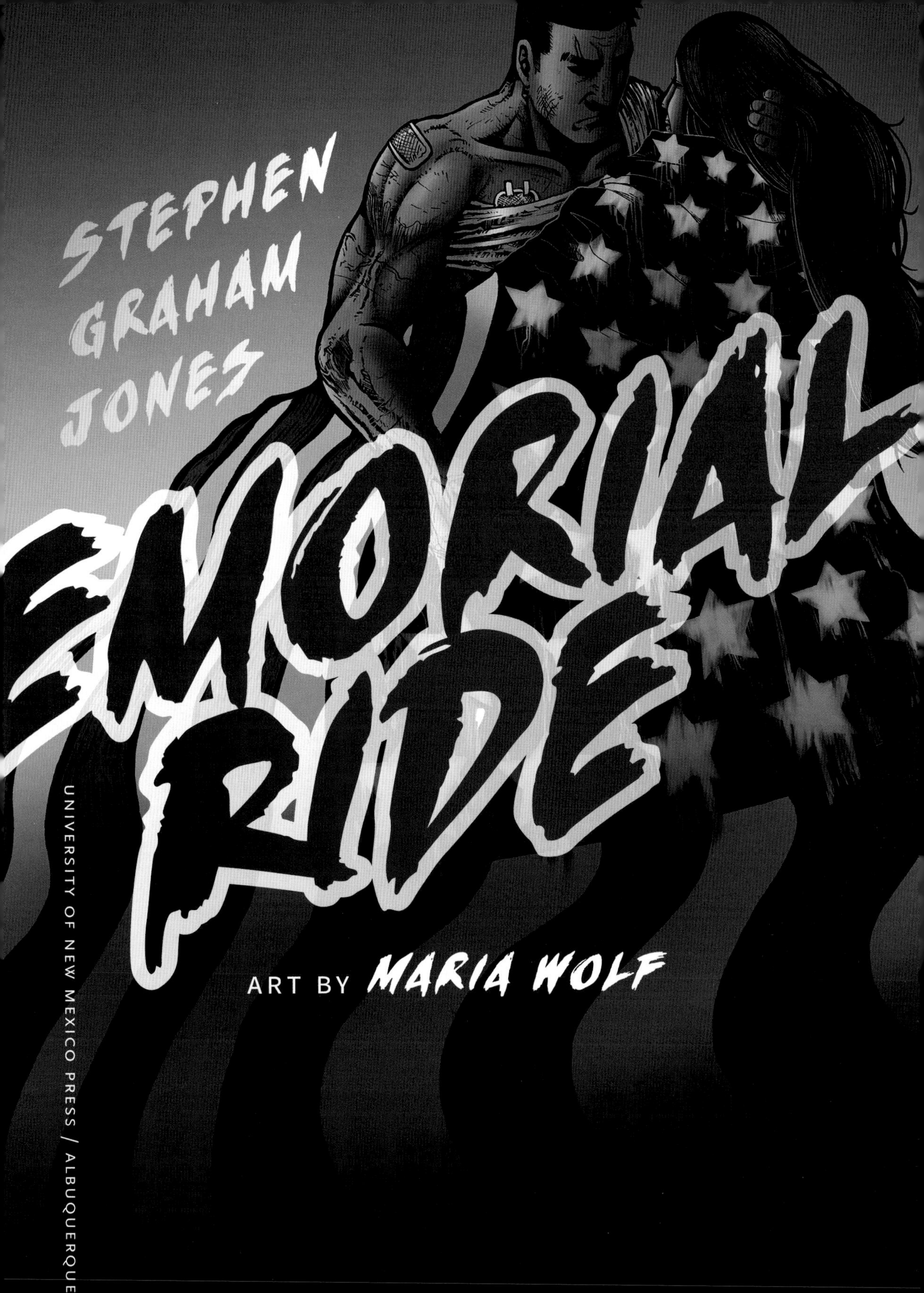

STEPHEN GRAHAM JONES

MEMORIAL RIDE

ART BY MARIA WOLF

UNIVERSITY OF NEW MEXICO PRESS / ALBUQUERQUE

ISBN 978-0-8263-6323-7 (paper)

ISBN 978-0-8263-6324-4 (e-book)

Library of Congress Cataloging-in-Publication data

is on file with the Library of Congress.

Founded in 1889, the University of New Mexico sits on the
traditional homelands of the Pueblo of Sandia. The original
peoples of New Mexico—Pueblo, Navajo, and Apache—since time
immemorial have deep connections to the land and have made
significant contributions to the broader community statewide.
We honor the land itself and those who remain stewards of this
land throughout the generations and also acknowledge our
committed relationship to Indigenous peoples. We gratefully
recognize our history.

Cover illustration by Maria Wolf

Inking by Dale Deforest

Lettering by Lee Francis 4

Part title image colorization by Gabrielle Hill

Cover design by Mindy Basinger Hill

PART ONE

IT STARTS WITH A FUNERAL. IT'LL END WITH A WAR.

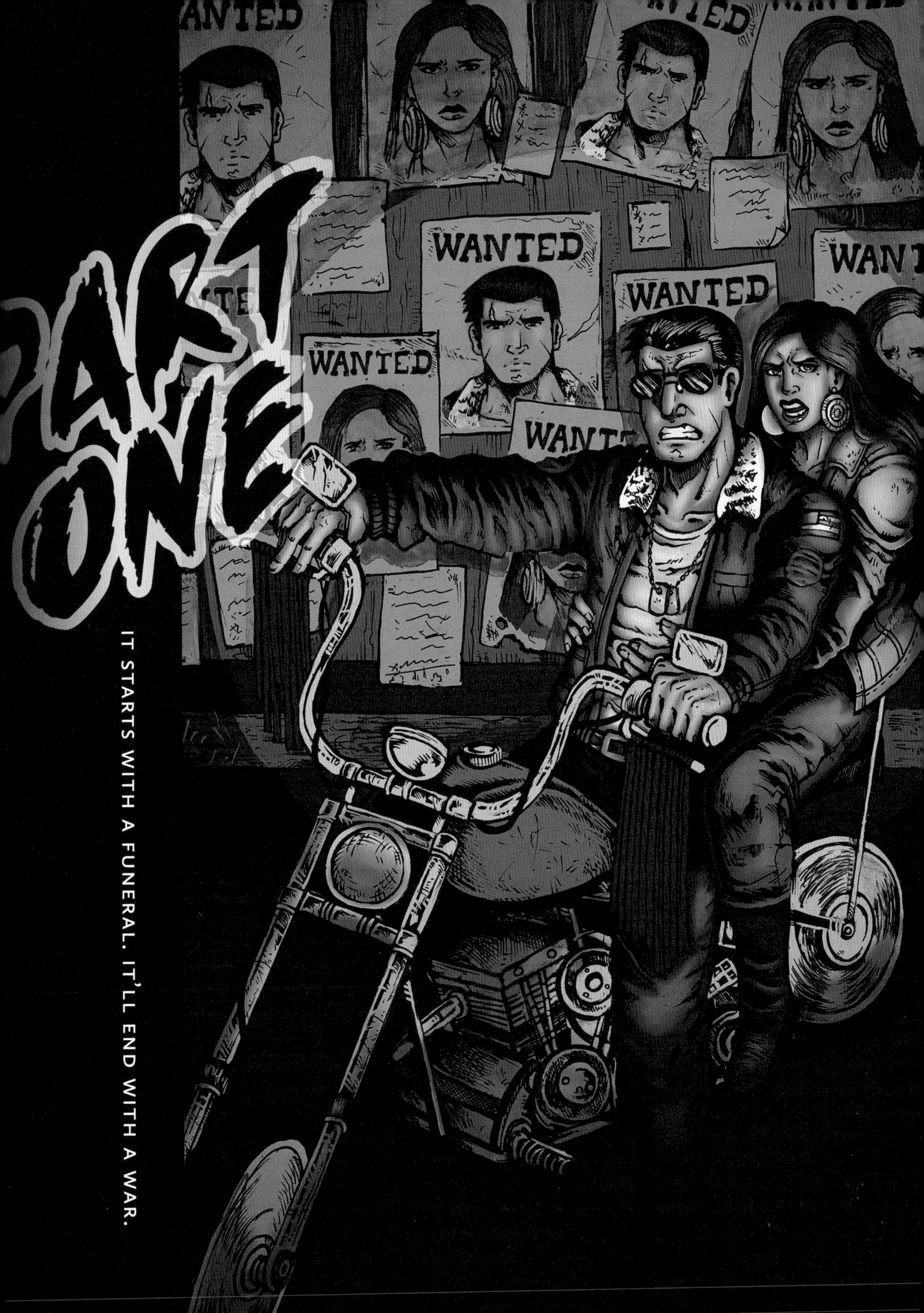
WANTED
WANTED
WANTED
WANTED

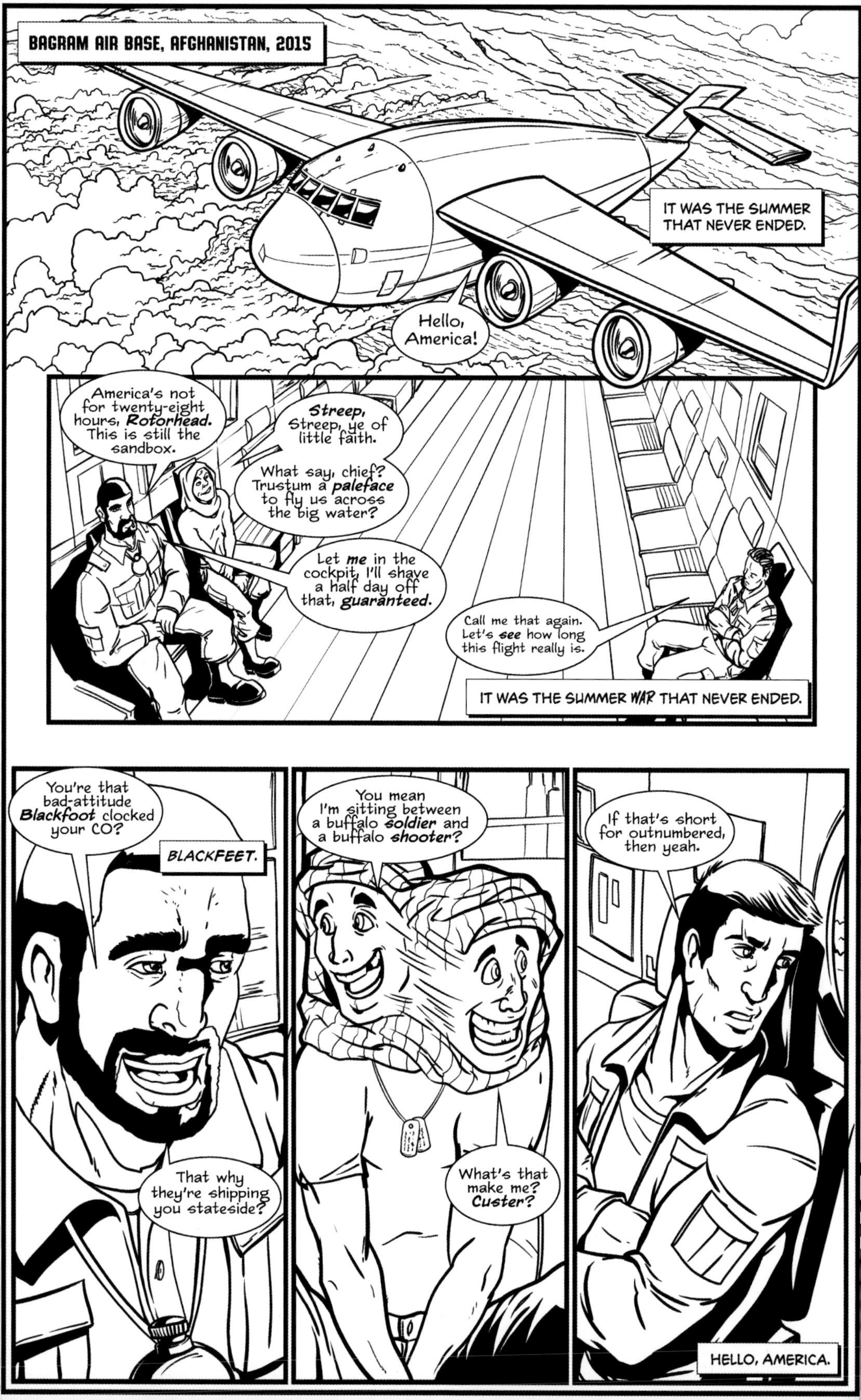
BAGRAM AIR BASE, AFGHANISTAN, 2015
IT WAS THE SUMMER THAT NEVER ENDED.
Hello, America!
America's not for twenty-eight hours, Rotorhead. This is still the sandbox.
Streep, Streep, ye of little faith.
What say, chief? Trustum a paleface to fly us across the big water?
Let me in the cockpit, I'll shave a half day off that, guaranteed.
Call me that again. Let's see how long this flight really is.
IT WAS THE SUMMER WAR THAT NEVER ENDED.
You're that bad-attitude Blackfoot clocked your CO?
BLACKFEET.
That why they're shipping you stateside?
You mean I'm sitting between a buffalo soldier and a buffalo shooter?
What's that make me? Custer?
If that's short for outnumbered, then yeah.
HELLO, AMERICA.

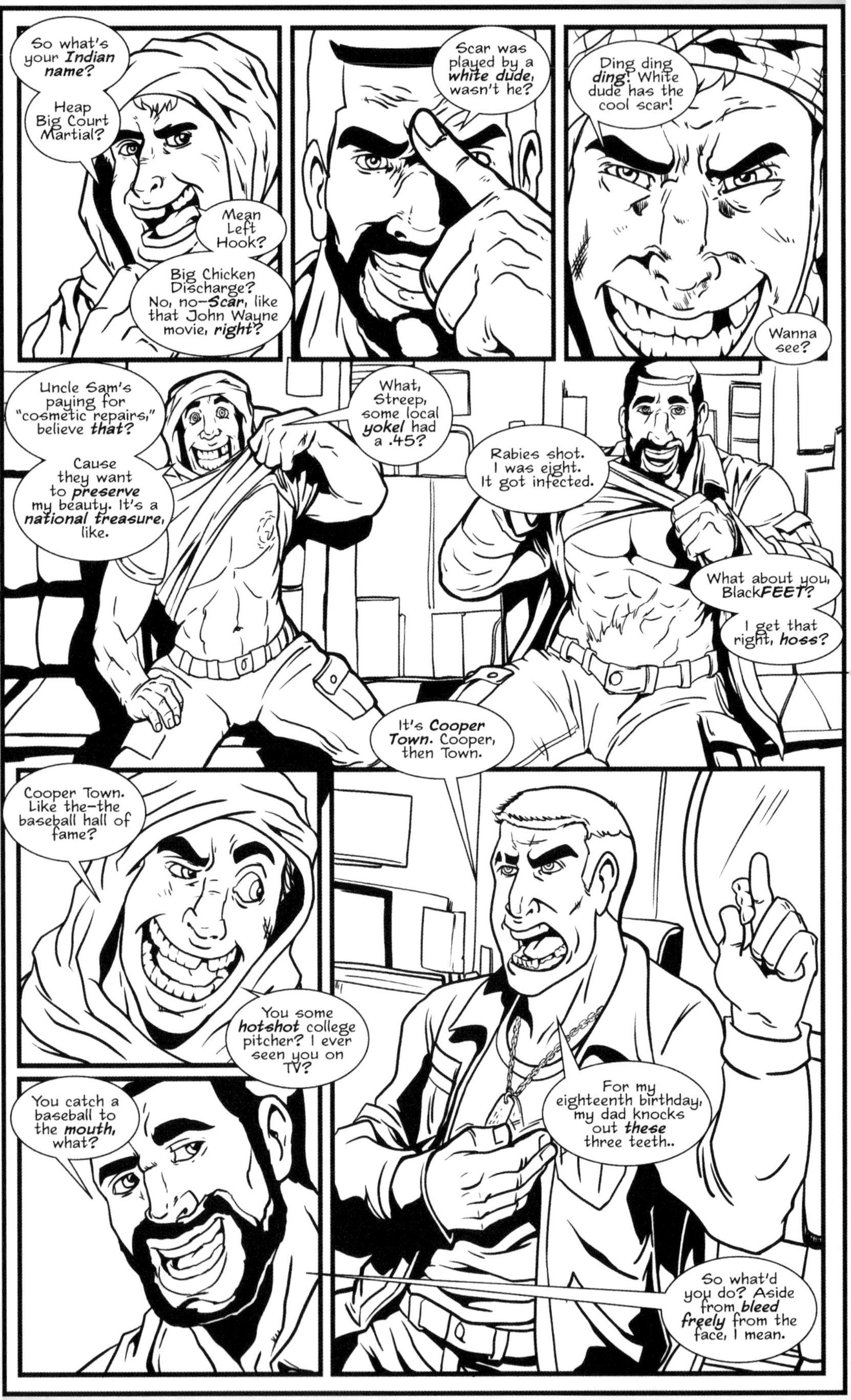
So what's your *Indian name*?
Heap Big Court Martial?
Mean Left Hook?
Big Chicken Discharge? No, no—*Scar*, like that John Wayne movie, *right*?
Scar was played by a *white dude*, wasn't he?
Ding ding *ding*! White dude has the cool scar!
Wanna see?
Uncle Sam's paying for "cosmetic repairs," believe *that*?
Cause they want to *preserve* my beauty. It's a *national treasure*, like.
What, Streep, some local *yokel* had a .45?
Rabies shot. I was eight. It got infected.
What about you, Black*FEET*?
I get that right, *hoss*?
It's *Cooper Town*. Cooper, then Town.
Cooper Town. Like the—the baseball hall of fame?
You some *hotshot* college pitcher? I ever seen you on TV?
You catch a baseball to the *mouth*, what?
For my eighteenth birthday, my dad knocks out *these* three teeth..
So what'd you do? Aside from *bleed freely* from the face, I mean.

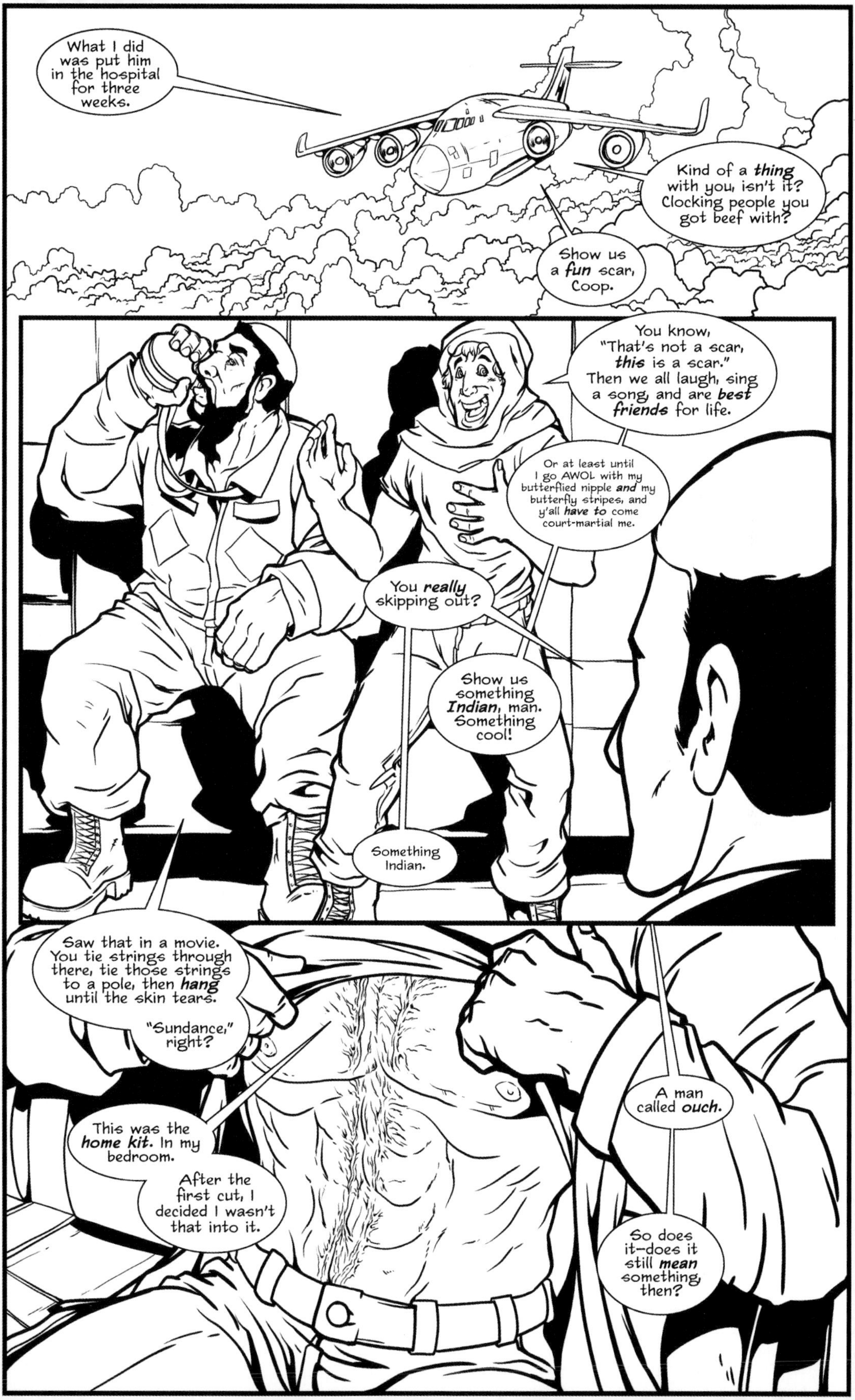
What I did was put him in the hospital for three weeks.
Kind of a thing with you, isn't it? Clocking people you got beef with?
Show us a fun scar, Coop.
You know, "That's not a scar, this is a scar." Then we all laugh, sing a song, and are best friends for life.
Or at least until I go AWOL with my butterflied nipple and my butterfly stripes, and y'all have to come court-martial me.
You really skipping out?
Show us something Indian, man. Something cool!
Something Indian.
Saw that in a movie. You tie strings through there, tie those strings to a pole, then hang until the skin tears.
"Sundance," right?
This was the home kit. In my bedroom.
After the first cut, I decided I wasn't that into it.
A man called ouch.
So does it—does it still mean something, then?

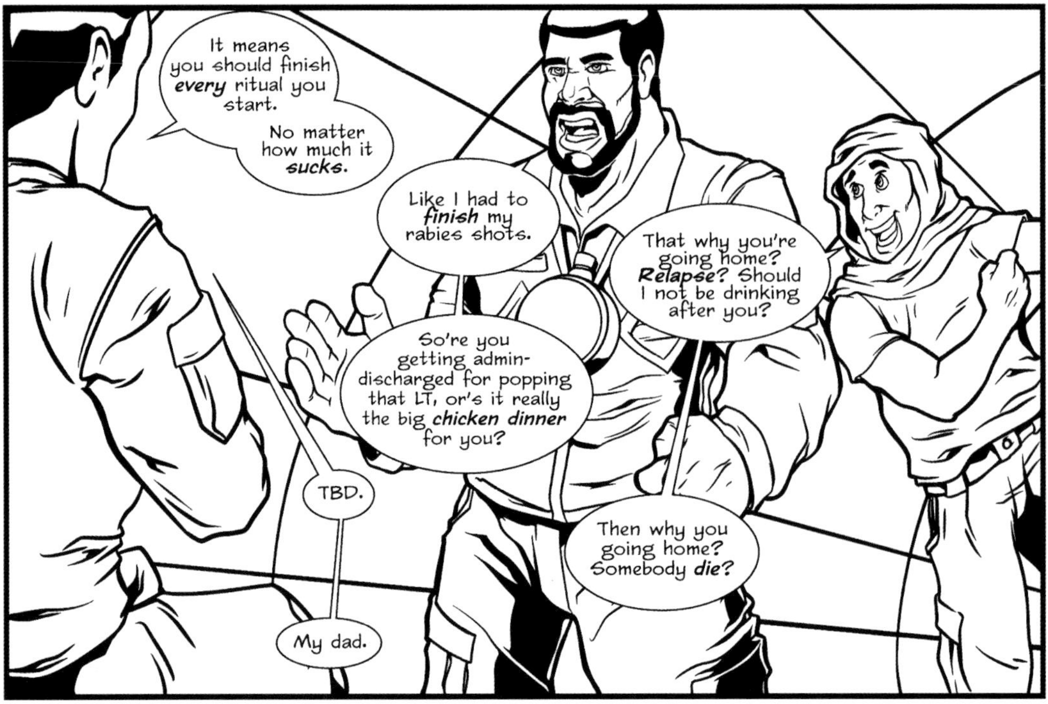
It means you should finish *every* ritual you start.
No matter how much it *sucks.*
Like I had to *finish* my rabies shots.
So're you getting admin-discharged for popping that LT, or's it really the big *chicken dinner* for you?
TBD.
That why you're going home? *Relapse?* Should I not be drinking after you?
Then why you going home? Somebody *die?*
My dad.

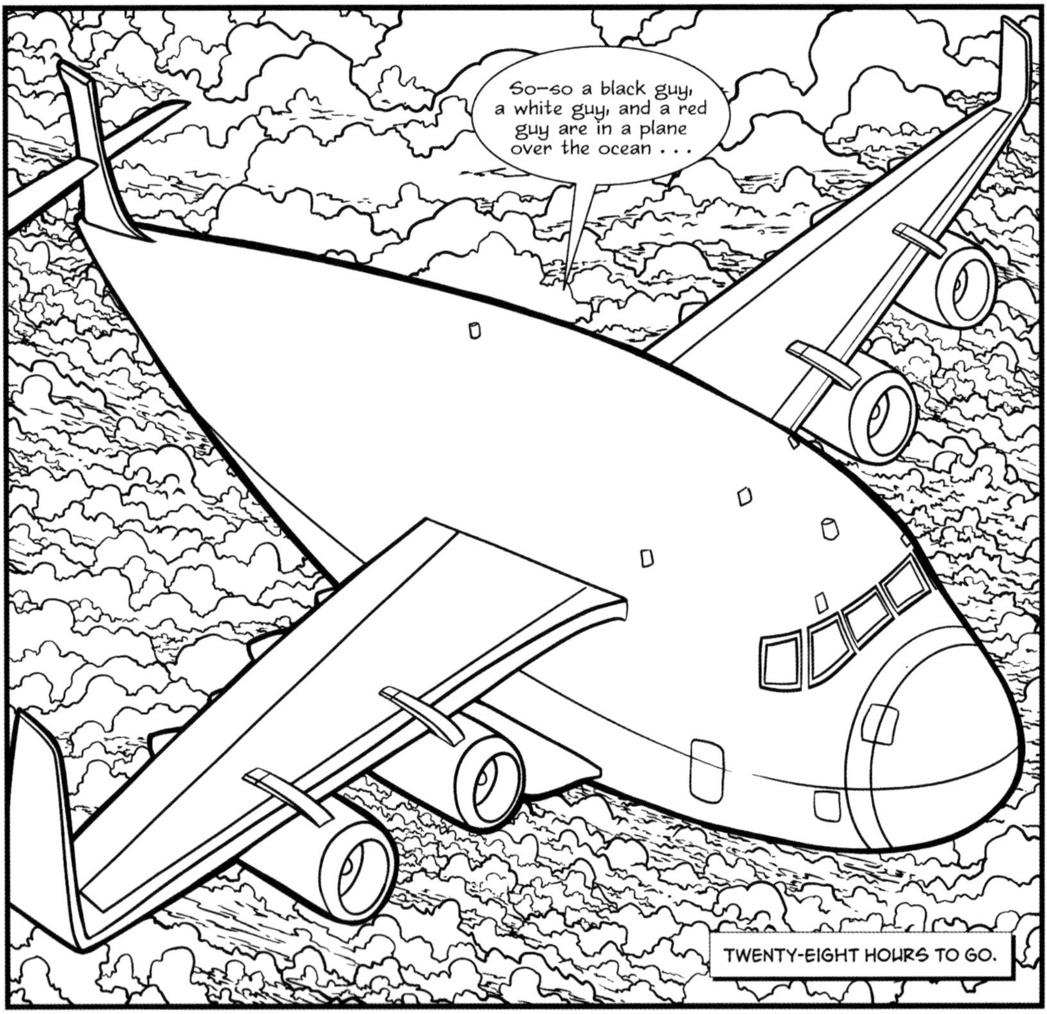
So-so a black guy, a white guy, and a red guy are in a plane over the ocean . . .
TWENTY-EIGHT HOURS TO GO.

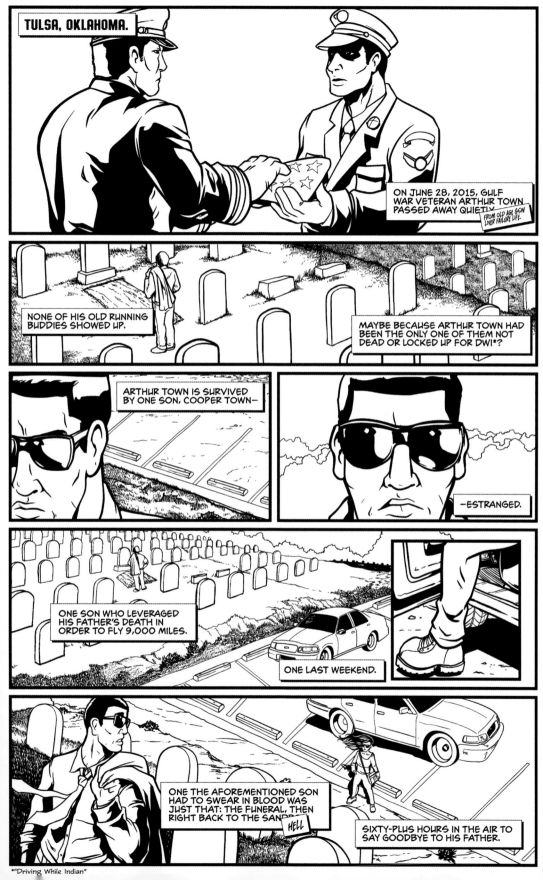

TULSA, OKLAHOMA.

ON JUNE 28, 2015, GULF WAR VETERAN ARTHUR TOWN PASSED AWAY QUIETLY. FROM OLD AGE GSW LIVER FAILURE LIFE.

NONE OF HIS OLD RUNNING BUDDIES SHOWED UP.

MAYBE BECAUSE ARTHUR TOWN HAD BEEN THE ONLY ONE OF THEM NOT DEAD OR LOCKED UP FOR DWI*?

ARTHUR TOWN IS SURVIVED BY ONE SON, COOPER TOWN—

—ESTRANGED.

ONE SON WHO LEVERAGED HIS FATHER'S DEATH IN ORDER TO FLY 9,000 MILES.

ONE LAST WEEKEND.

ONE THE AFOREMENTIONED SON HAD TO SWEAR IN BLOOD WAS JUST THAT: THE FUNERAL, THEN RIGHT BACK TO THE SAND. HELL

SIXTY-PLUS HOURS IN THE AIR TO SAY GOODBYE TO HIS FATHER.

*"Driving While Indian"

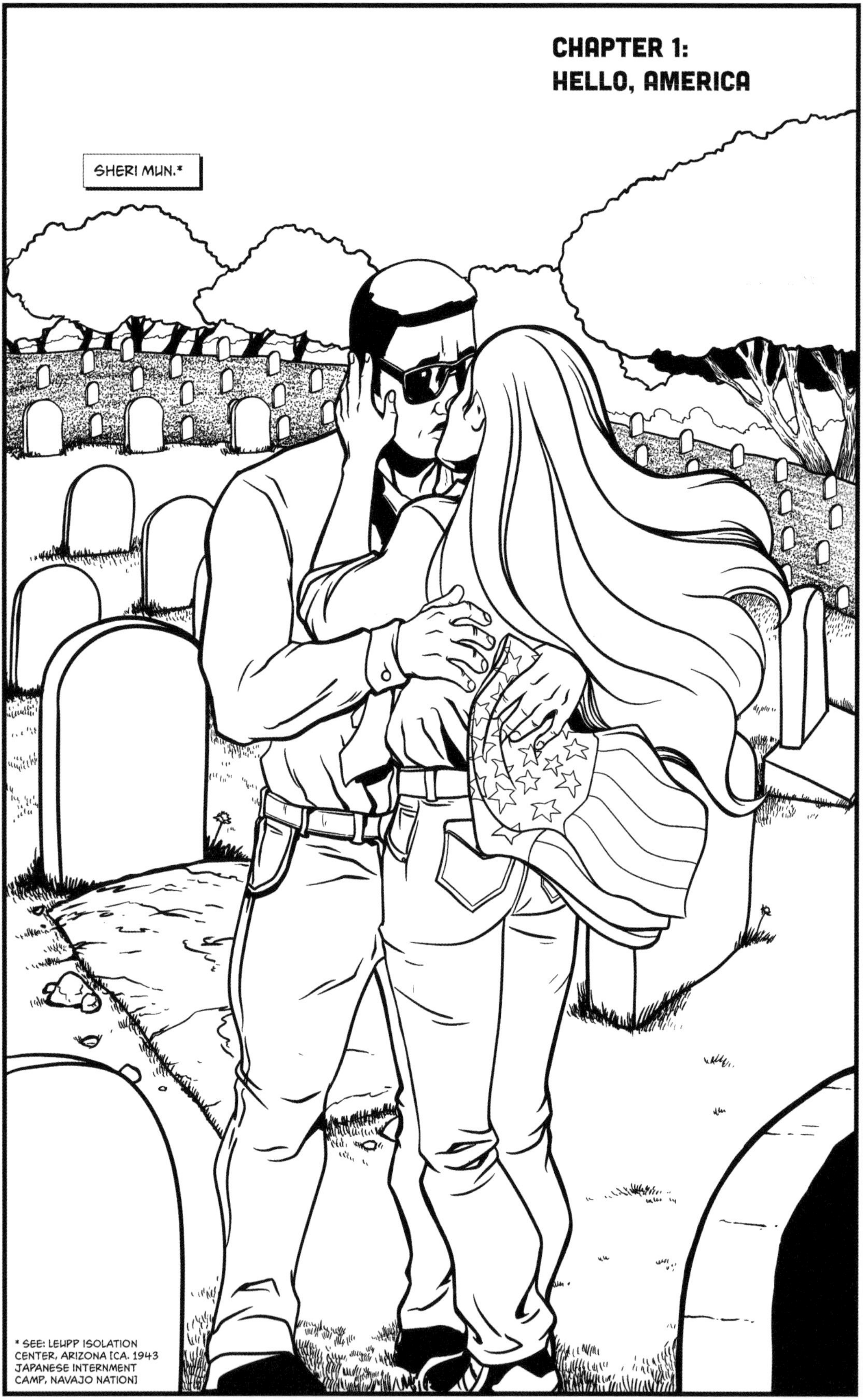
CHAPTER 1:
HELLO, AMERICA
SHERI MUN.*
* SEE: LEUPP ISOLATION CENTER, ARIZONA [CA. 1943 JAPANESE INTERNMENT CAMP, NAVAJO NATION]

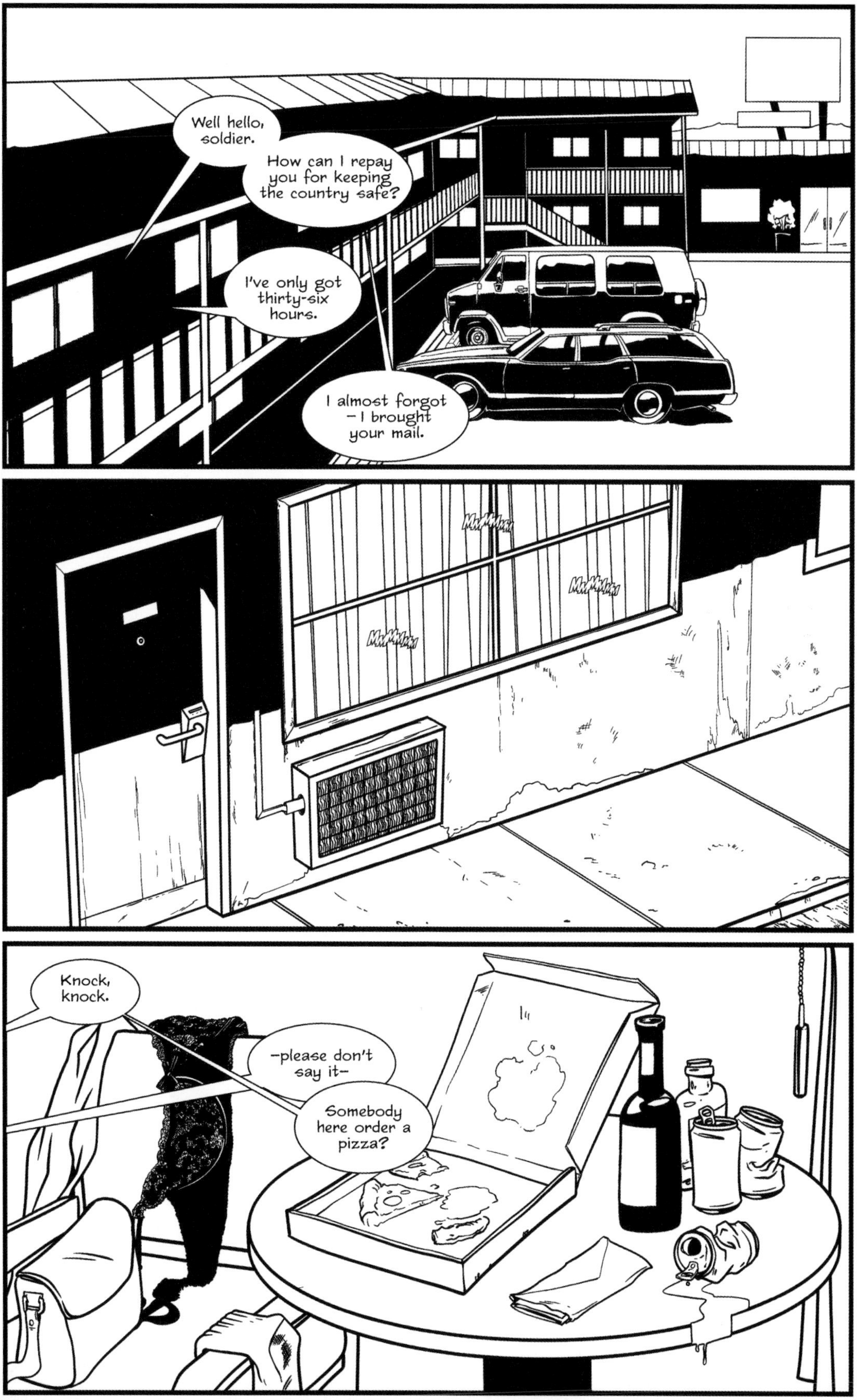
Well hello, soldier.
How can I repay you for keeping the country safe?
I've only got thirty-six hours.
I almost forgot —I brought your mail.
MMMMMM
MMMMMM
MMMMMM
Knock, knock.
-please don't say it-
Somebody here order a pizza?

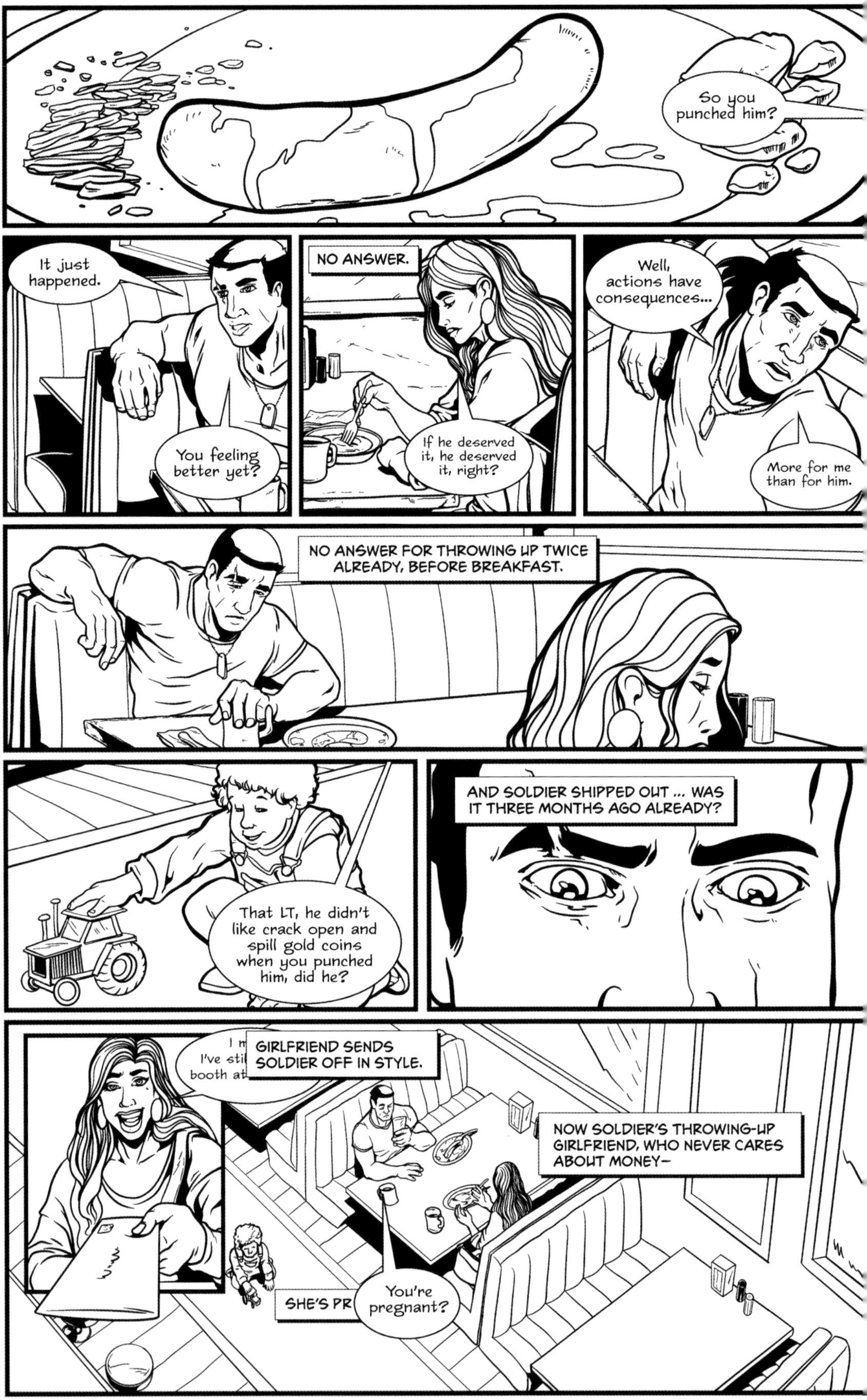
So you punched him?
It just happened.
You feeling better yet?
NO ANSWER.
If he deserved it, he deserved it, right?
Well, actions have consequences...
More for me than for him.
NO ANSWER FOR THROWING UP TWICE ALREADY, BEFORE BREAKFAST.
That LT, he didn't like crack open and spill gold coins when you punched him, did he?
AND SOLDIER SHIPPED OUT ... WAS IT THREE MONTHS AGO ALREADY?
GIRLFRIEND SENDS SOLDIER OFF IN STYLE.
NOW SOLDIER'S THROWING-UP GIRLFRIEND, WHO NEVER CARES ABOUT MONEY—
You're pregnant?

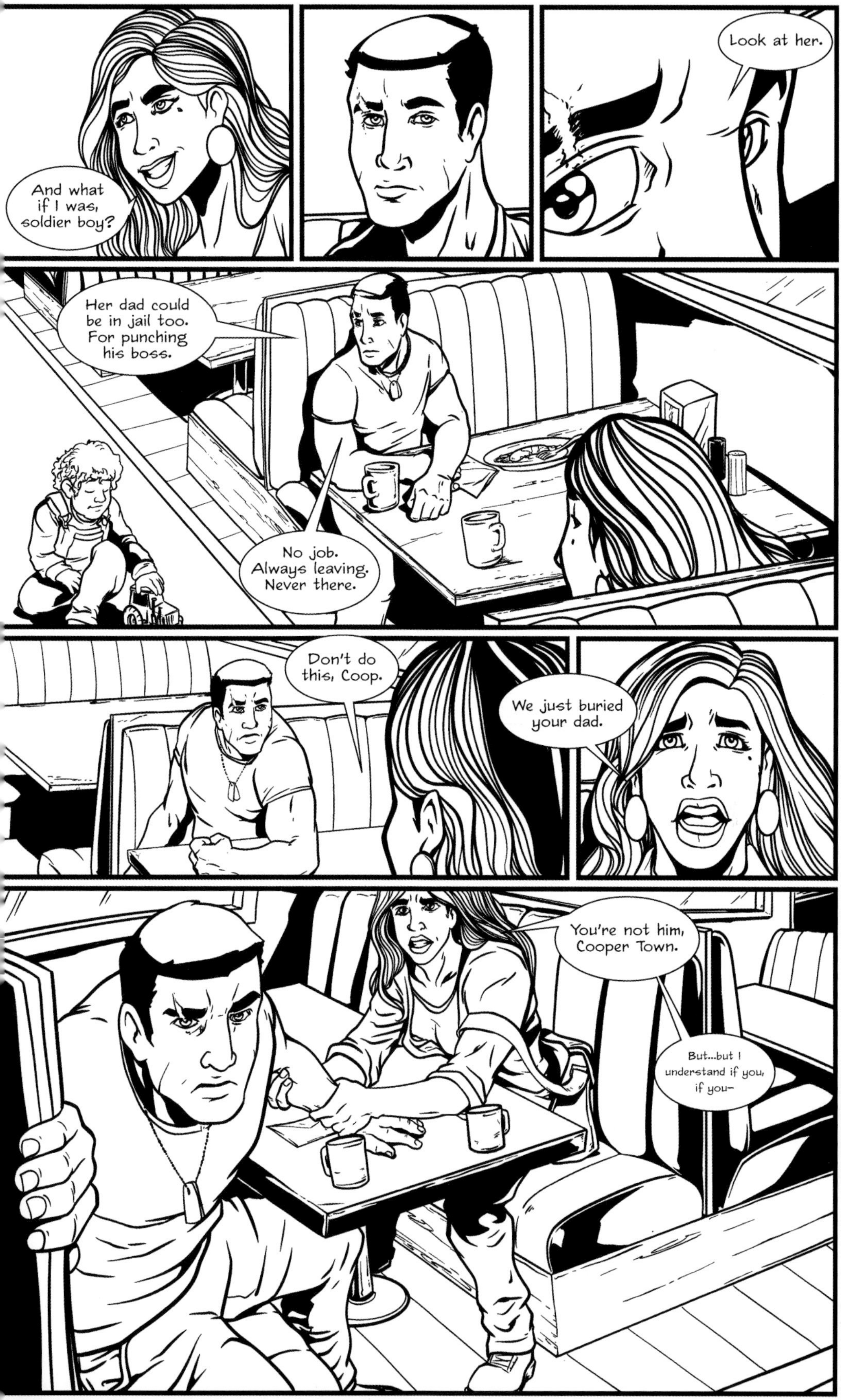
And what if I was, soldier boy?
Look at her.
Her dad could be in jail too. For punching his boss.
No job. Always leaving. Never there.
Don't do this, Coop.
We just buried your dad.
You're not him, Cooper Town.
But...but I understand if you, if you–

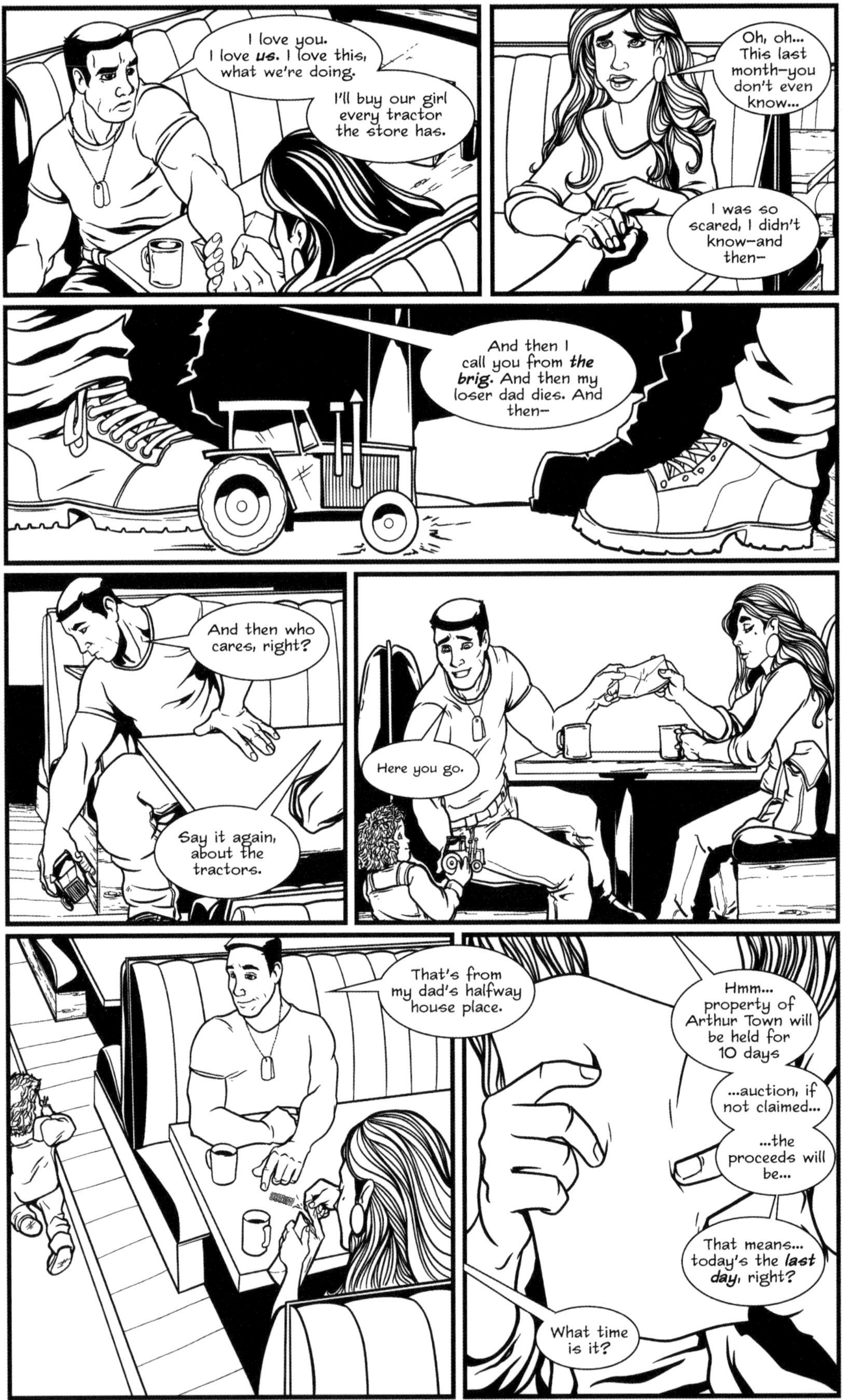
I love you. I love *us.* I love this, what we're doing.
I'll buy our girl every tractor the store has.
Oh, oh... This last month—you don't even know...
I was so scared, I didn't know—and then—
And then I call you from ***the brig.*** And then my loser dad dies. And then—
And then who cares, right?
Say it again, about the tractors.
Here you go.
That's from my dad's halfway house place.
Hmm... property of Arthur Town will be held for 10 days
...auction, if not claimed...
...the proceeds will be...
That means... today's the ***last day***, right?
What time is it?

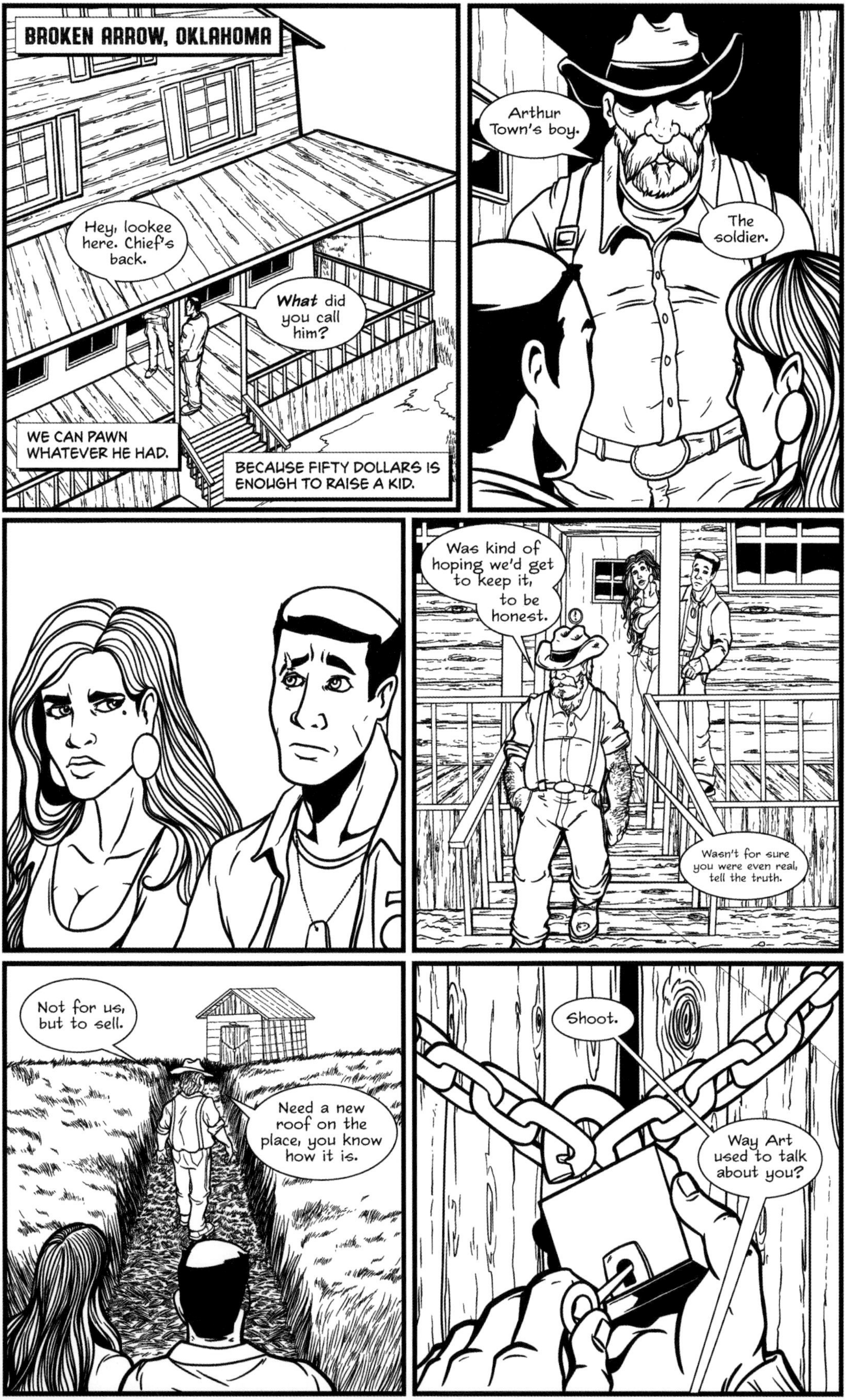
BROKEN ARROW, OKLAHOMA
Hey, lookee here. Chief's back.
What did you call him?
WE CAN PAWN WHATEVER HE HAD.
BECAUSE FIFTY DOLLARS IS ENOUGH TO RAISE A KID.
Arthur Town's boy.
The soldier.
Was kind of hoping we'd get to keep it, to be honest.
!
Wasn't for sure you were even real, tell the truth.
Not for us, but to sell.
Need a new roof on the place, you know how it is.
Shoot.
Way Art used to talk about you?

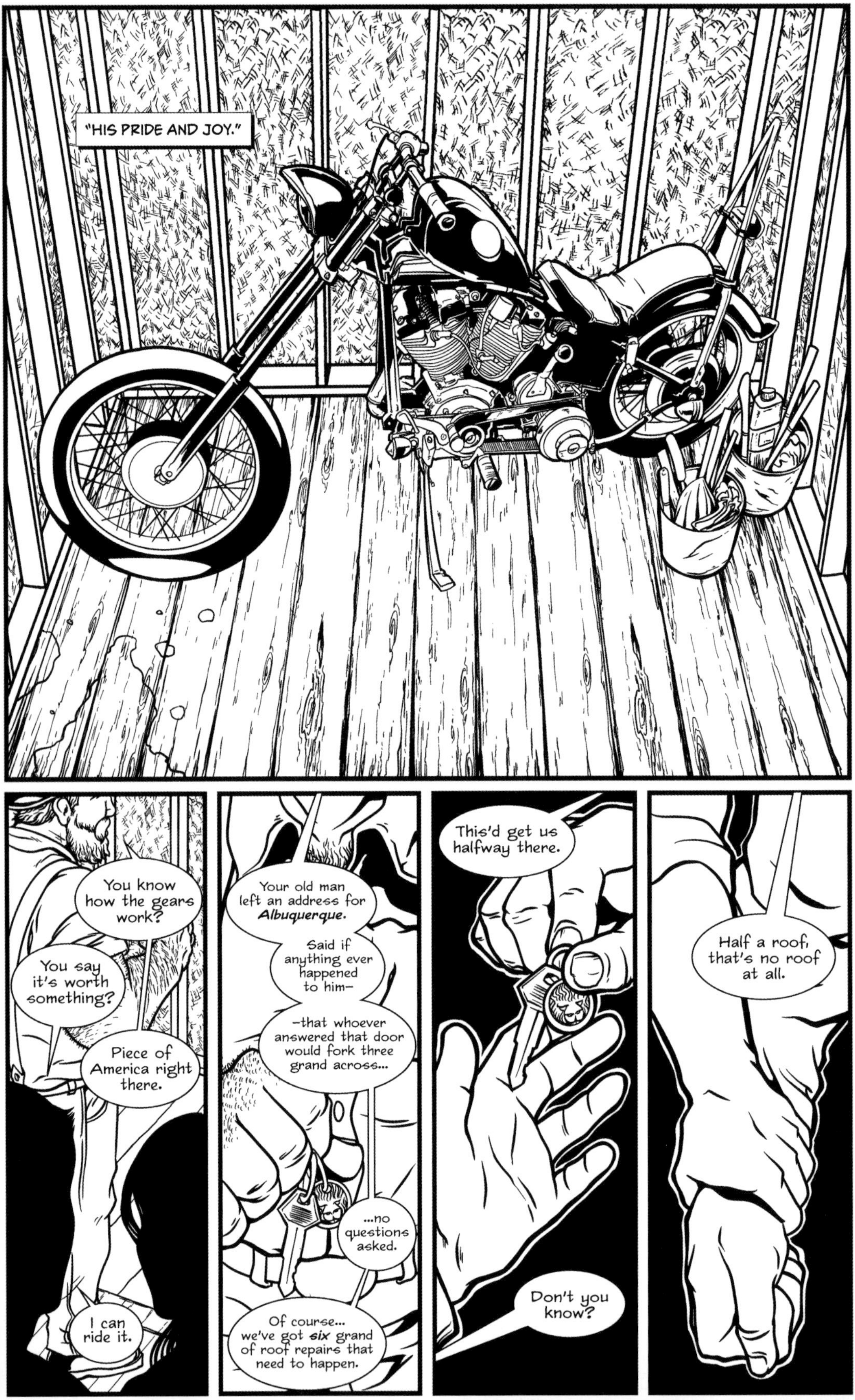
"HIS PRIDE AND JOY."
You know how the gears work?
You say it's worth something?
Piece of America right there.
I can ride it.
Your old man left an address for *Albuquerque*.
Said if anything ever happened to him–
–that whoever answered that door would fork three grand across...
...no questions asked.
Of course... we've got *six* grand of roof repairs that need to happen.
This'd get us halfway there.
Don't you know?
Half a roof, that's no roof at all.

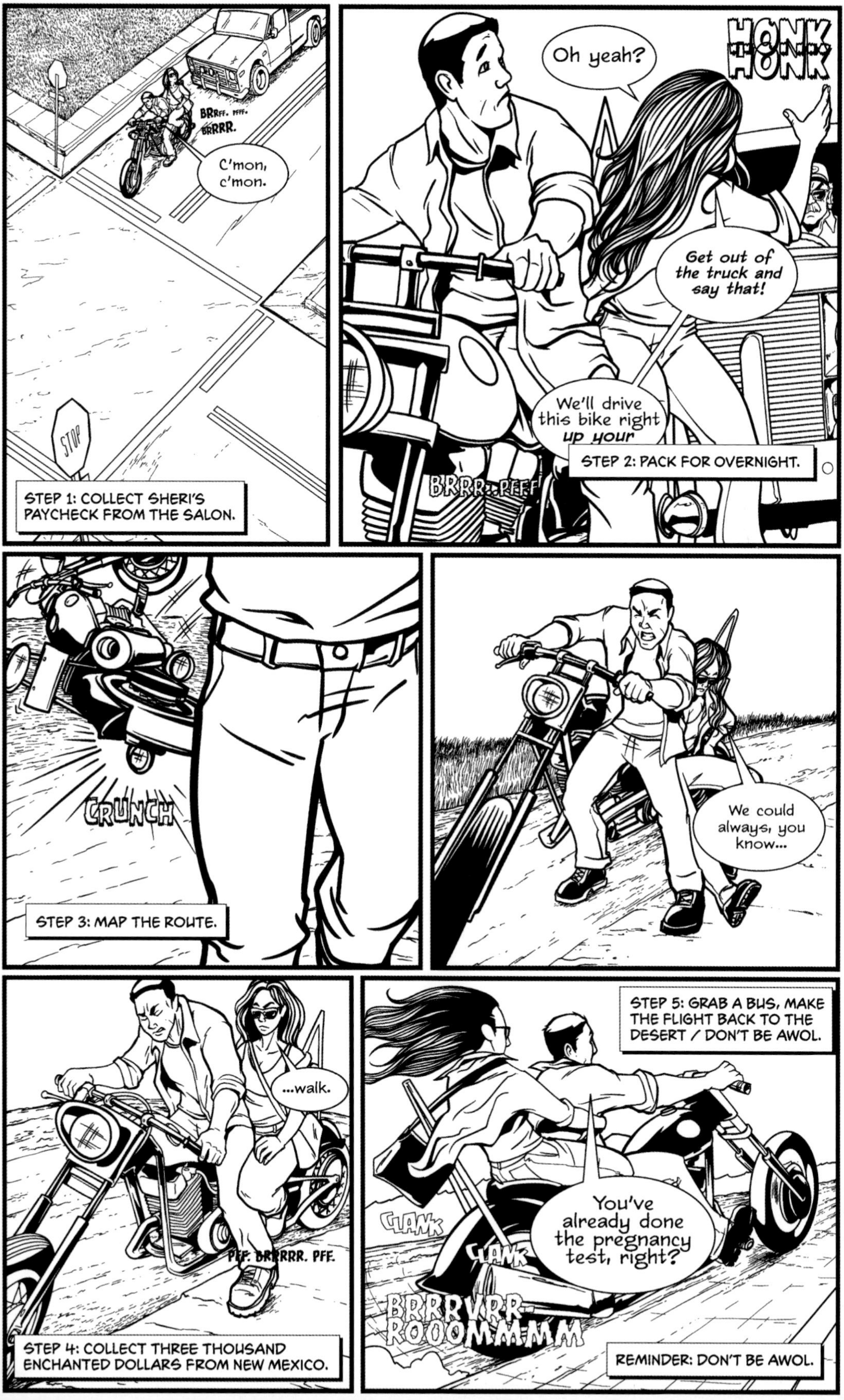
BRRFF. PFFF.
BRRRR.
C'mon, c'mon.
STOP
STEP 1: COLLECT SHERI'S PAYCHECK FROM THE SALON.
HONK HONK
Oh yeah?
Get out of the truck and say that!
We'll drive this bike right *up your*
STEP 2: PACK FOR OVERNIGHT.
BRRR..PFFF
CRUNCH
STEP 3: MAP THE ROUTE.
We could always, you know...
...walk.
PFF. BRRRRR. PFF.
STEP 4: COLLECT THREE THOUSAND ENCHANTED DOLLARS FROM NEW MEXICO.
STEP 5: GRAB A BUS, MAKE THE FLIGHT BACK TO THE DESERT / DON'T BE AWOL.
CLANK
CLANK
You've already done the pregnancy test, right?
BRRRVRR ROOOMMMM
REMINDER: DON'T BE AWOL.

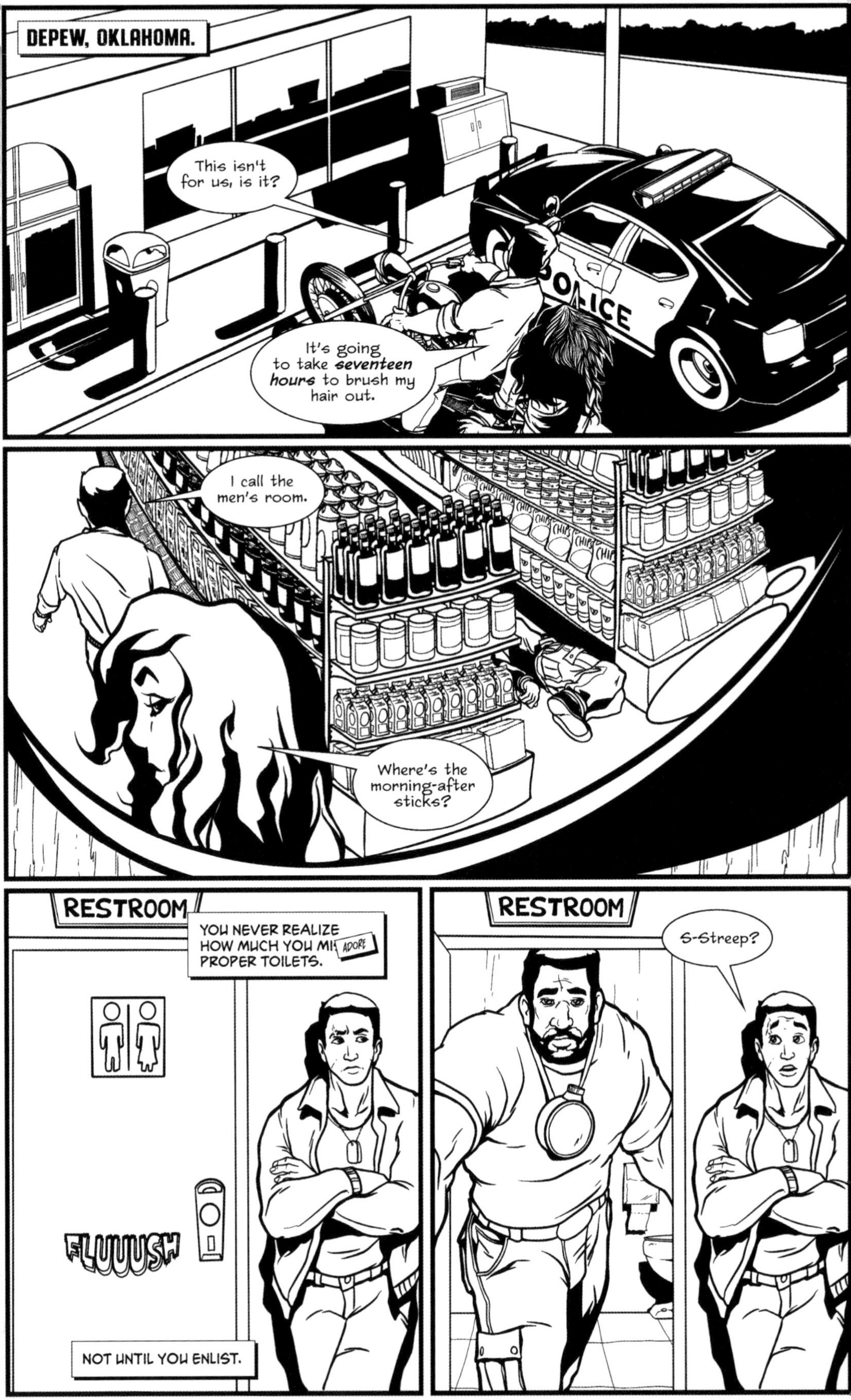

DEPEW, OKLAHOMA.
This isn't for us, is it?
It's going to take **seventeen hours** to brush my hair out.
I call the men's room.
Where's the morning-after sticks?
RESTROOM
YOU NEVER REALIZE HOW MUCH YOU MIS ADORE PROPER TOILETS.
FLUUUSH
NOT UNTIL YOU ENLIST.
RESTROOM
S-Streep?

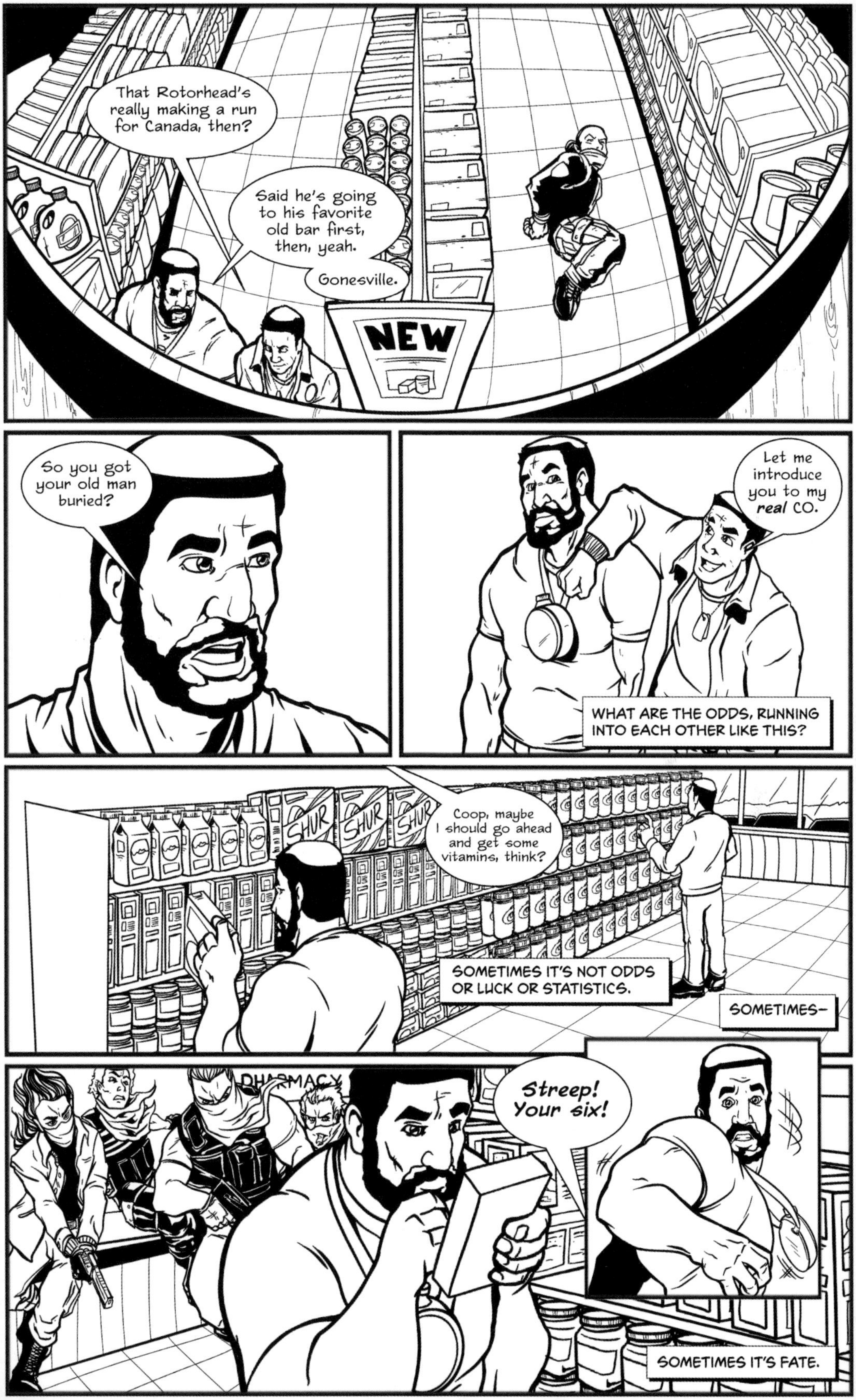
That Rotorhead's really making a run for Canada, then?
Said he's going to his favorite old bar first, then, yeah.
Gonesville.
NEW
So you got your old man buried?
Let me introduce you to my *real* CO.
WHAT ARE THE ODDS, RUNNING INTO EACH OTHER LIKE THIS?
SHUR
SHUR
SHUR
Coop, maybe I should go ahead and get some vitamins, think?
SOMETIMES IT'S NOT ODDS OR LUCK OR STATISTICS.
SOMETIMES–
PHARMACY
Streep! Your six!
SOMETIMES IT'S FATE.

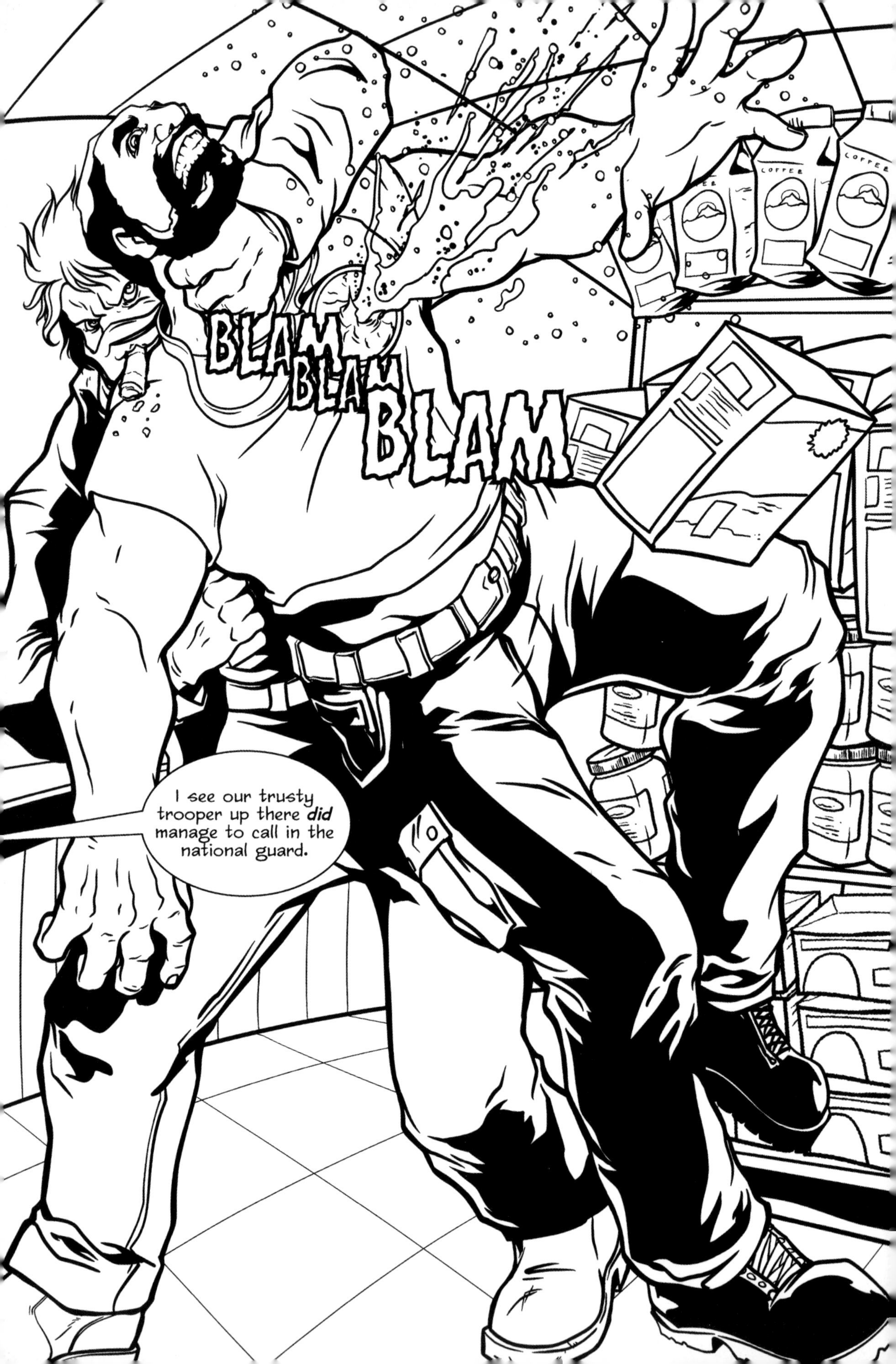
BLAM
BLAM
BLAM
COFFEE
COFFEE
I see our trusty trooper up there *did* manage to call in the national guard.

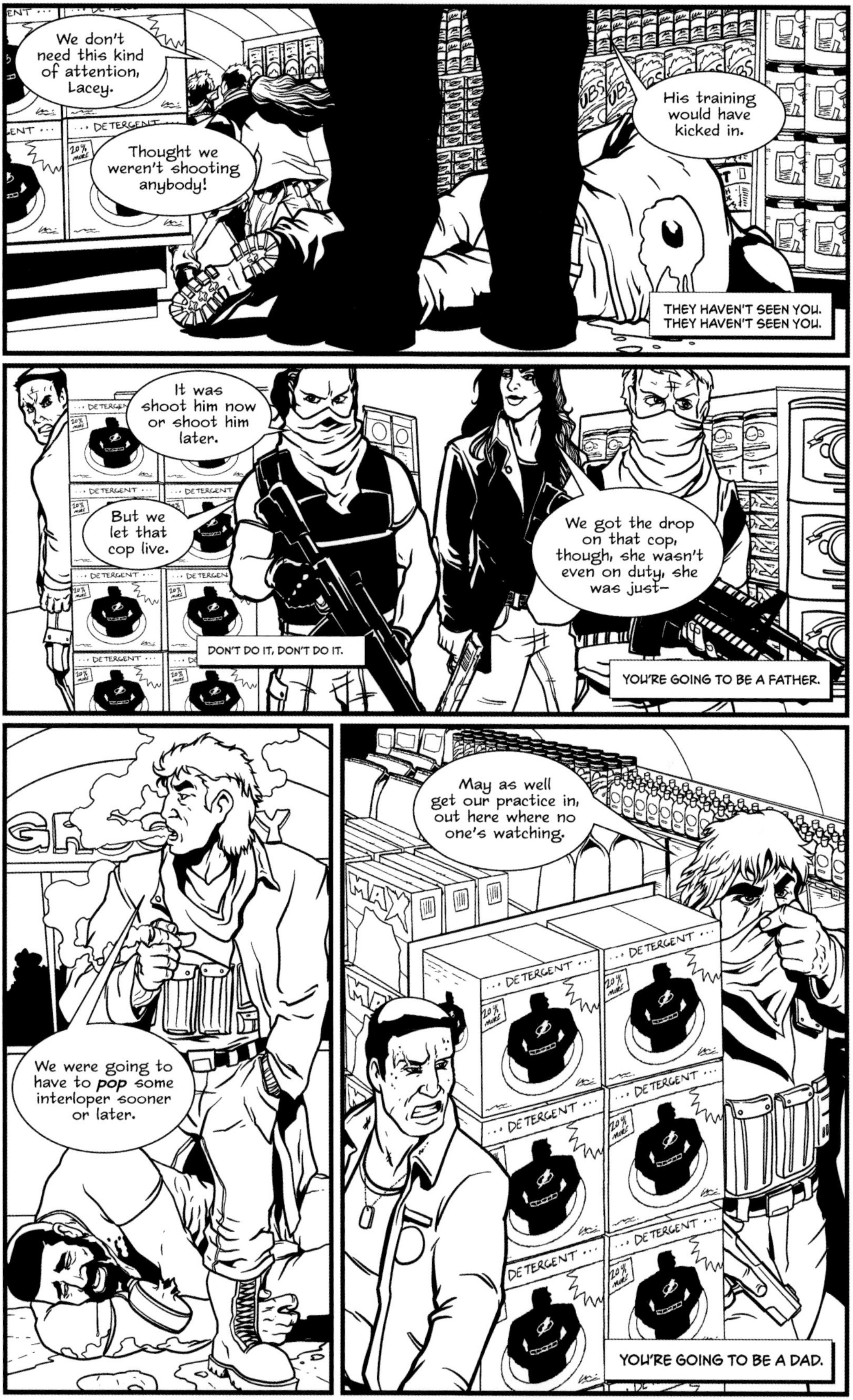
We don't need this kind of attention, Lacey.
Thought we weren't shooting anybody!
His training would have kicked in.
THEY HAVEN'T SEEN YOU. THEY HAVEN'T SEEN YOU.
It was shoot him now or shoot him later.
But we let that cop live.
DON'T DO IT, DON'T DO IT.
We got the drop on that cop, though, she wasn't even on duty, she was just–
YOU'RE GOING TO BE A FATHER.
We were going to have to *pop* some interloper sooner or later.
May as well get our practice in, out here where no one's watching.
YOU'RE GOING TO BE A DAD.

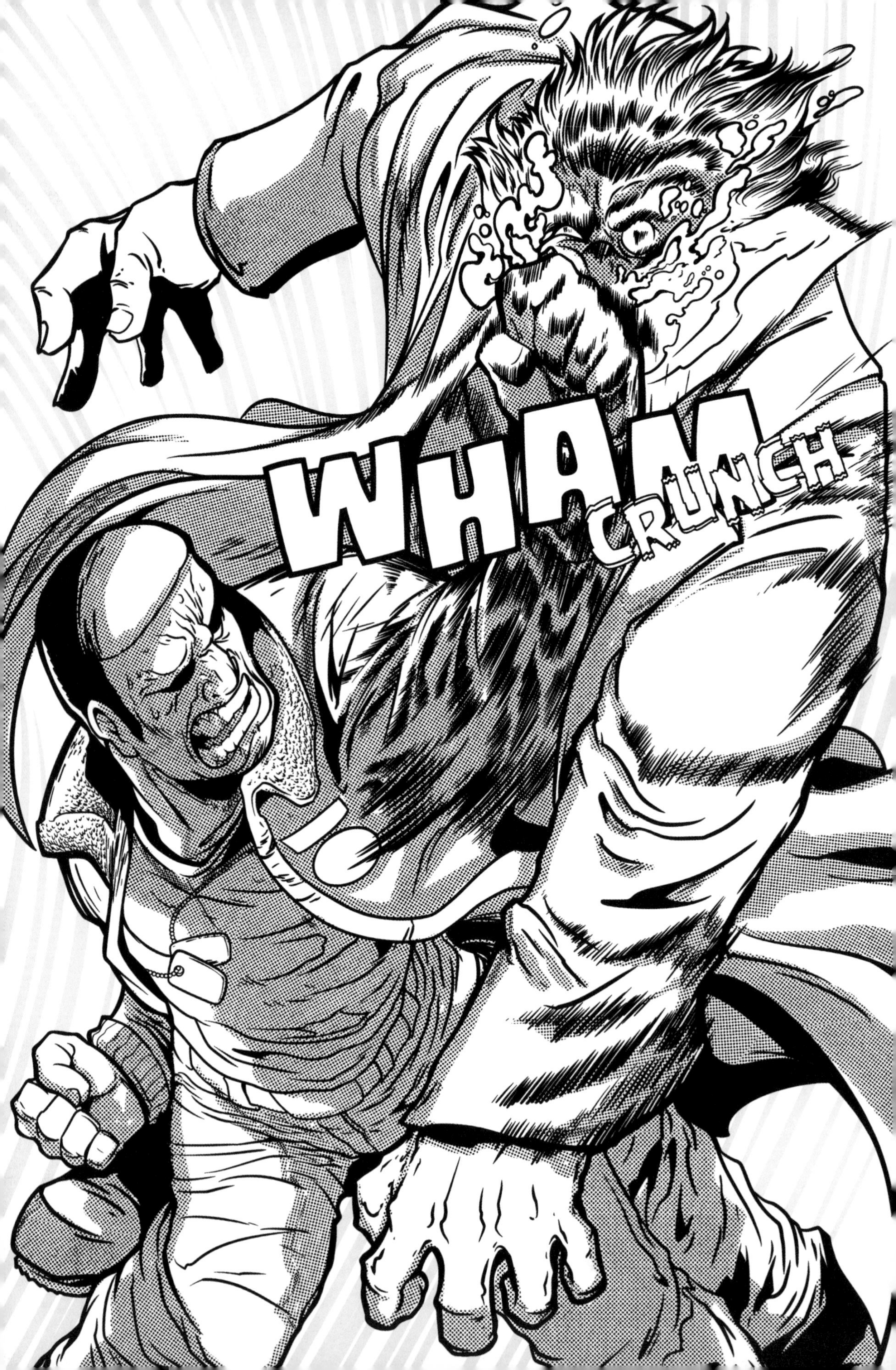
WHAM
CRUNCH

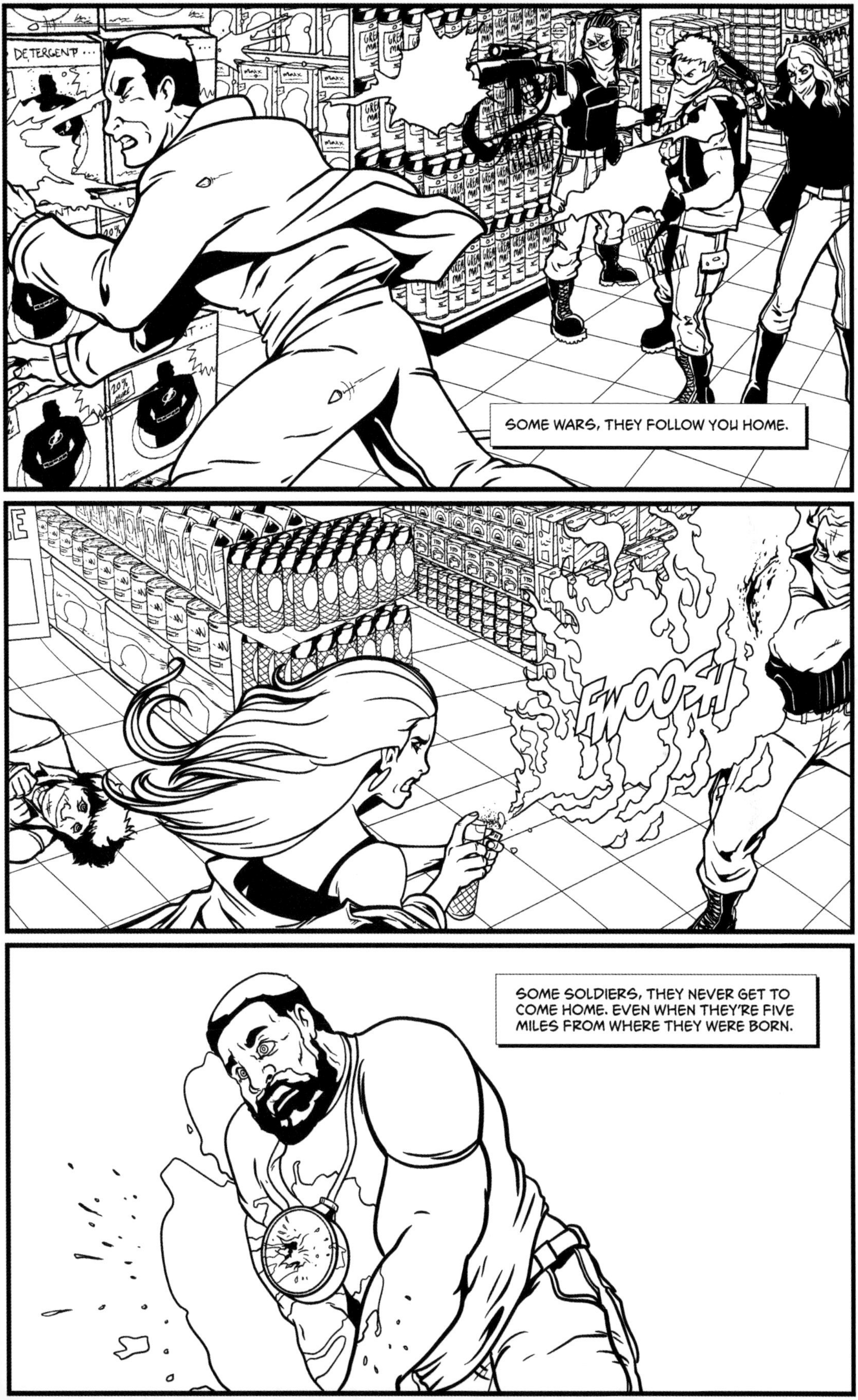
DETERGENT...
20% MORE
SOME WARS, THEY FOLLOW YOU HOME.
FWOOSH
SOME SOLDIERS, THEY NEVER GET TO COME HOME. EVEN WHEN THEY'RE FIVE MILES FROM WHERE THEY WERE BORN.

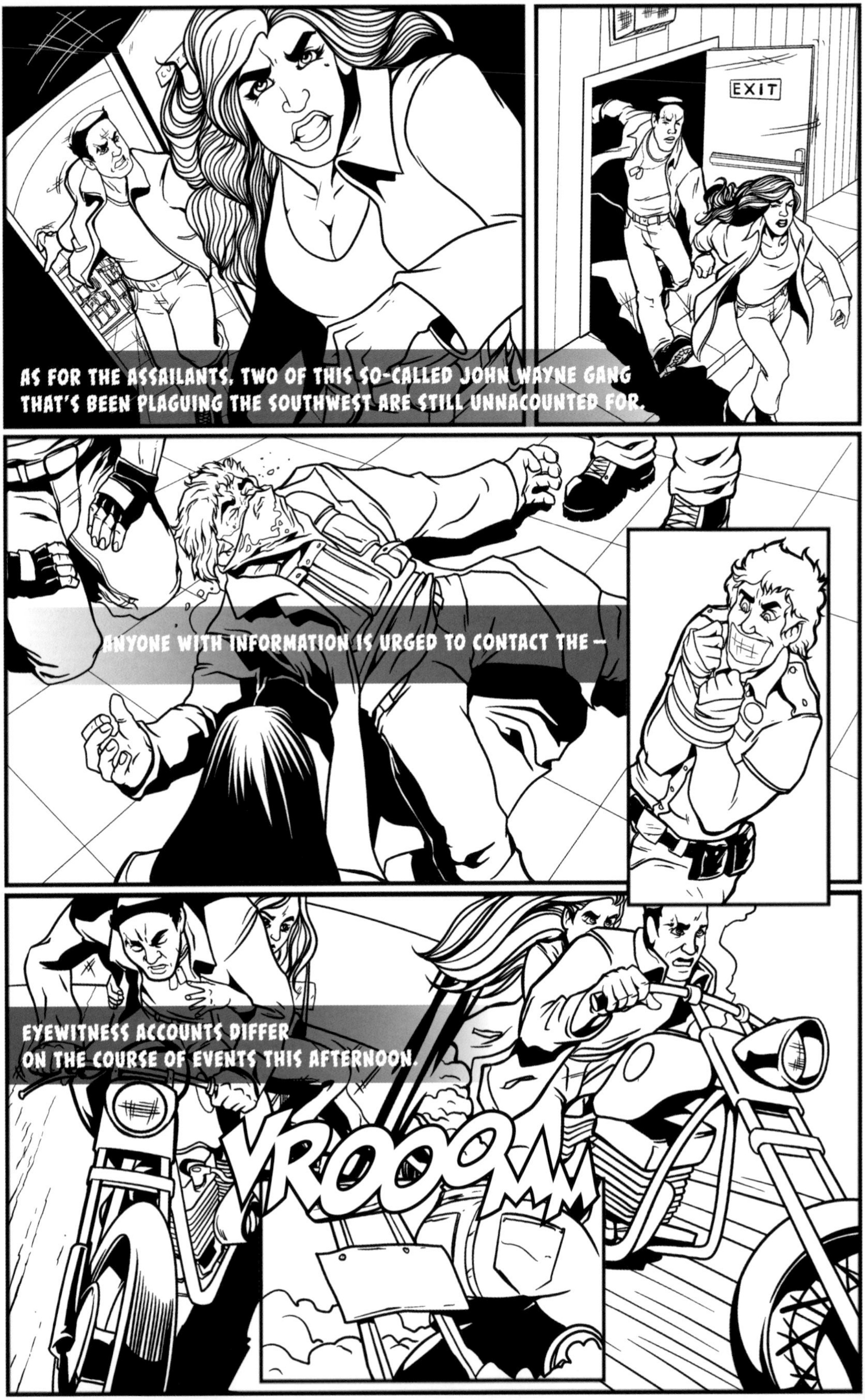
AS FOR THE ASSAILANTS, TWO OF THIS SO-CALLED JOHN WAYNE GANG THAT'S BEEN PLAGUING THE SOUTHWEST ARE STILL UNNACOUNTED FOR.
ANYONE WITH INFORMATION IS URGED TO CONTACT THE—
EXIT
EYEWITNESS ACCOUNTS DIFFER ON THE COURSE OF EVENTS THIS AFTERNOON.
VROOOMMM

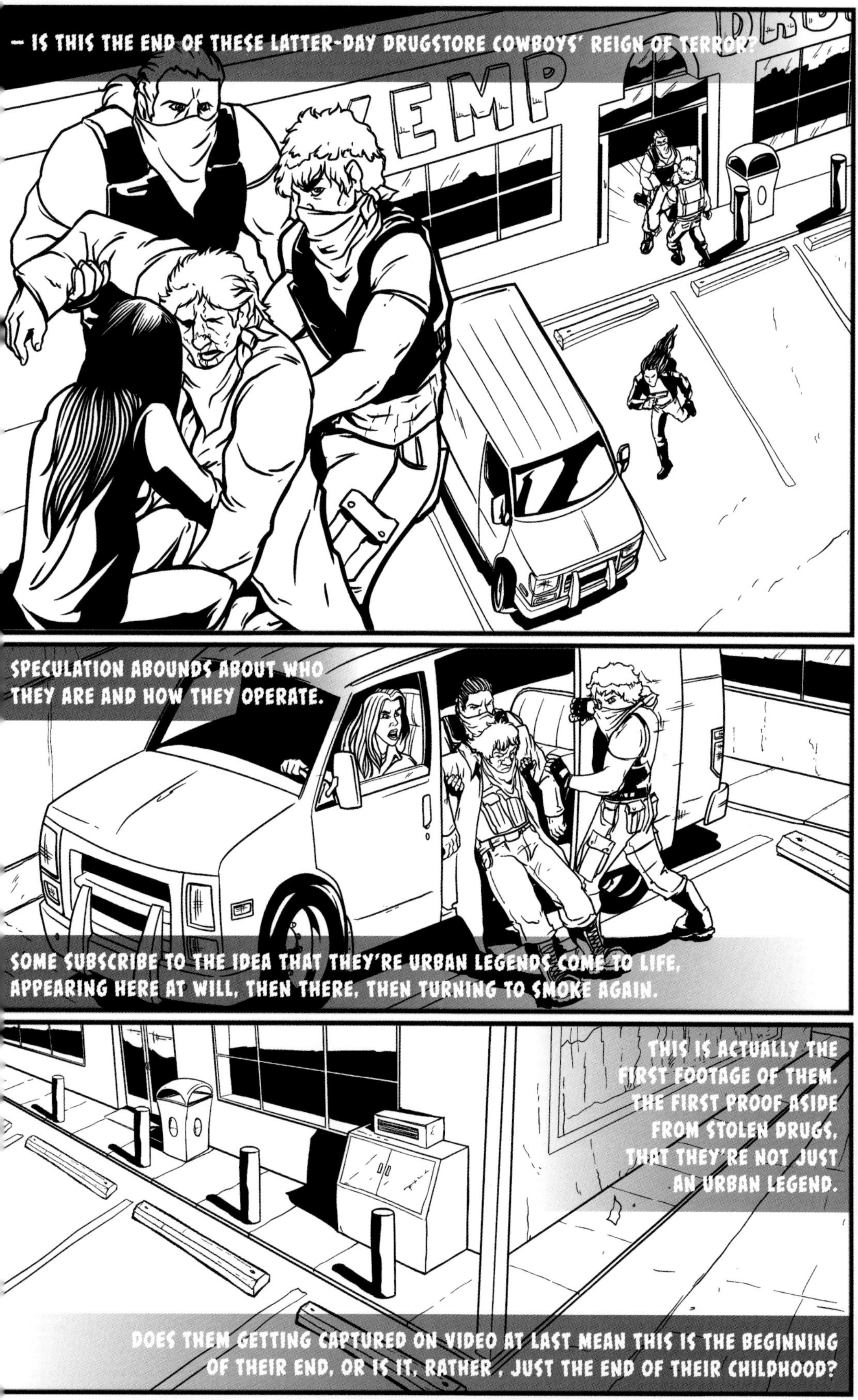
– IS THIS THE END OF THESE LATTER-DAY DRUGSTORE COWBOYS' REIGN OF TERROR?
EMP
SPECULATION ABOUNDS ABOUT WHO THEY ARE AND HOW THEY OPERATE.
SOME SUBSCRIBE TO THE IDEA THAT THEY'RE URBAN LEGENDS COME TO LIFE, APPEARING HERE AT WILL, THEN THERE, THEN TURNING TO SMOKE AGAIN.
THIS IS ACTUALLY THE FIRST FOOTAGE OF THEM. THE FIRST PROOF ASIDE FROM STOLEN DRUGS, THAT THEY'RE NOT JUST AN URBAN LEGEND.
DOES THEM GETTING CAPTURED ON VIDEO AT LAST MEAN THIS IS THE BEGINNING OF THEIR END, OR IS IT, RATHER , JUST THE END OF THEIR CHILDHOOD?

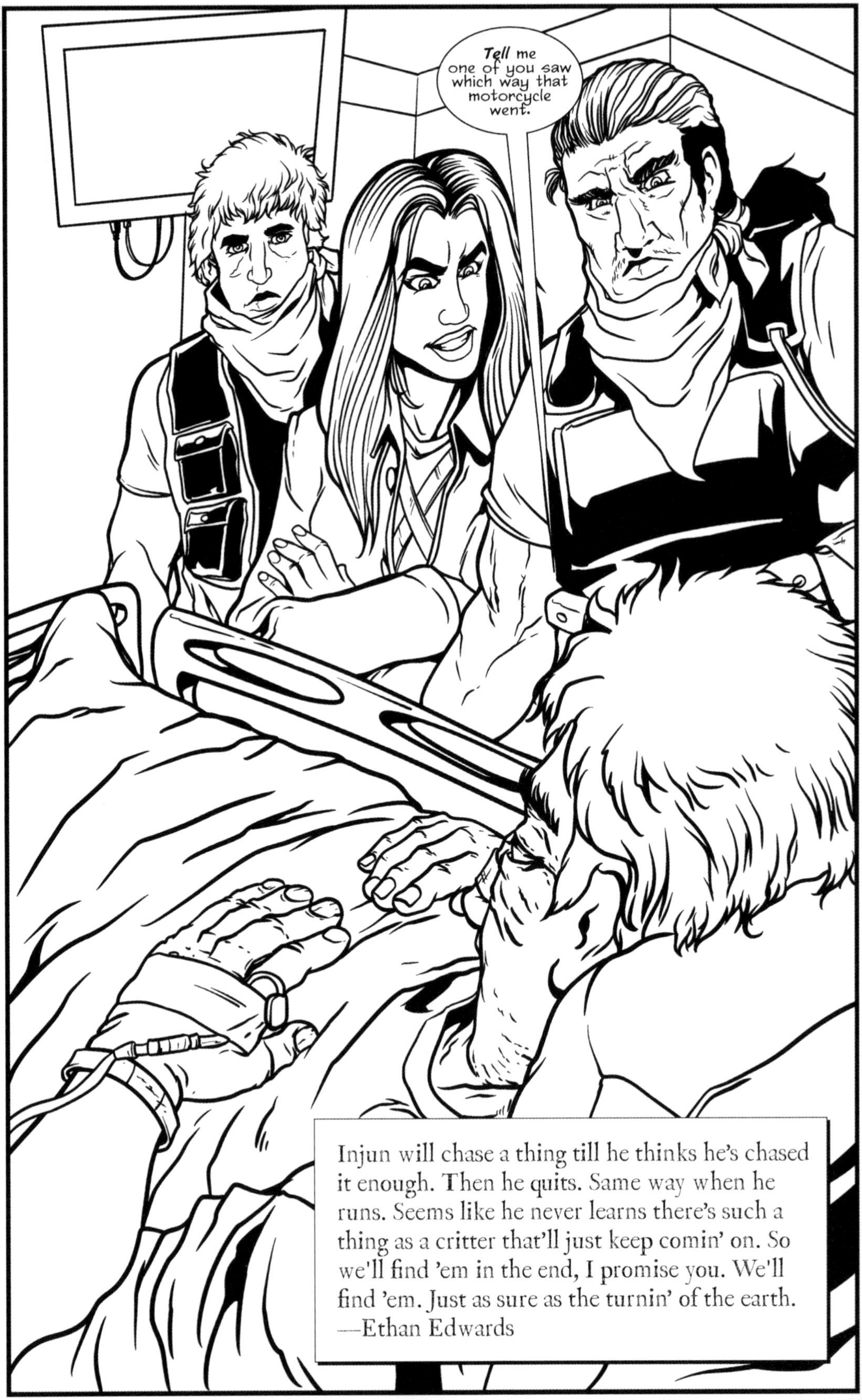
Tell me one of you saw which way that motorcycle went.
Injun will chase a thing till he thinks he's chased it enough. Then he quits. Same way when he runs. Seems like he never learns there's such a thing as a critter that'll just keep comin' on. So we'll find 'em in the end, I promise you. We'll find 'em. Just as sure as the turnin' of the earth.
—Ethan Edwards

PART TWO

SOME RIDES YOU HAVE TO MAKE.

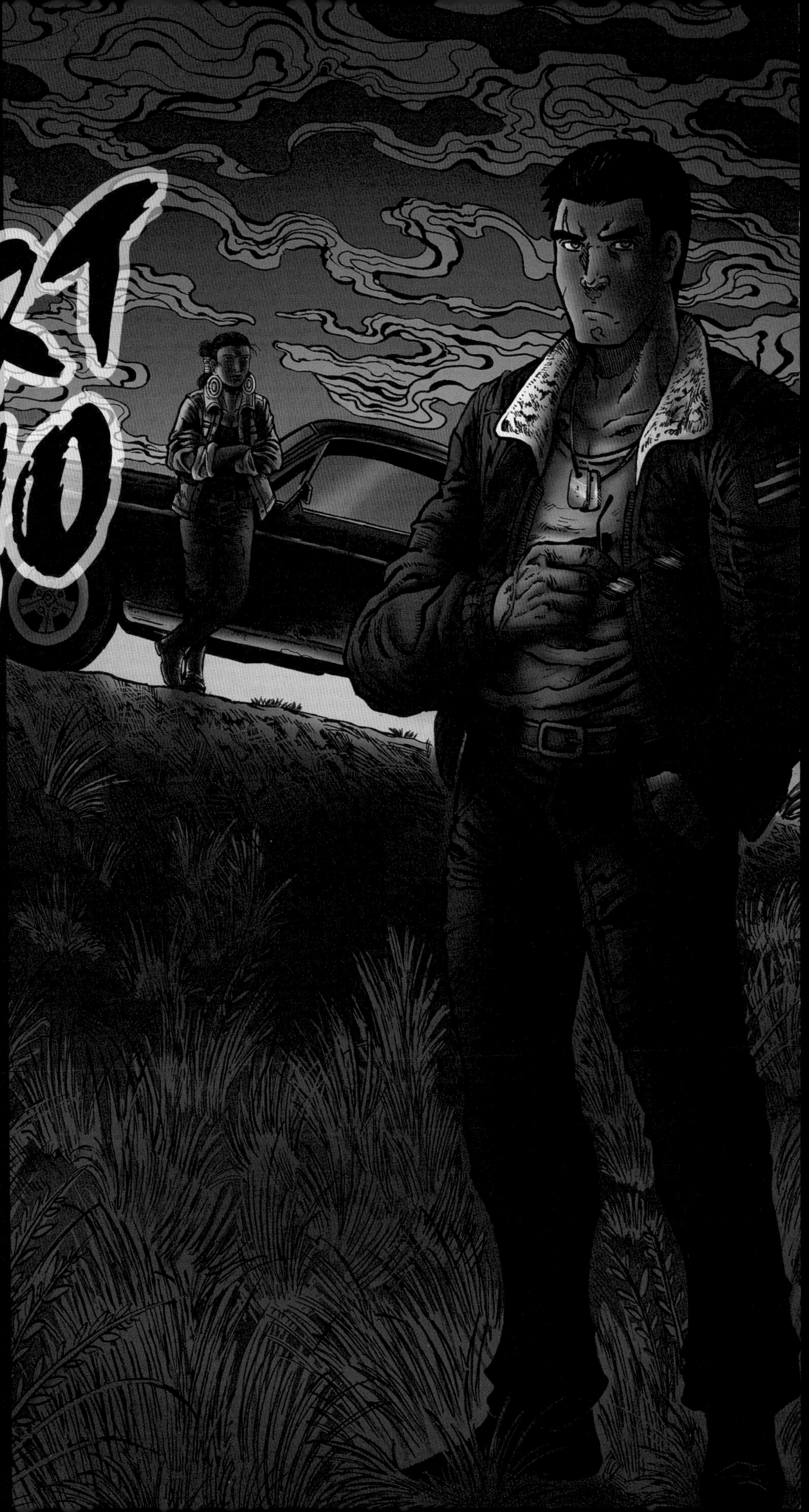

HOME FROM THE WAR FOR HIS ESTRANGED FATHER'S FUNERAL, COOPER TOWN AND HIS GIRLFRIEND SHERI MUN STUMBLED INTO A DRUGSTORE HEIST WHERE COOPER TOWN BECAME A HERO. NOW THEY NEED TO: DELIVER HIS FATHER'S HARLEY FOR A FISTFUL OF CASH, AVOID BOTH THE FEARED JOHN WAYNES GANG AND THE STATE POLICE, AND MAKE IT BACK TO THE PLANE ON TIME, TO KEEP COOP FROM GOING AWOL.

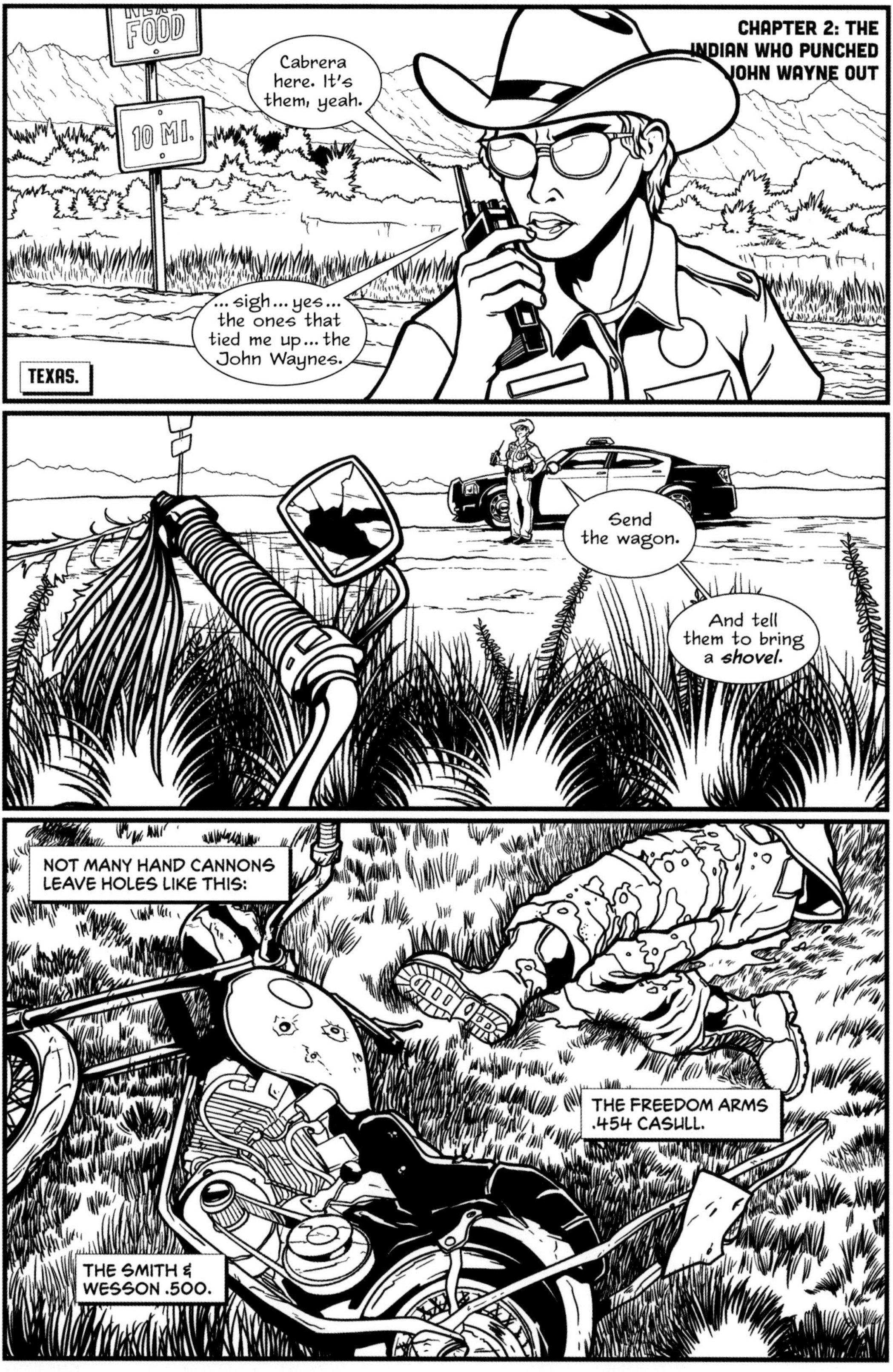
FOOD
10 MI.
Cabrera here. It's them, yeah.
CHAPTER 2: THE INDIAN WHO PUNCHED JOHN WAYNE OUT
... sigh ... yes ... the ones that tied me up ... the John Waynes.
TEXAS.
Send the wagon.
And tell them to bring a *shovel.*
NOT MANY HAND CANNONS LEAVE HOLES LIKE THIS:
THE FREEDOM ARMS .454 CASULL.
THE SMITH & WESSON .500.

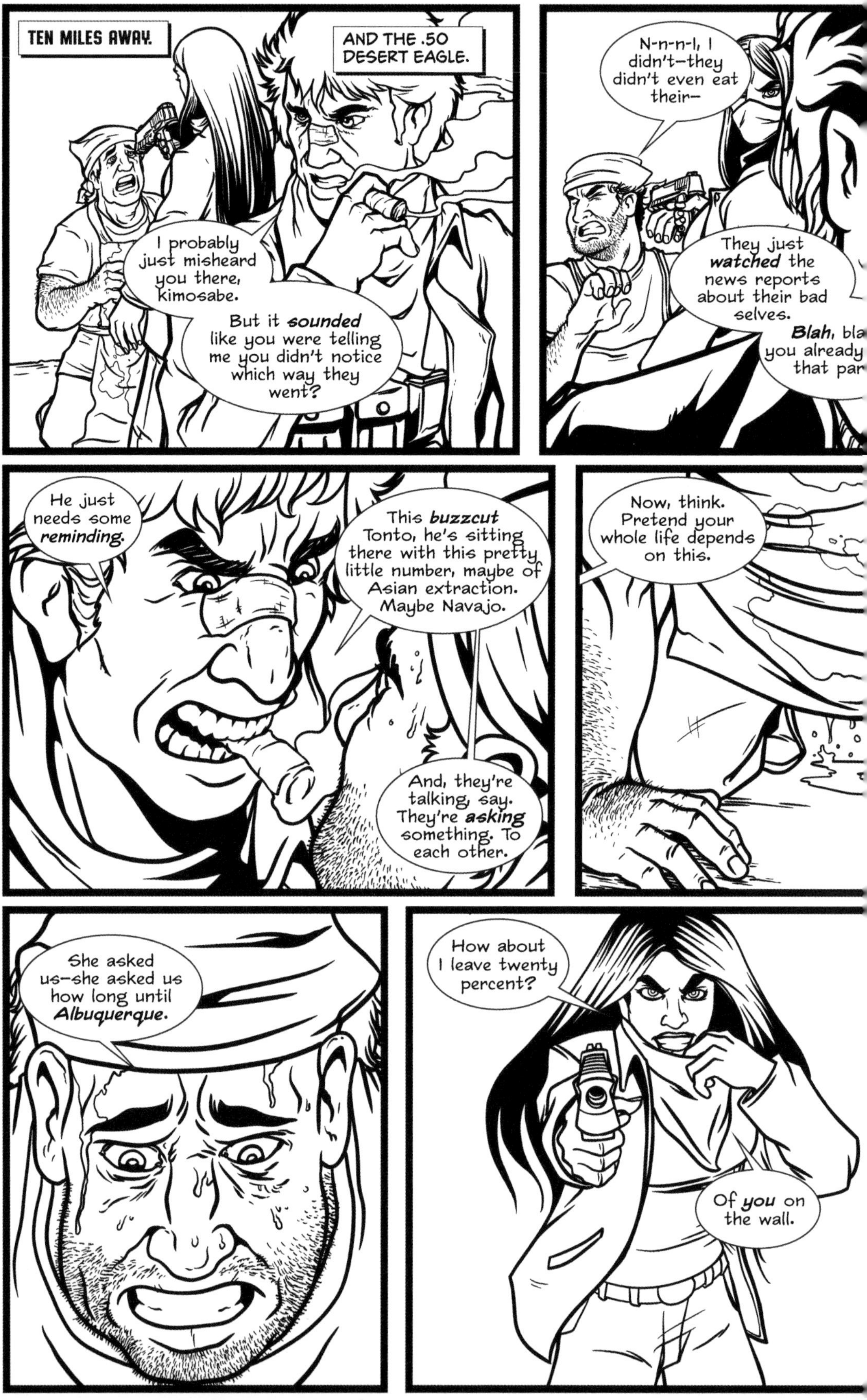
TEN MILES AWAY.
AND THE .50 DESERT EAGLE.
I probably just misheard you there, kimosabe.
But it *sounded* like you were telling me you didn't notice which way they went?
N-n-n-I, I didn't—they didn't even eat their—
They just *watched* the news reports about their bad selves.
Blah, bla you already that par
He just needs some *reminding*.
This *buzzcut* Tonto, he's sitting there with this pretty little number, maybe of Asian extraction. Maybe Navajo.
And, they're talking, say. They're *asking* something. To each other.
Now, think. Pretend your whole life depends on this.
She asked us—she asked us how long until *Albuquerque*.
How about I leave twenty percent?
Of *you* on the wall.

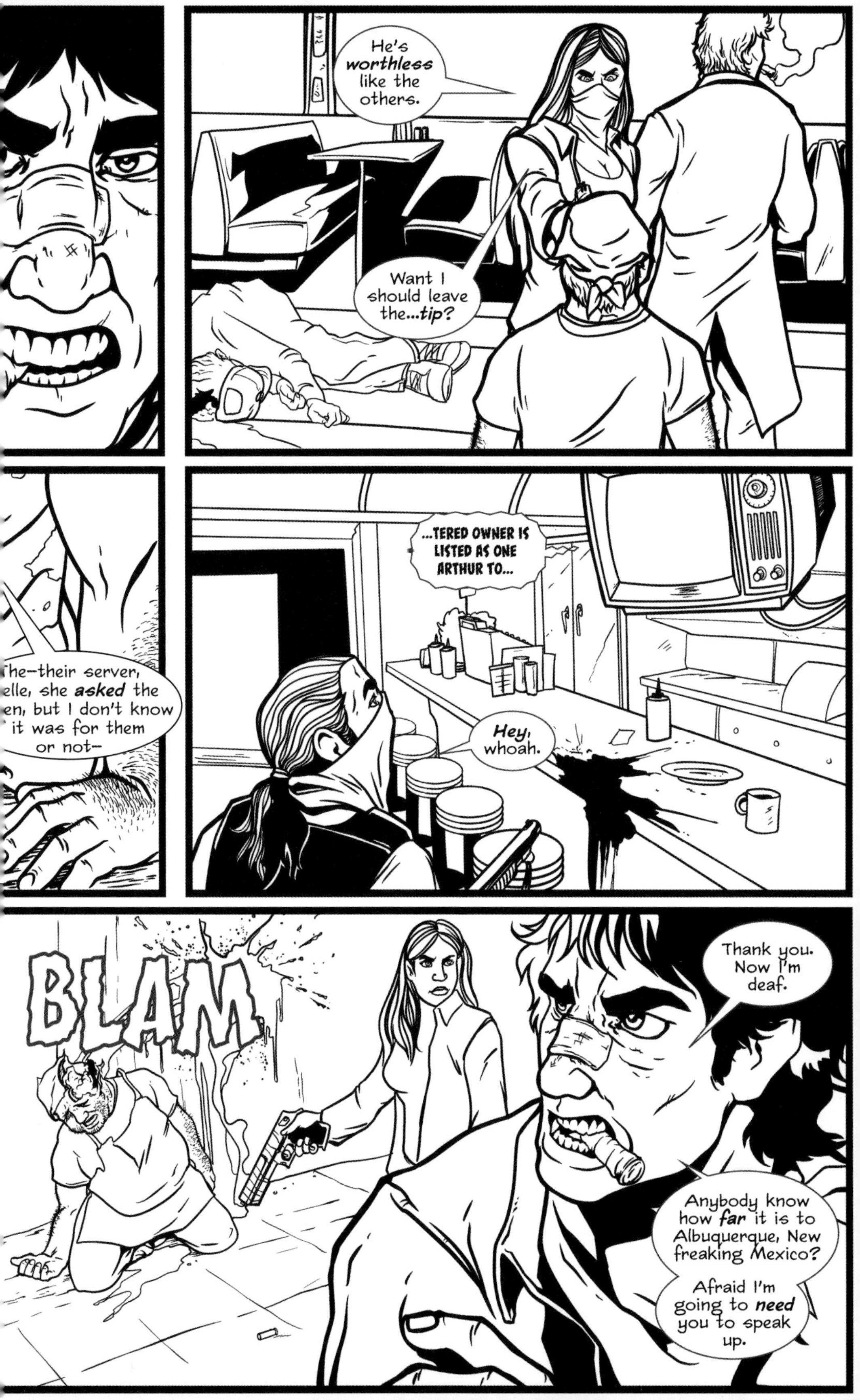
He's *worthless* like the others.
Want I should leave the...*tip*?
...TERED OWNER IS LISTED AS ONE ARTHUR TO...
he—their server, elle, she *asked* the en, but I don't know it was for them or not—
Hey, whoah.
BLAM
Thank you. Now I'm deaf.
Anybody know how *far* it is to Albuquerque, New freaking Mexico?
Afraid I'm going to *need* you to speak up.

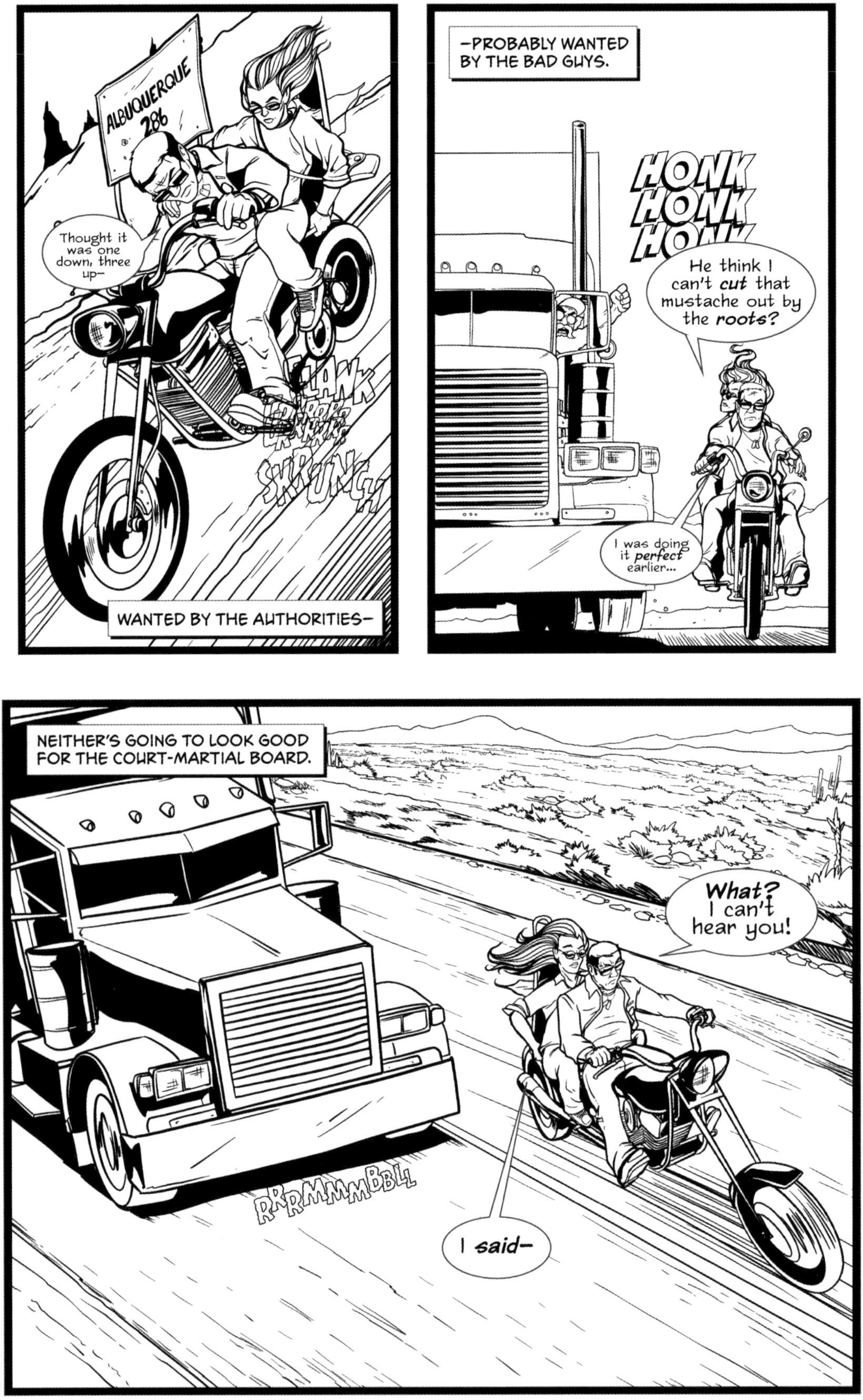
ALBUQUERQUE 286
Thought it was one down, three up–
CLANK
SKRUNCH
WANTED BY THE AUTHORITIES–
–PROBABLY WANTED BY THE BAD GUYS.
HONK HONK HONK
He think I can't *cut* that mustache out by the *roots*?
I was doing it *perfect* earlier...
NEITHER'S GOING TO LOOK GOOD FOR THE COURT-MARTIAL BOARD.
What? I can't hear you!
RRRMMMMBBLL
I *said*–

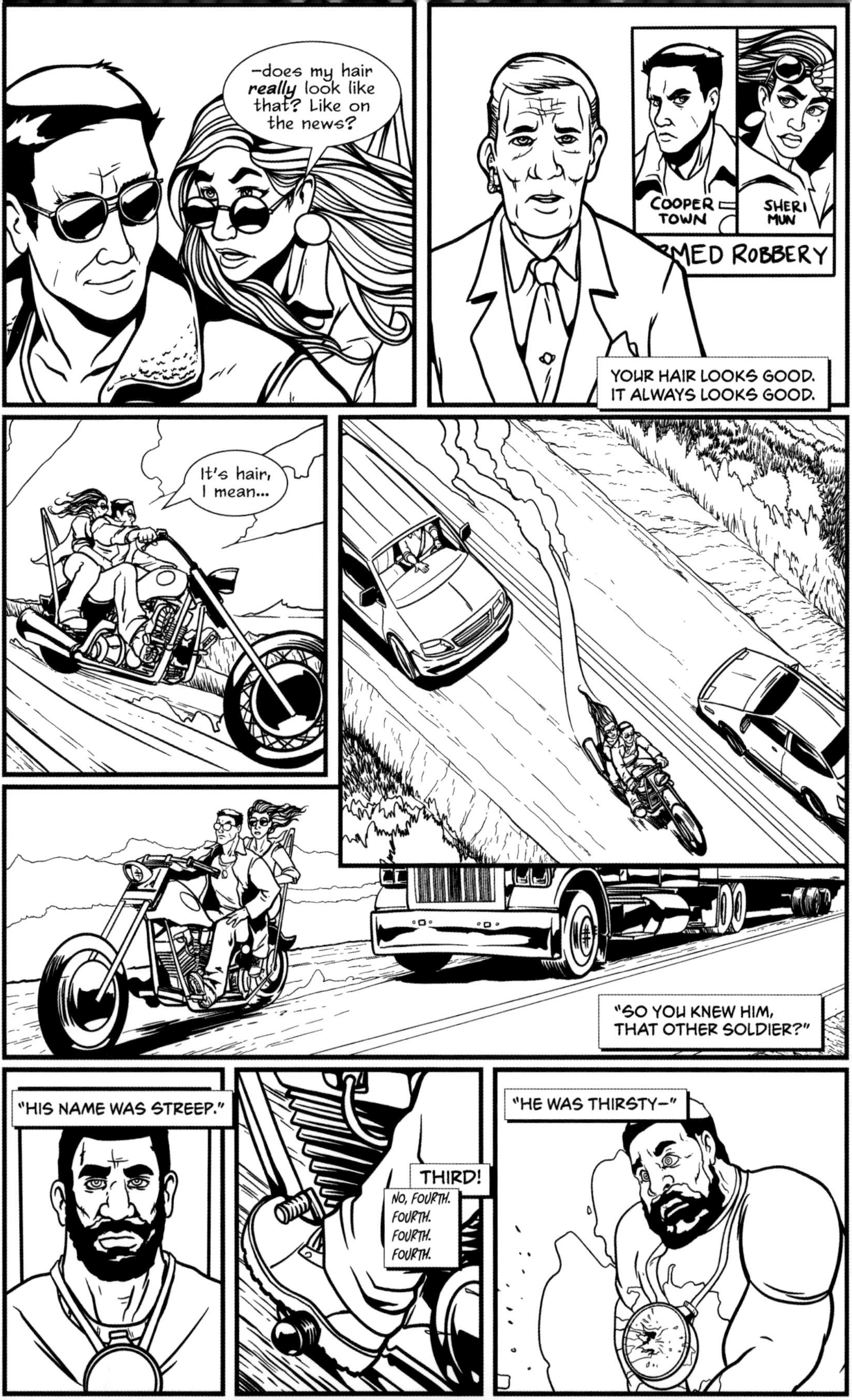
–does my hair *really* look like that? Like on the news?
COOPER TOWN
SHERI MUN
RMED ROBBERY
YOUR HAIR LOOKS GOOD. IT ALWAYS LOOKS GOOD.
It's hair, I mean...
"SO YOU KNEW HIM, THAT OTHER SOLDIER?"
"HIS NAME WAS STREEP."
THIRD!
NO, FOURTH. FOURTH. FOURTH. FOURTH.
"HE WAS THIRSTY–"

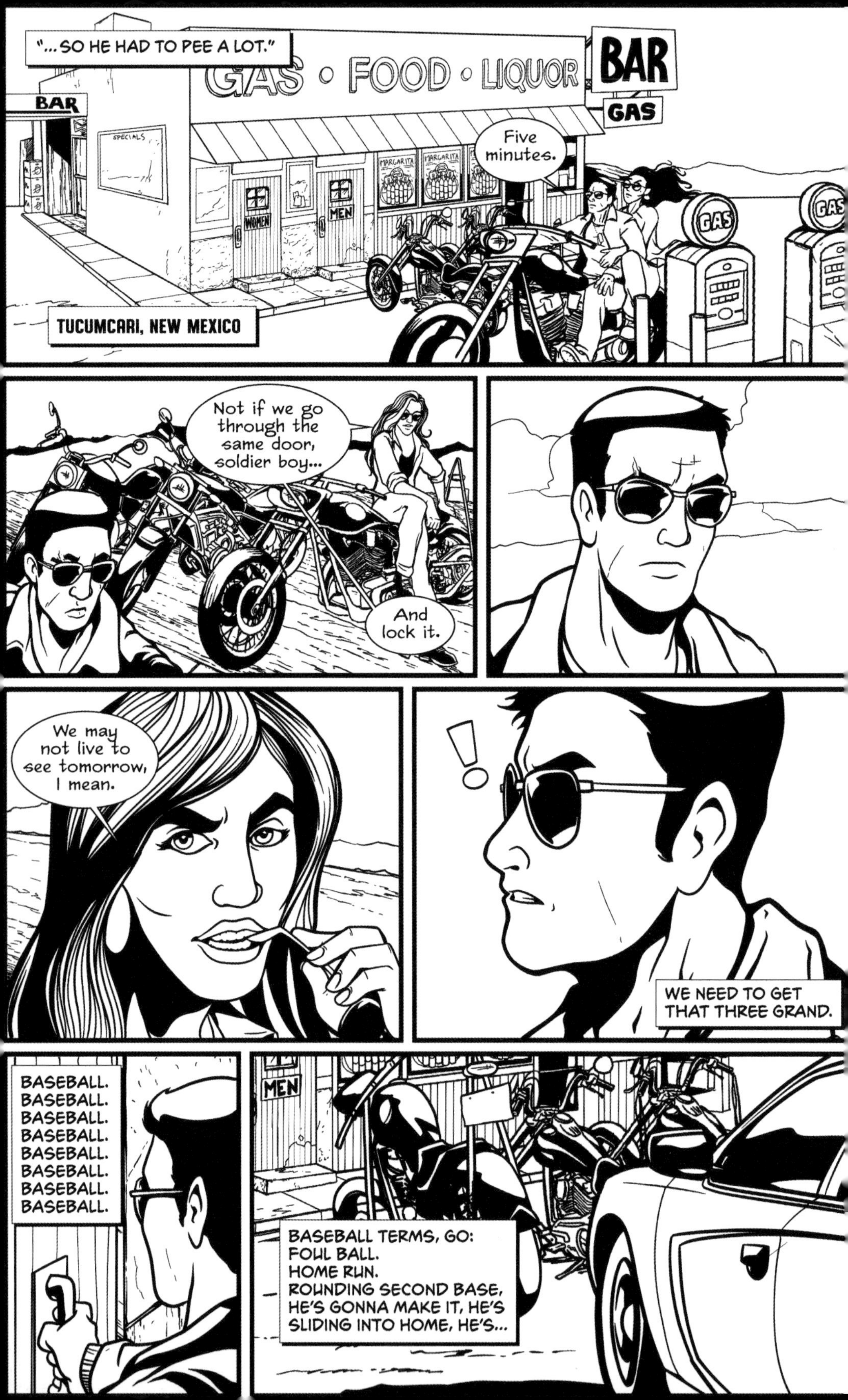
"...SO HE HAD TO PEE A LOT."
GAS • FOOD • LIQUOR
BAR
GAS
BAR
SPECIALS
WOMEN
MEN
MARGARITA
MARGARITA
Five minutes.
GAS
GAS
TUCUMCARI, NEW MEXICO
Not if we go through the same door, soldier boy...
And lock it.
We may not live to see tomorrow, I mean.
!
WE NEED TO GET THAT THREE GRAND.
BASEBALL.
BASEBALL.
BASEBALL.
BASEBALL.
BASEBALL.
BASEBALL.
BASEBALL.
BASEBALL.
MEN
BASEBALL TERMS, GO:
FOUL BALL.
HOME RUN.
ROUNDING SECOND BASE, HE'S GONNA MAKE IT, HE'S SLIDING INTO HOME, HE'S...

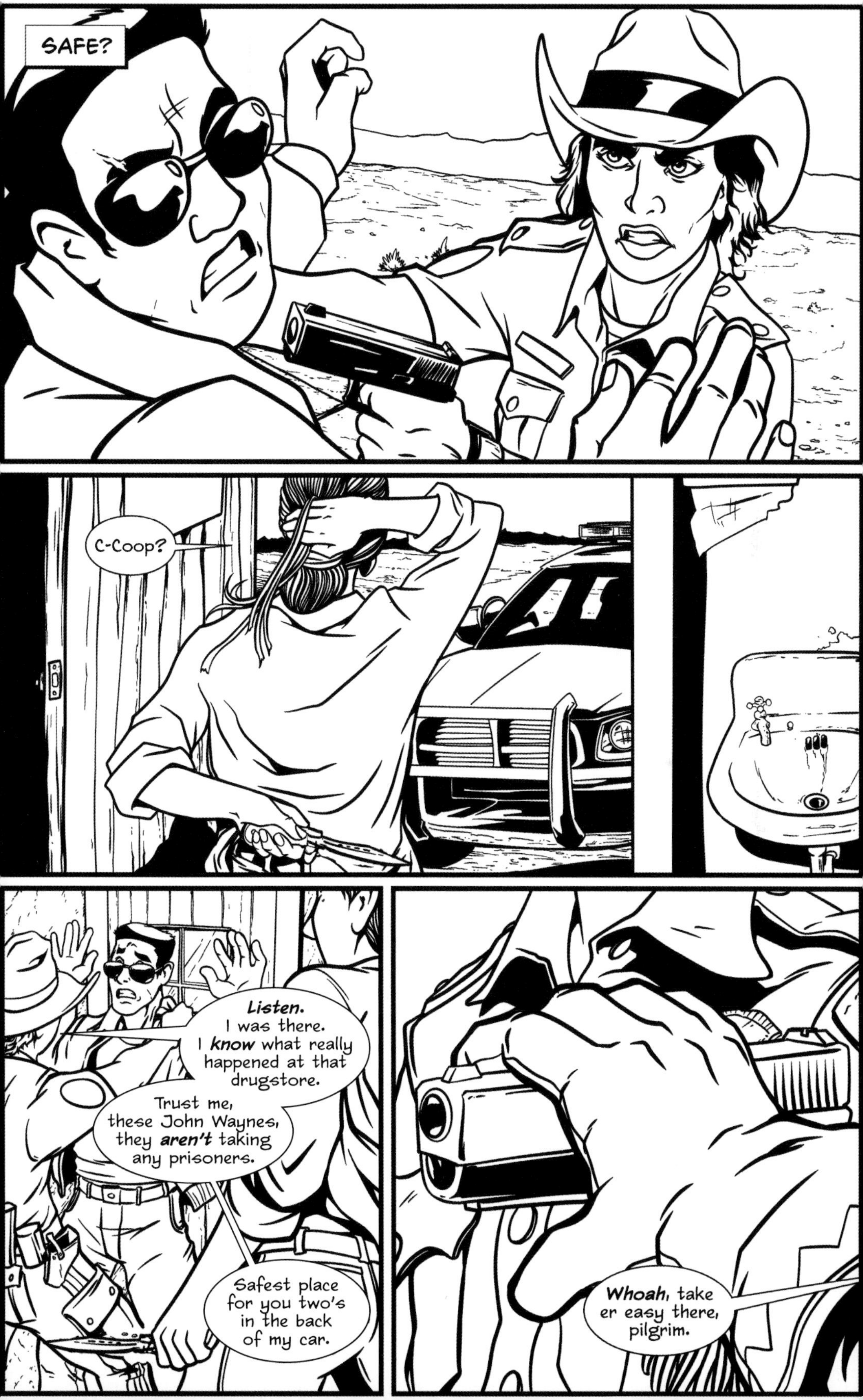
SAFE?
C-Coop?
Listen. I was there. I know what really happened at that drugstore.
Trust me, these John Waynes, they aren't taking any prisoners.
Safest place for you two's in the back of my car.
Whoah, take er easy there, pilgrim.

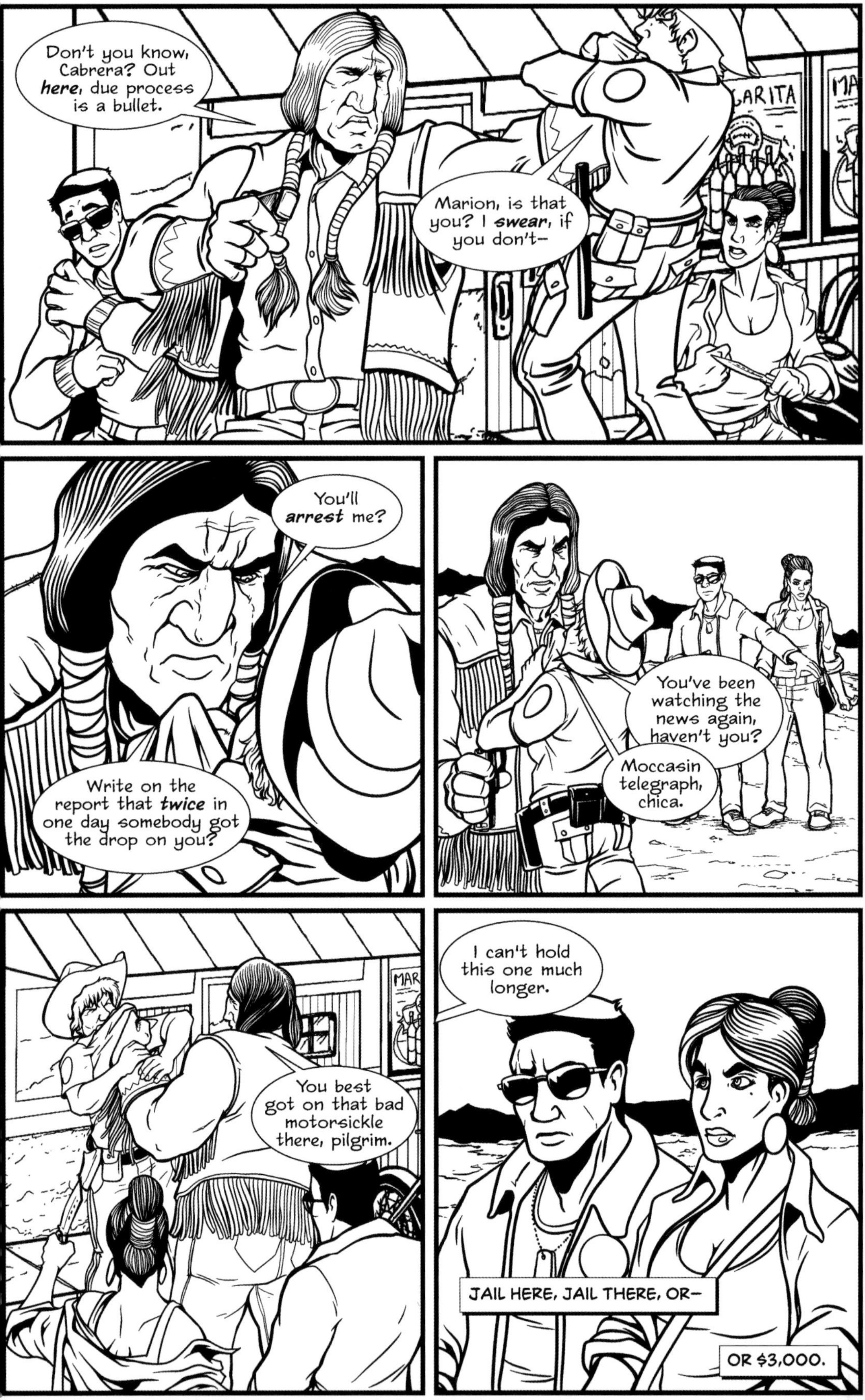
Don't you know, Cabrera? Out here, due process is a bullet.
Marion, is that you? I swear, if you don't–
You'll arrest me?
Write on the report that twice in one day somebody got the drop on you?
You've been watching the news again, haven't you?
Moccasin telegraph, chica.
You best get on that bad motorsickle there, pilgrim.
I can't hold this one much longer.
JAIL HERE, JAIL THERE, OR–
OR $3,000.

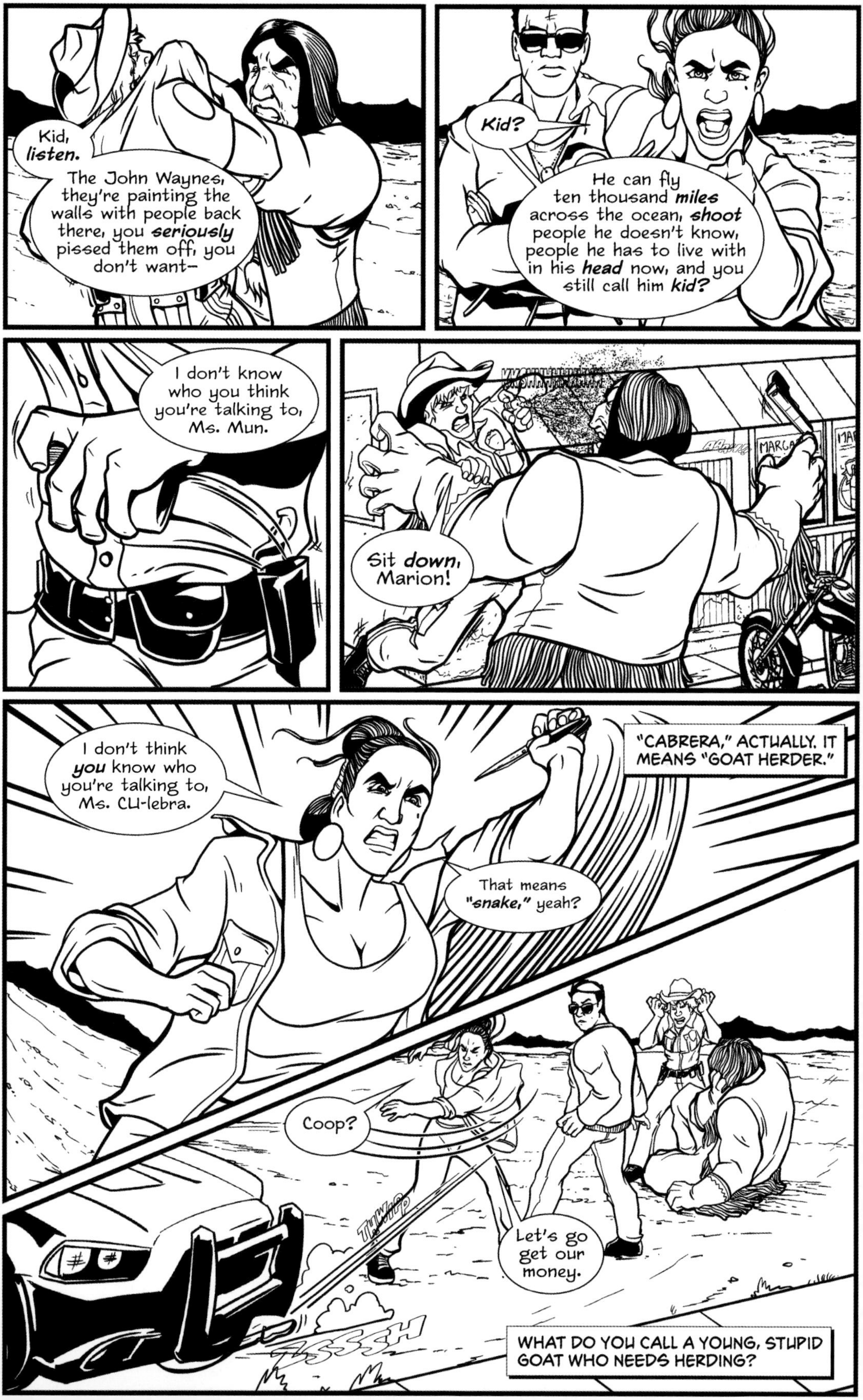

Kid, listen.
The John Waynes, they're painting the walls with people back there, you seriously pissed them off, you don't want–
Kid?
He can fly ten thousand miles across the ocean, shoot people he doesn't know, people he has to live with in his head now, and you still call him kid?
I don't know who you think you're talking to, Ms. Mun.
Sit down, Marion!
I don't think you know who you're talking to, Ms. CU-lebra.
"CABRERA," ACTUALLY. IT MEANS "GOAT HERDER."
That means "snake," yeah?
Coop?
Let's go get our money.
WHAT DO YOU CALL A YOUNG, STUPID GOAT WHO NEEDS HERDING?

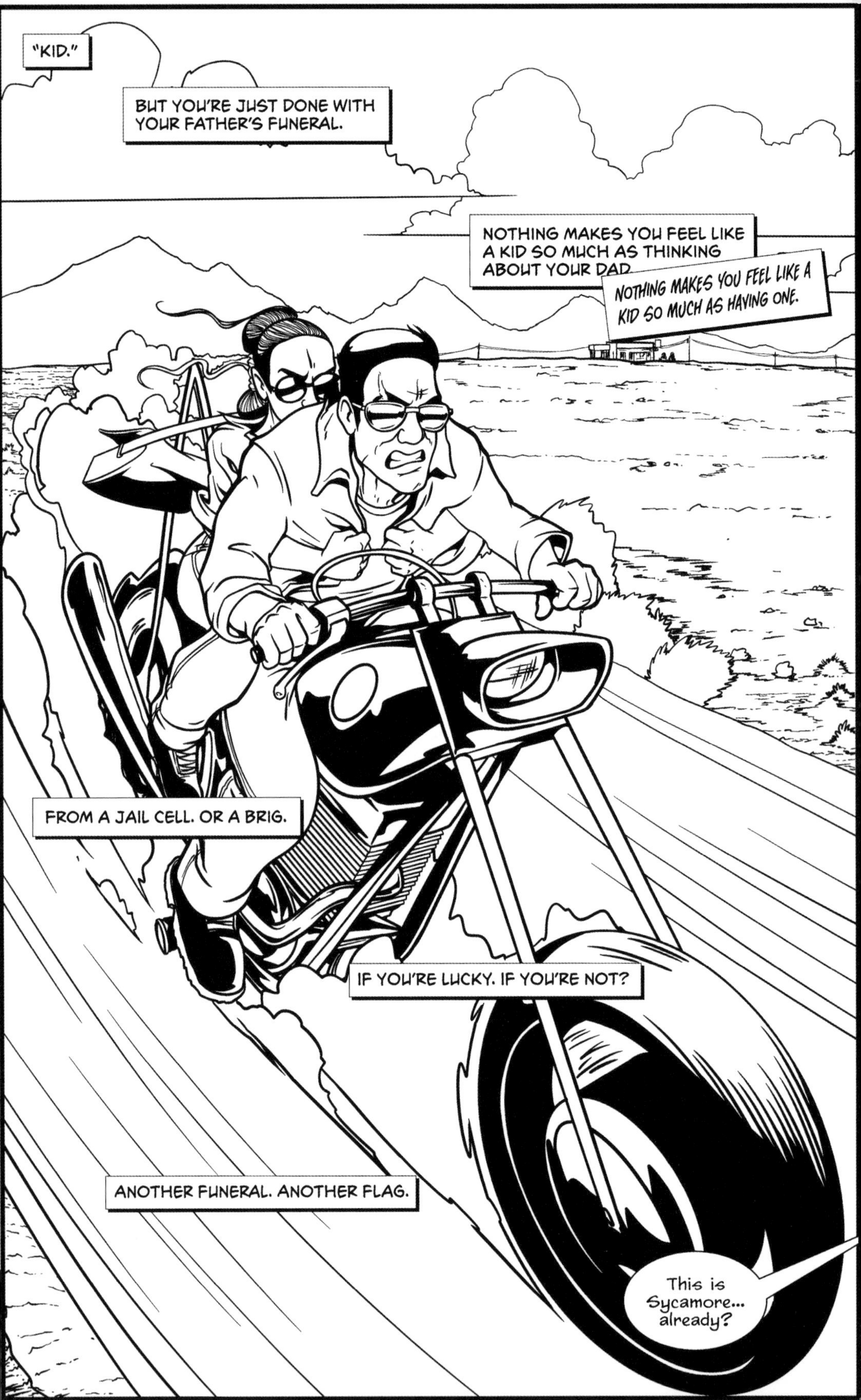
"KID."
BUT YOU'RE JUST DONE WITH YOUR FATHER'S FUNERAL.
NOTHING MAKES YOU FEEL LIKE A KID SO MUCH AS THINKING ABOUT YOUR DAD.
NOTHING MAKES YOU FEEL LIKE A KID SO MUCH AS HAVING ONE.
FROM A JAIL CELL. OR A BRIG.
IF YOU'RE LUCKY. IF YOU'RE NOT?
ANOTHER FUNERAL. ANOTHER FLAG.
This is Sycamore... already?

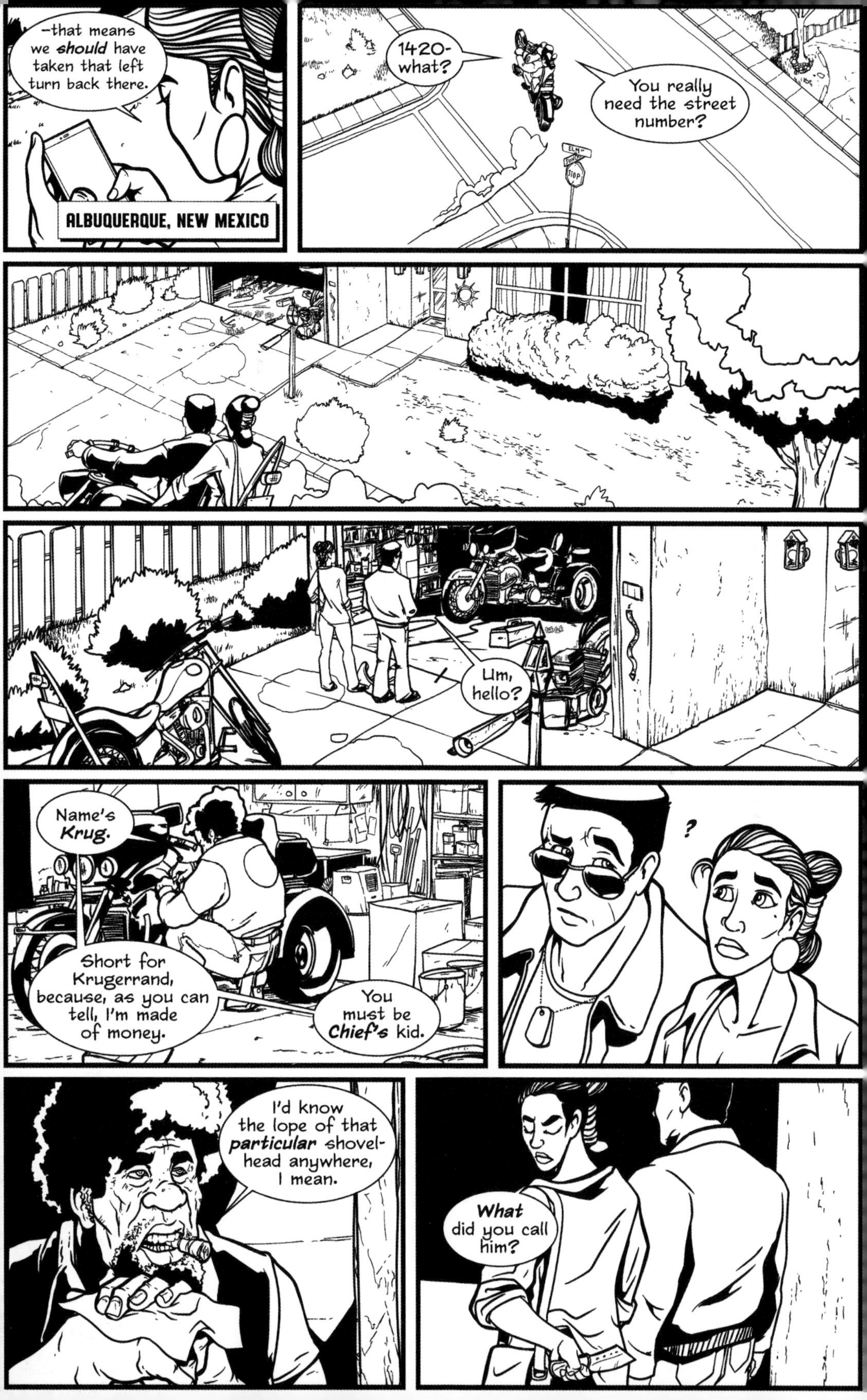
–that means we *should* have taken that left turn back there.
ALBUQUERQUE, NEW MEXICO
1420-what?
You really need the street number?
Um, hello?
Name's *Krug.*
Short for Krugerrand, because, as you can tell, I'm made of money.
You must be *Chief's* kid.
?
I'd know the lope of that *particular* shovel-head anywhere, I mean.
What did you call him?

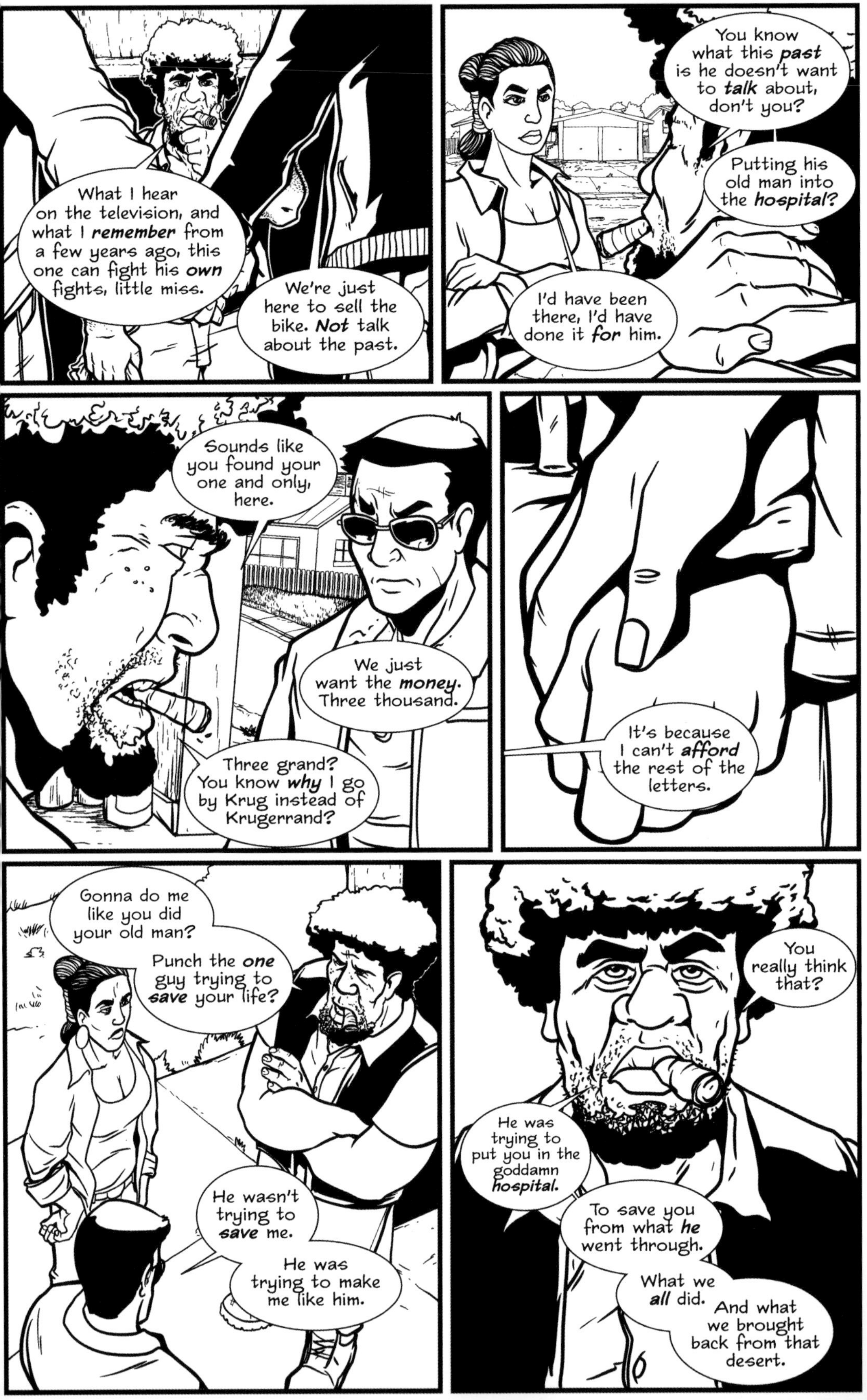
What I hear on the television, and what I *remember* from a few years ago, this one can fight his *own* fights, little miss.
We're just here to sell the bike. *Not* talk about the past.
You know what this *past* is he doesn't want to *talk* about, don't you?
Putting his old man into the *hospital?*
I'd have been there, I'd have done it *for* him.
Sounds like you found your one and only, here.
We just want the *money*. Three thousand.
Three grand? You know *why* I go by Krug instead of Krugerrand?
It's because I can't *afford* the rest of the letters.
Gonna do me like you did your old man?
Punch the *one* guy trying to *save* your life?
He wasn't trying to *save* me.
He was trying to make me like him.
You really think that?
He was trying to put you in the goddamn *hospital.*
To save you from what *he* went through.
What we *all* did.
And what we brought back from that desert.

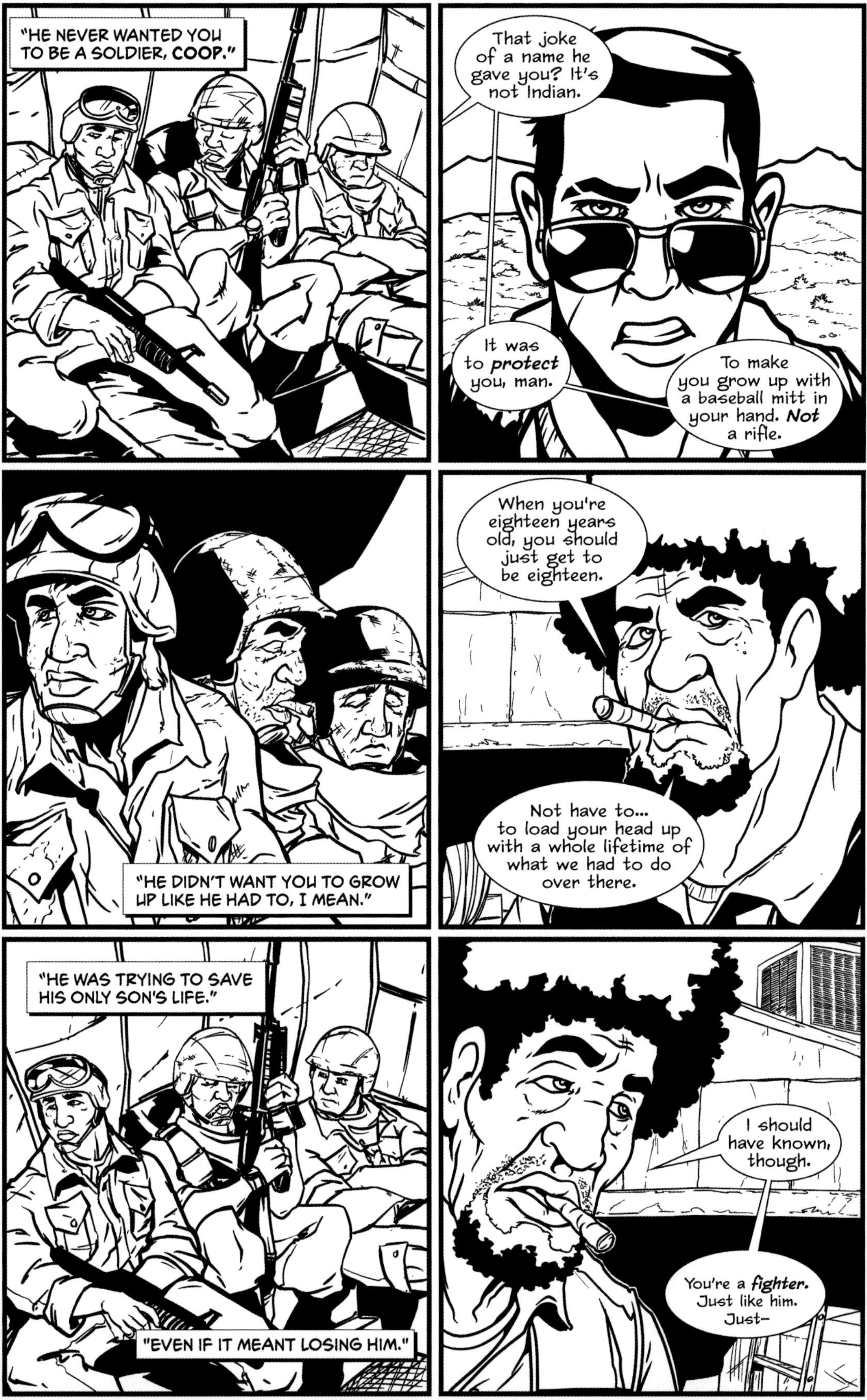
"HE NEVER WANTED YOU TO BE A SOLDIER, COOP."
That joke of a name he gave you? It's not Indian.
It was to *protect* you, man.
To make you grow up with a baseball mitt in your hand. *Not* a rifle.
"HE DIDN'T WANT YOU TO GROW UP LIKE HE HAD TO, I MEAN."
When you're eighteen years old, you should just get to be eighteen.
Not have to... to load your head up with a whole lifetime of what we had to do over there.
"HE WAS TRYING TO SAVE HIS ONLY SON'S LIFE."
"EVEN IF IT MEANT LOSING HIM."
I should have known, though.
You're a *fighter.* Just like him. Just–

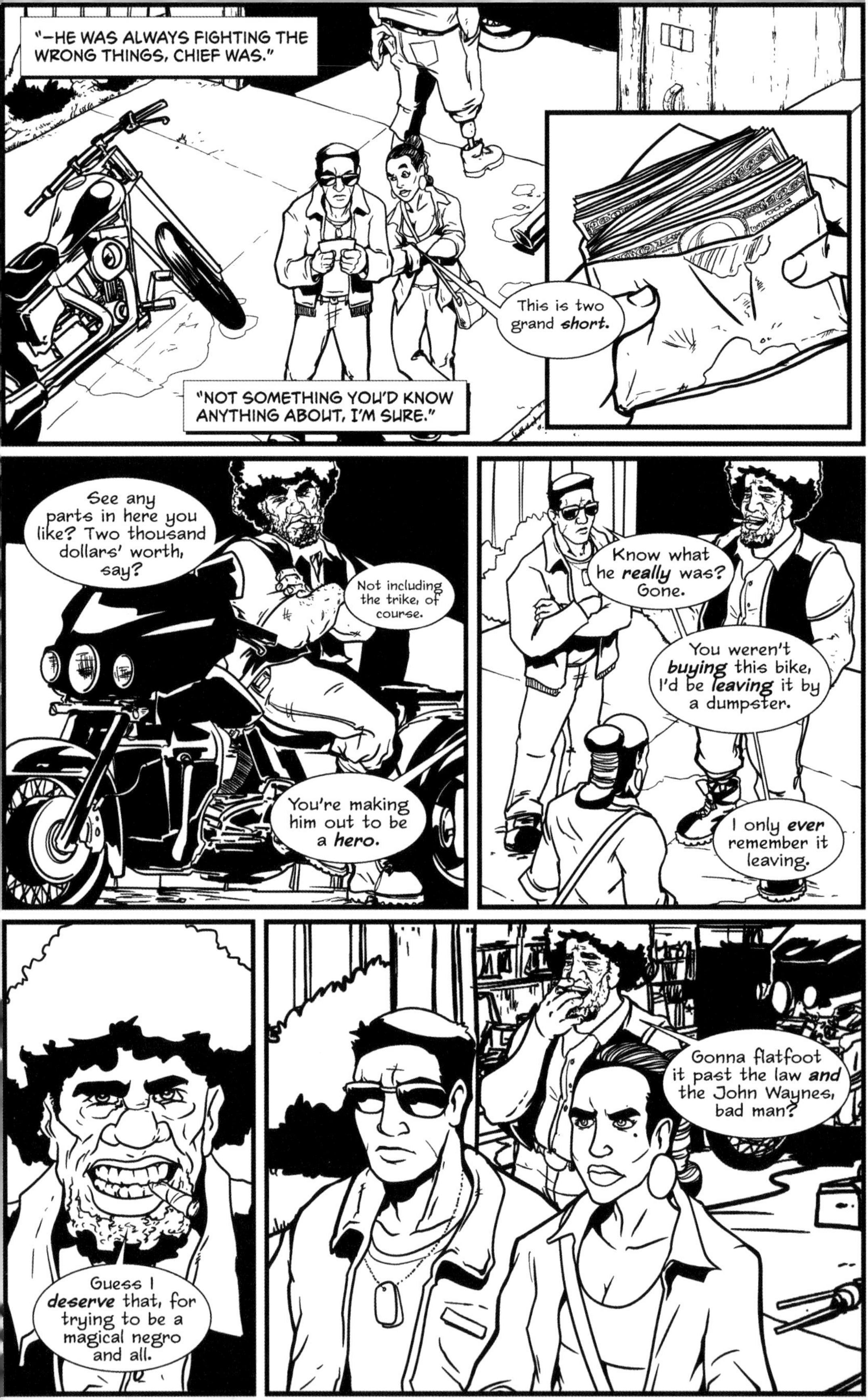
"—HE WAS ALWAYS FIGHTING THE WRONG THINGS, CHIEF WAS."
This is two grand short.
"NOT SOMETHING YOU'D KNOW ANYTHING ABOUT, I'M SURE."
See any parts in here you like? Two thousand dollars' worth, say?
Not including the trike, of course.
You're making him out to be a hero.
Know what he really was? Gone.
You weren't buying this bike, I'd be leaving it by a dumpster.
I only ever remember it leaving.
Guess I deserve that, for trying to be a magical negro and all.
Gonna flatfoot it past the law and the John Waynes, bad man?

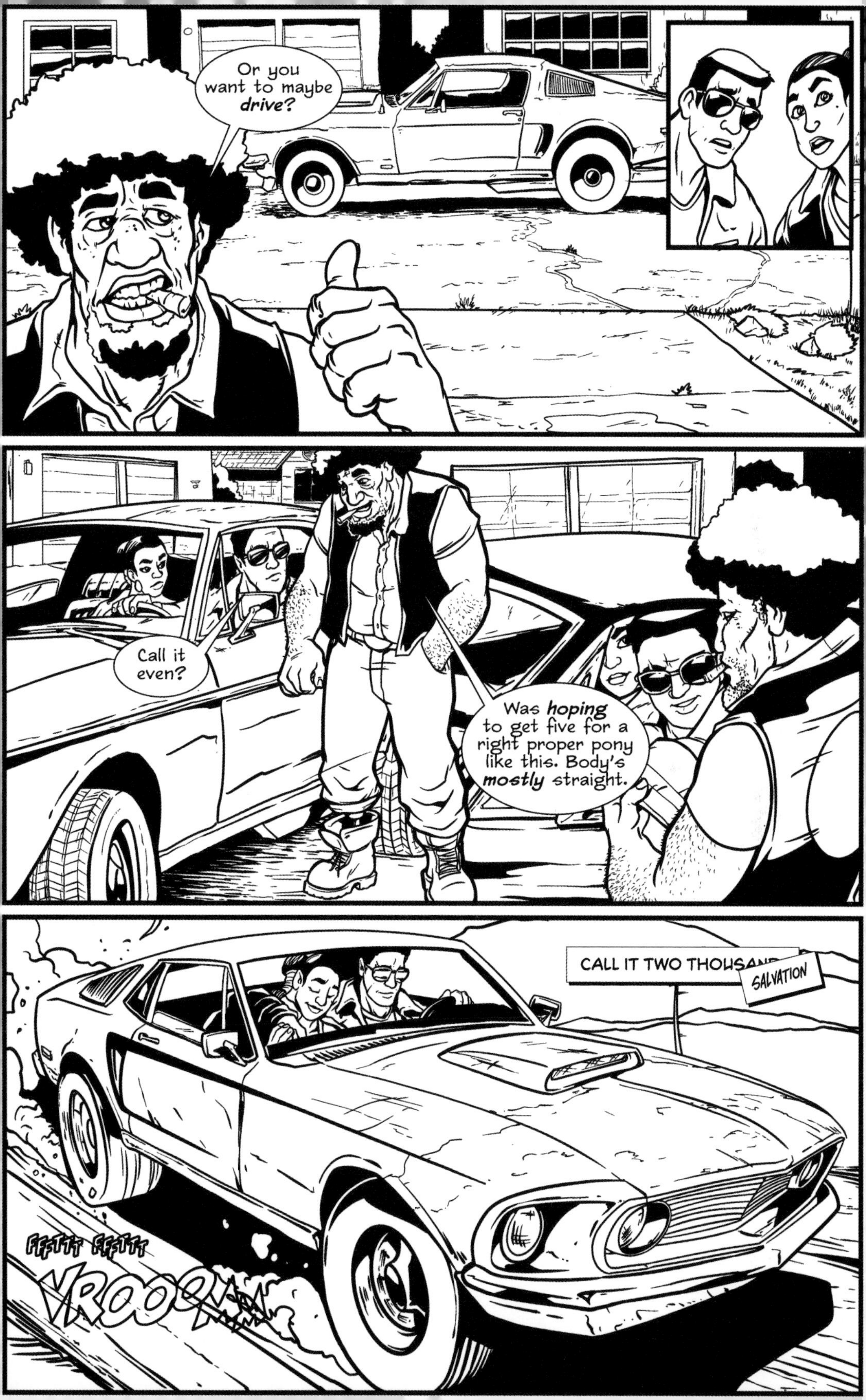
Or you want to maybe *drive?*
Call it even?
Was *hoping* to get five for a right proper pony like this. Body's *mostly* straight.
CALL IT TWO THOUSAND
SALVATION
FFSTTT FFSTTT
VROOOM

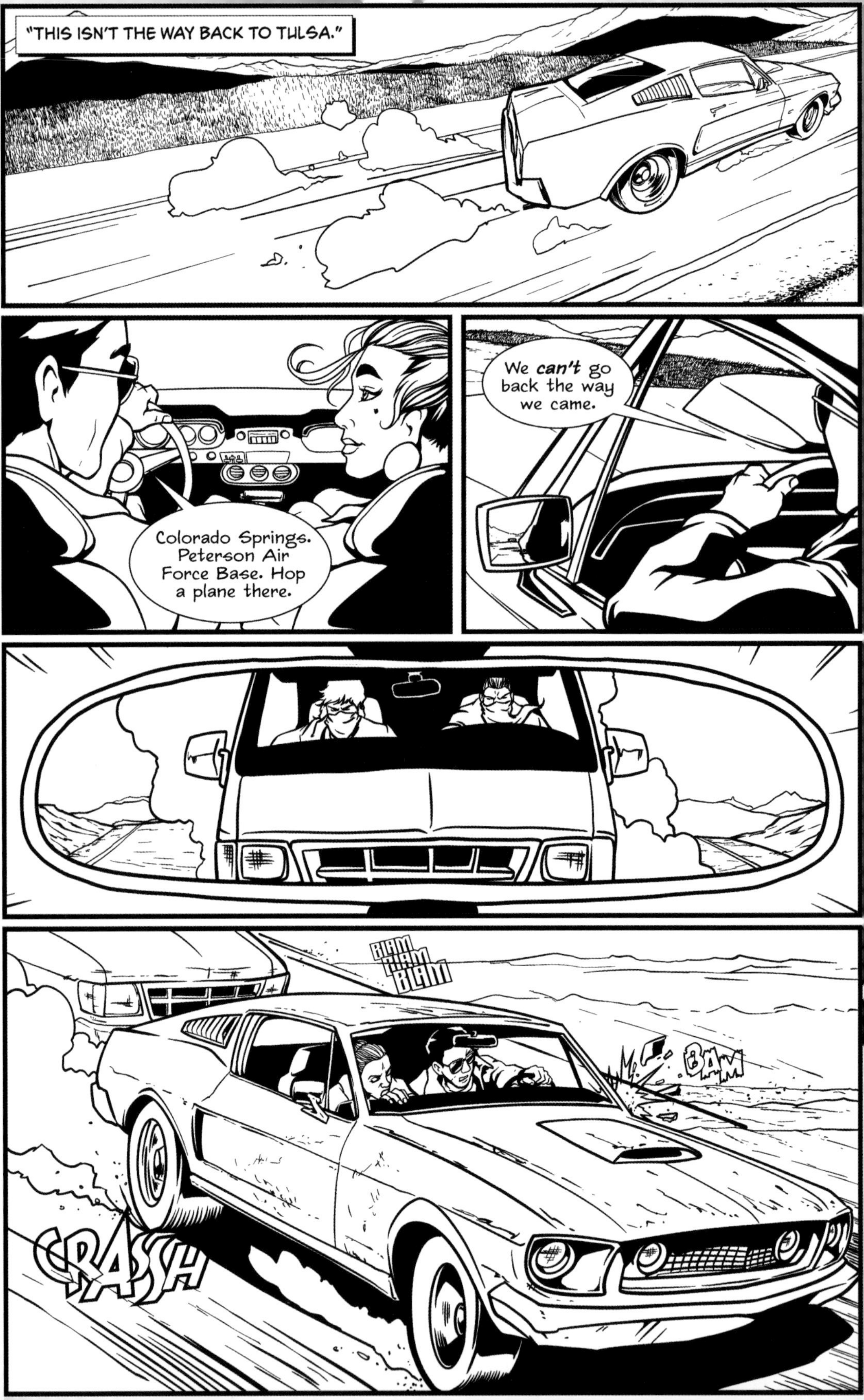
"THIS ISN'T THE WAY BACK TO TULSA."
Colorado Springs. Peterson Air Force Base. Hop a plane there.
We **can't** go back the way we came.
BLAM BLAM BLAM
BAM
CRASH

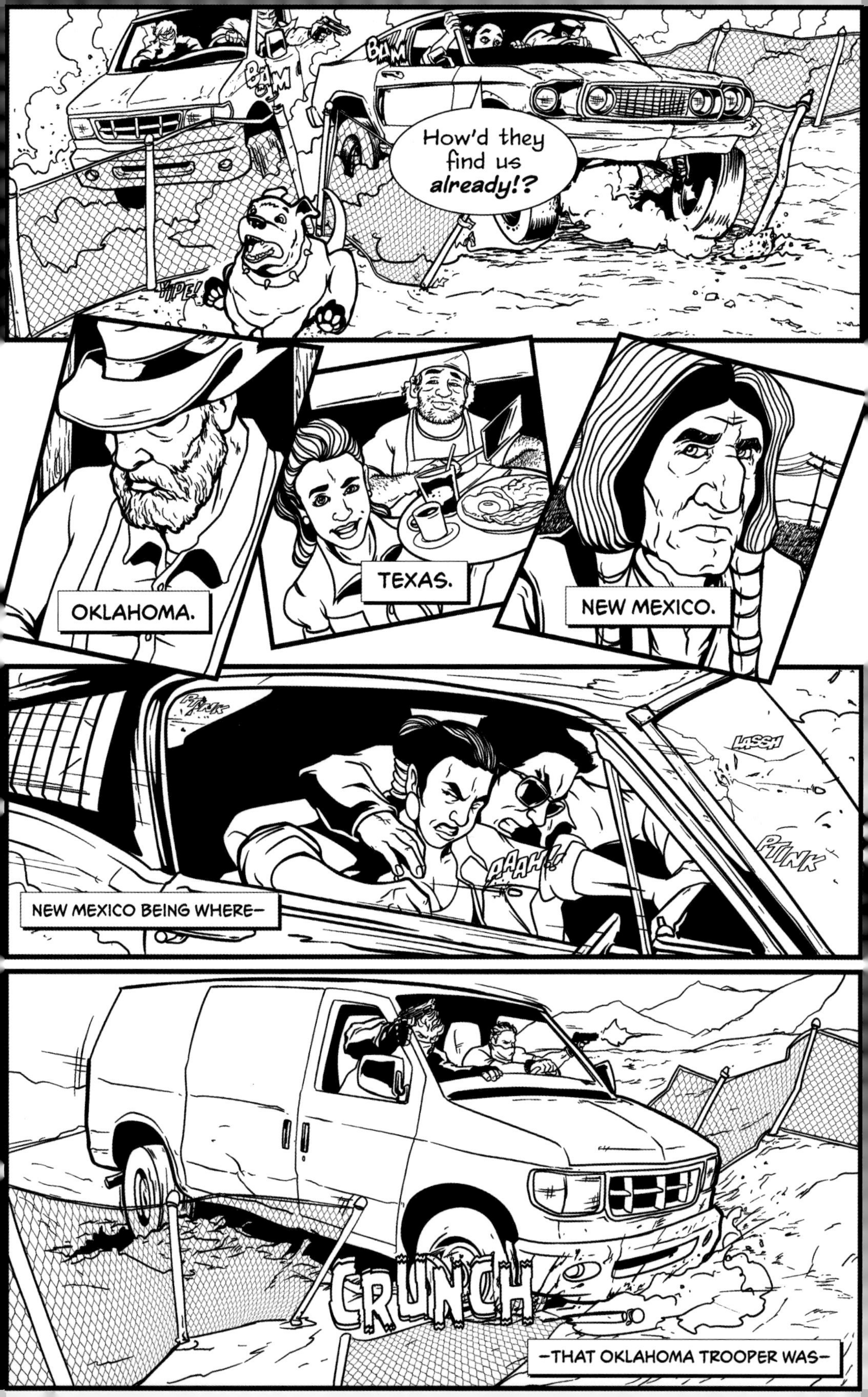
BAM
BAM
How'd they find us *already!?*
YIPE!
OKLAHOMA.
TEXAS.
NEW MEXICO.
AAAH!!
PTINK
NEW MEXICO BEING WHERE—
CRUNCH
—THAT OKLAHOMA TROOPER WAS—

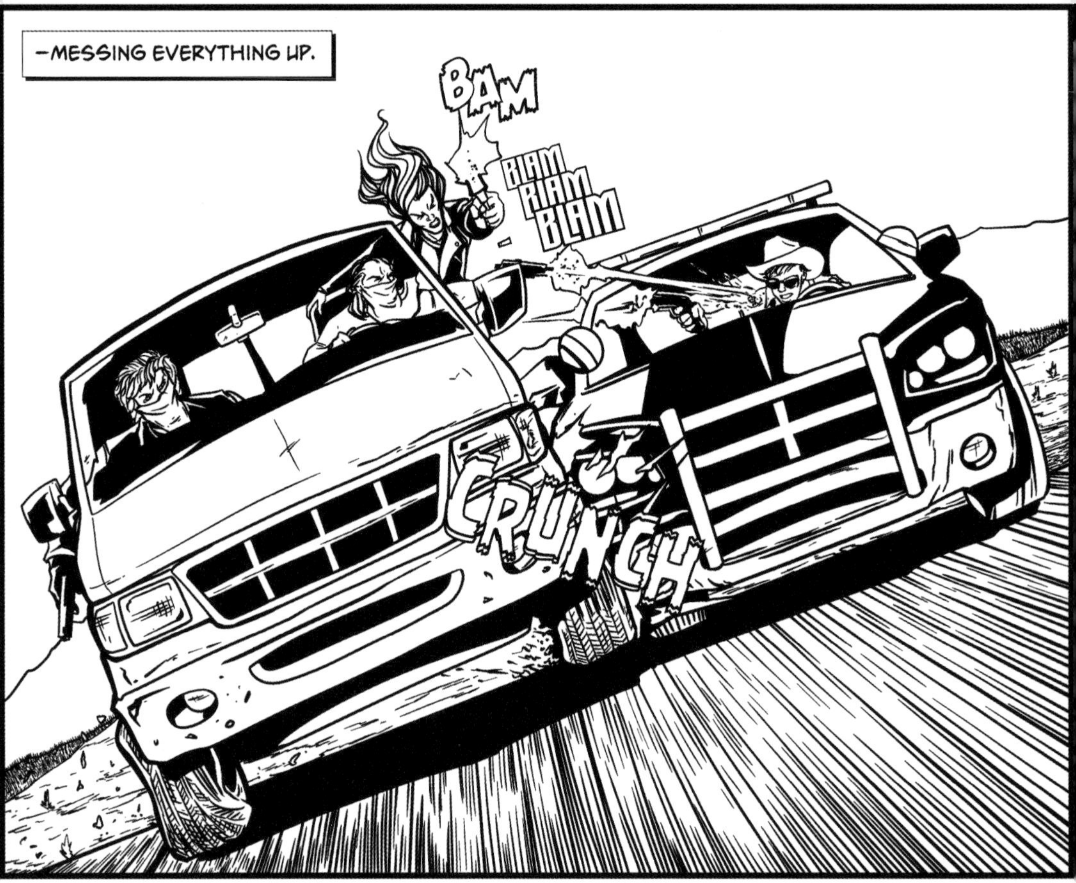
—MESSING EVERYTHING UP.
BAM
BLAM BLAM BLAM
CRUNCH
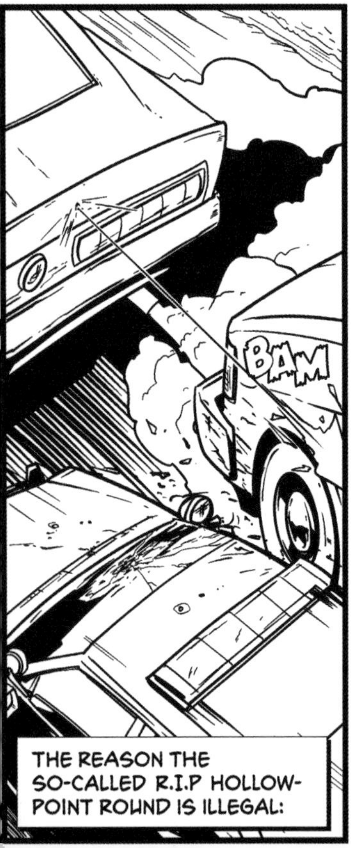
BAM
THE REASON THE SO-CALLED R.I.P HOLLOW-POINT ROUND IS ILLEGAL:
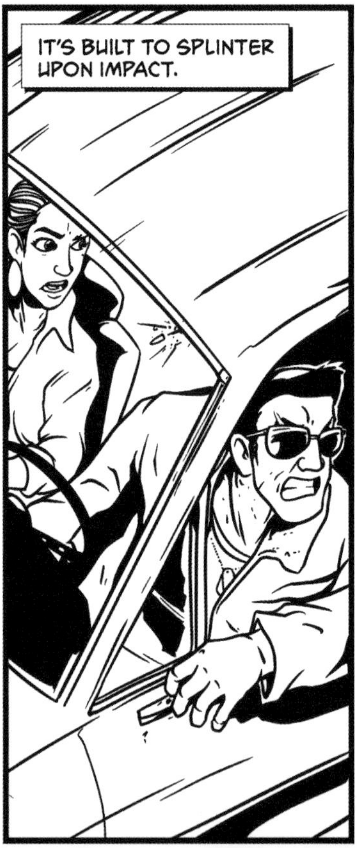
IT'S BUILT TO SPLINTER UPON IMPACT.
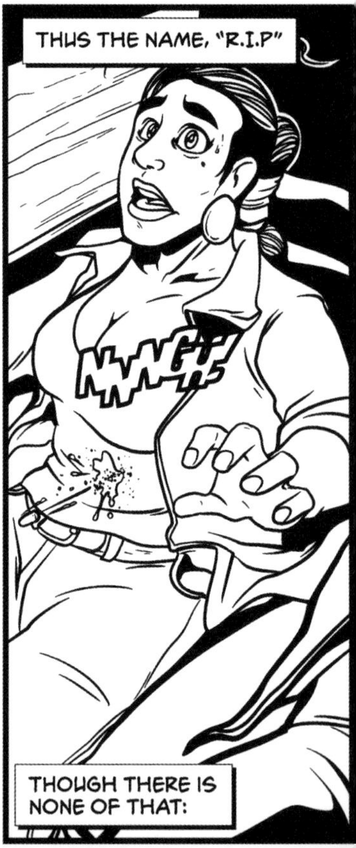
THUS THE NAME, "R.I.P"
NNNGH!
THOUGH THERE IS NONE OF THAT:

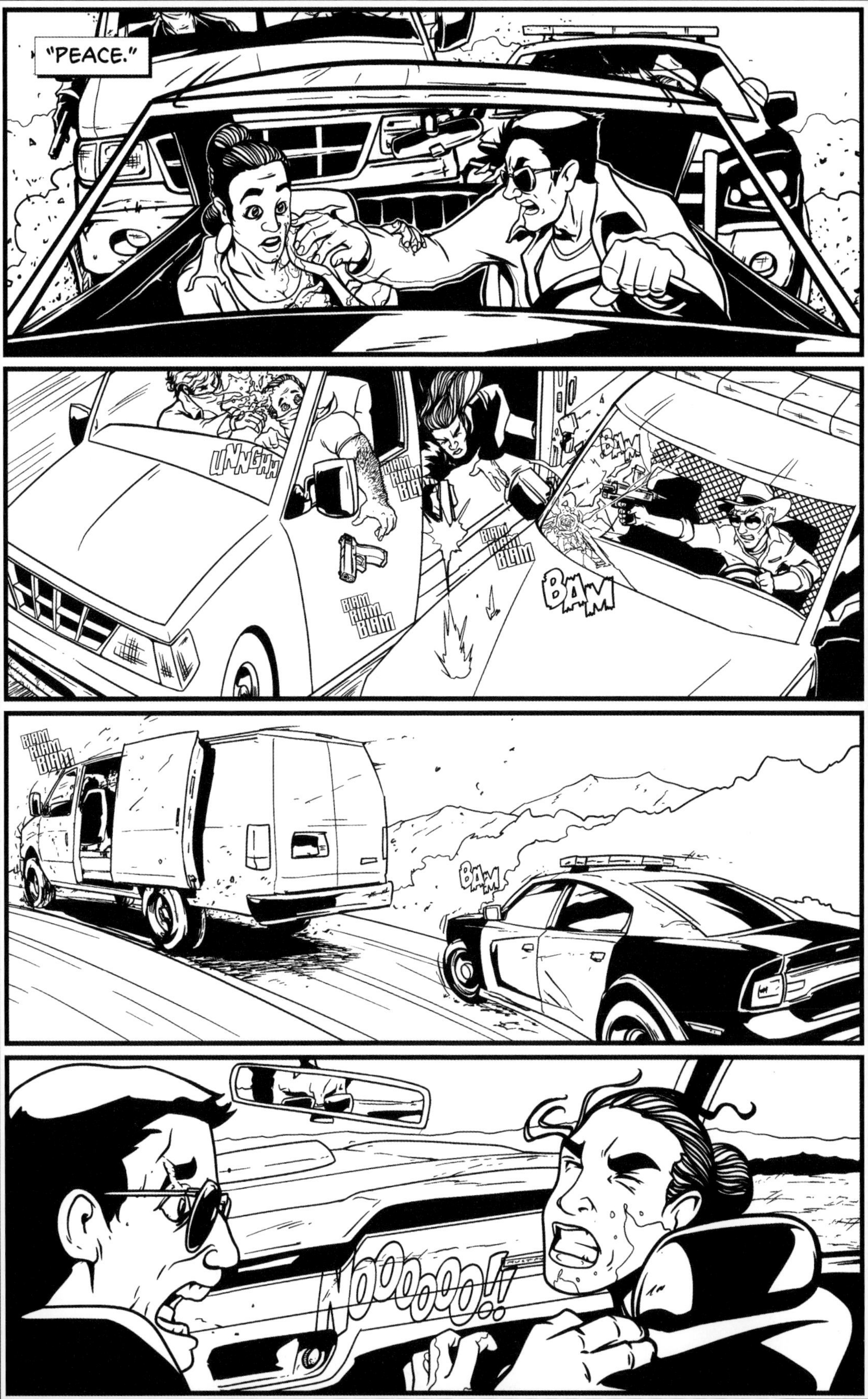
"PEACE."
UNNGHH
BLAM BLAM BLAM
BAM
BLAM BLAM BLAM
BLAM BLAM BLAM
BAM
BLAM BLAM BLAM
BAM
NOOOOOOO!!

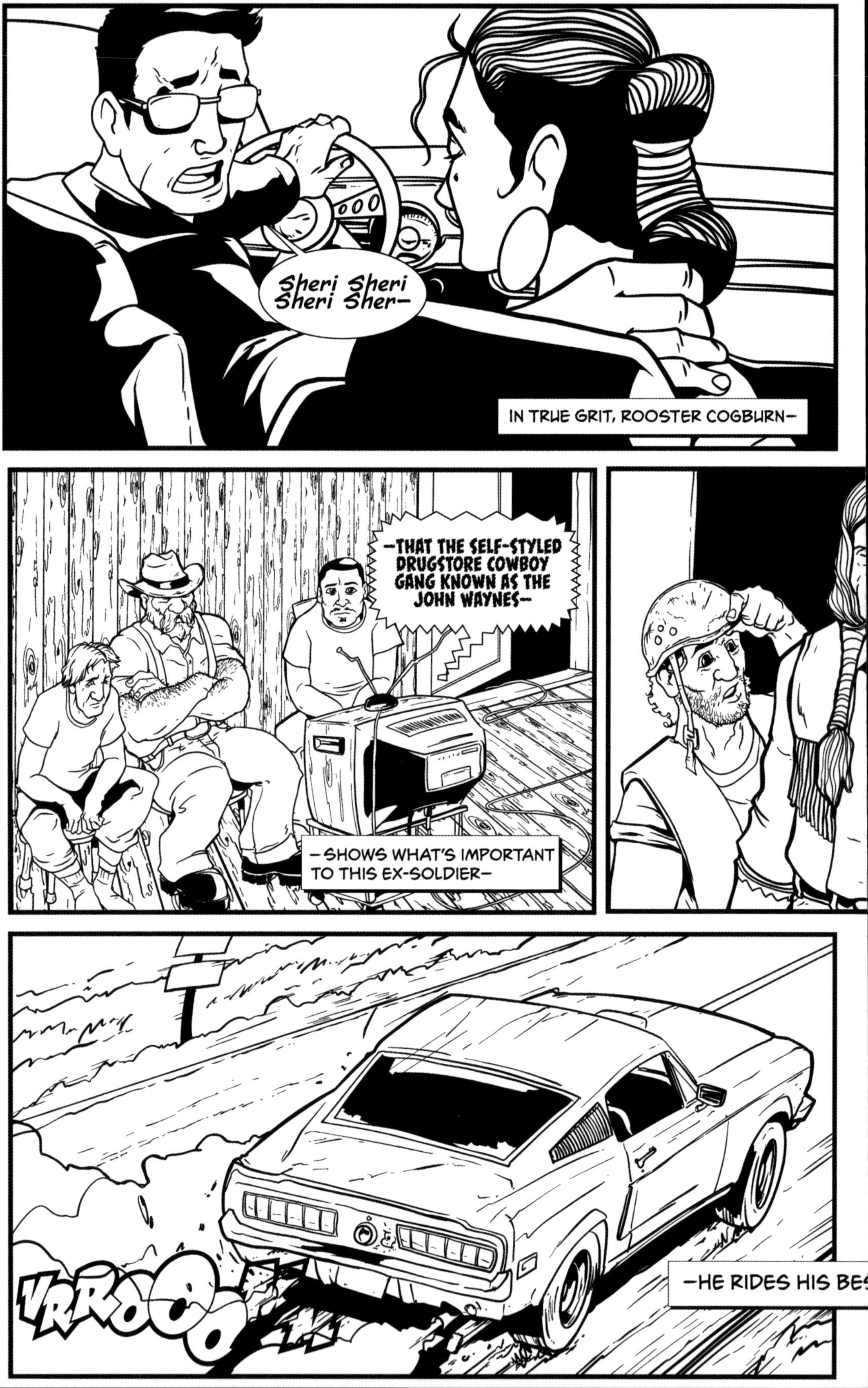
Sheri Sheri Sheri Sher—
IN TRUE GRIT, ROOSTER COGBURN—
—THAT THE SELF-STYLED DRUGSTORE COWBOY GANG KNOWN AS THE JOHN WAYNES—
—SHOWS WHAT'S IMPORTANT TO THIS EX-SOLDIER—
VRROOOO
—HE RIDES HIS BES

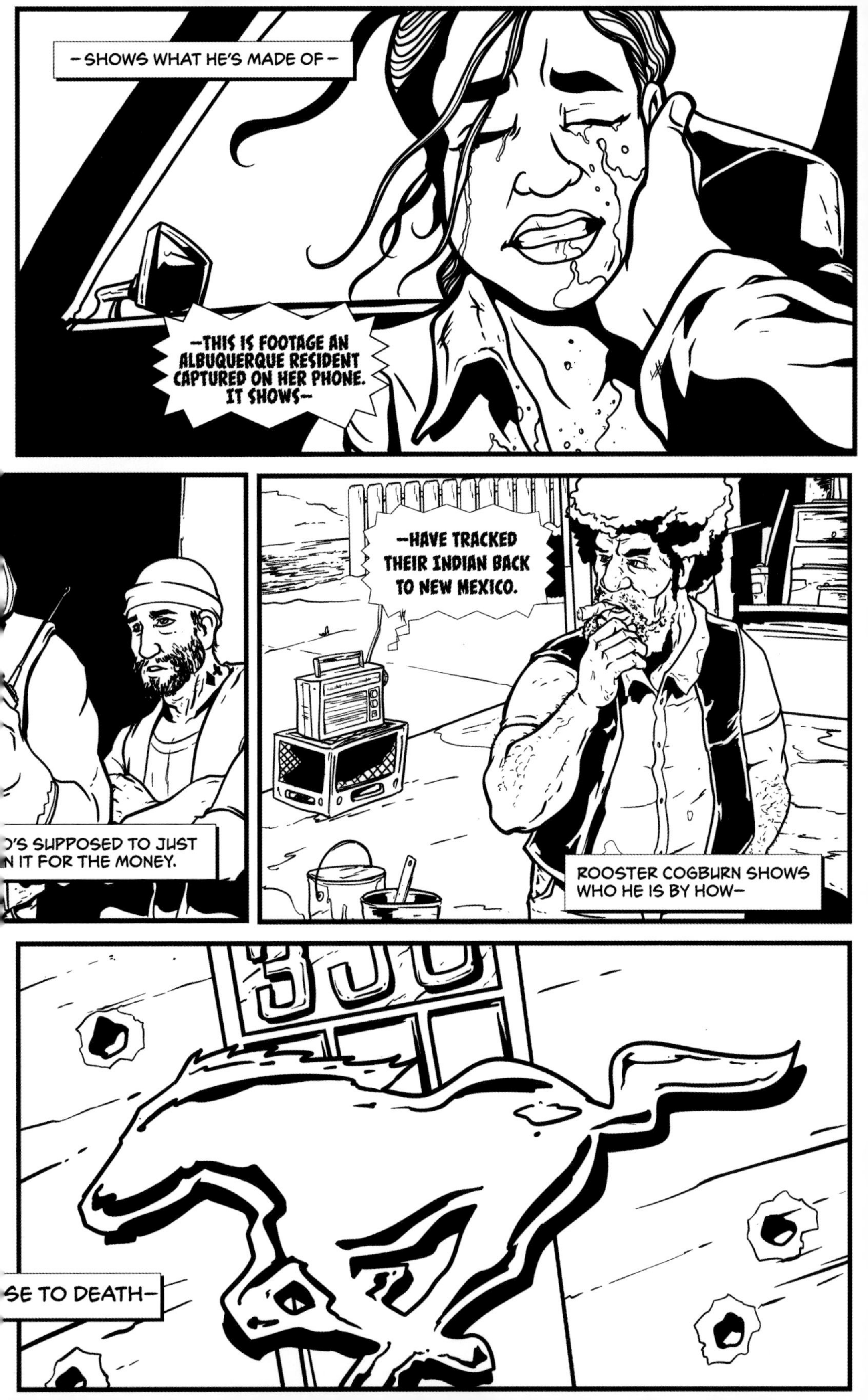
—SHOWS WHAT HE'S MADE OF—
—THIS IS FOOTAGE AN ALBUQUERQUE RESIDENT CAPTURED ON HER PHONE. IT SHOWS—
'S SUPPOSED TO JUST IT FOR THE MONEY.
—HAVE TRACKED THEIR INDIAN BACK TO NEW MEXICO.
ROOSTER COGBURN SHOWS WHO HE IS BY HOW—
SE TO DEATH—

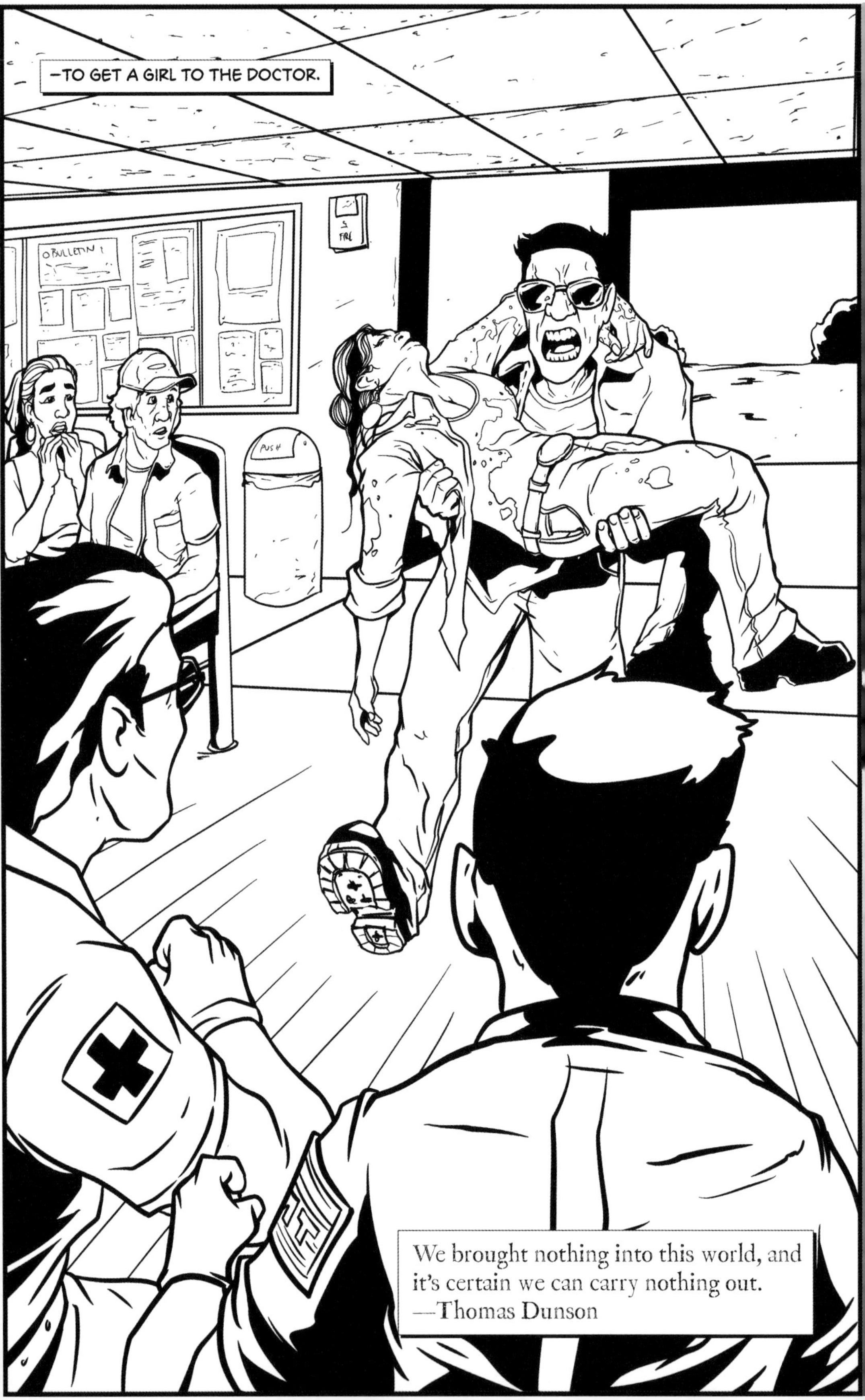
—TO GET A GIRL TO THE DOCTOR.
PUSH
We brought nothing into this world, and it's certain we can carry nothing out.
—Thomas Dunson

PART THREE

THE END OF THE TRAIL STARTS HERE.

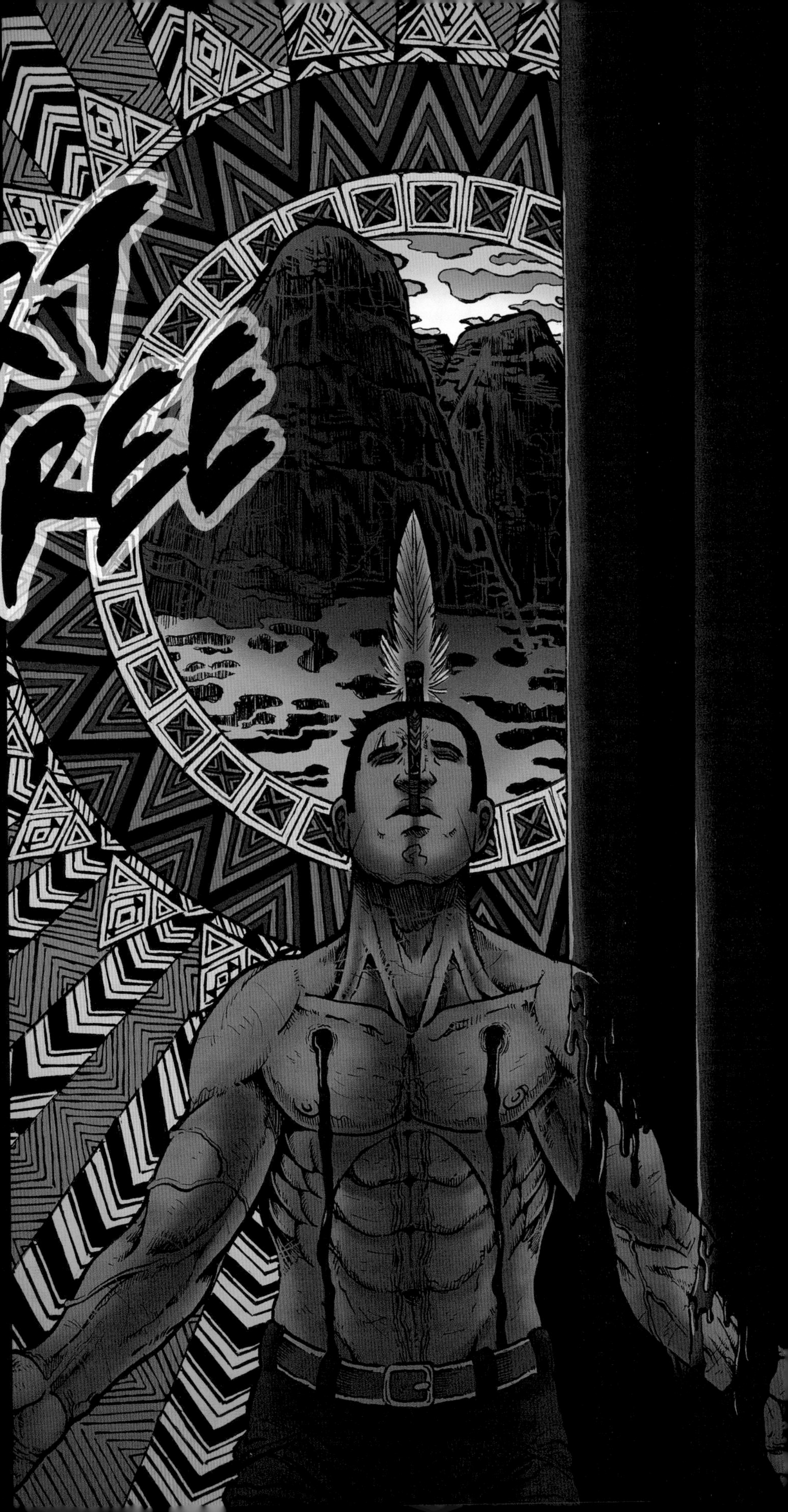

Home from the war for his estranged father's funeral, Cooper Town and his girlfriend Sheri Mun stumbled into a drugstore heist the John Waynes were pulling off, and, in trying to outrun them, Sheri Mun ended up shot, and is now in her third hour of surgery:

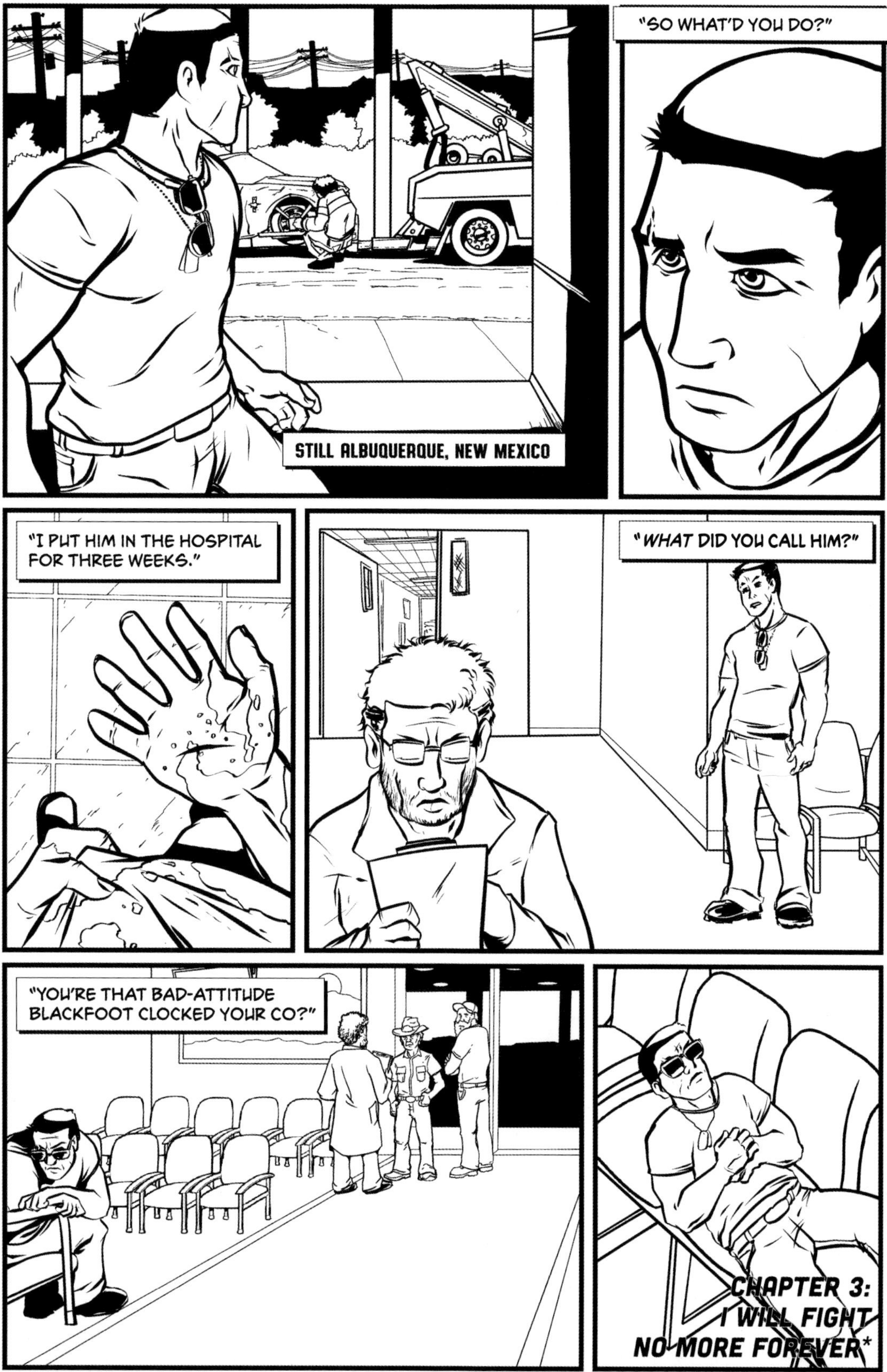
STILL ALBUQUERQUE, NEW MEXICO
"SO WHAT'D YOU DO?"
"I PUT HIM IN THE HOSPITAL FOR THREE WEEKS."
"*WHAT* DID YOU CALL HIM?"
"YOU'RE THAT BAD-ATTITUDE BLACKFOOT CLOCKED YOUR CO?"
CHAPTER 3:
I WILL FIGHT NO MORE FOREVER*

* UNLESS SHE DOESN'T MAKE IT

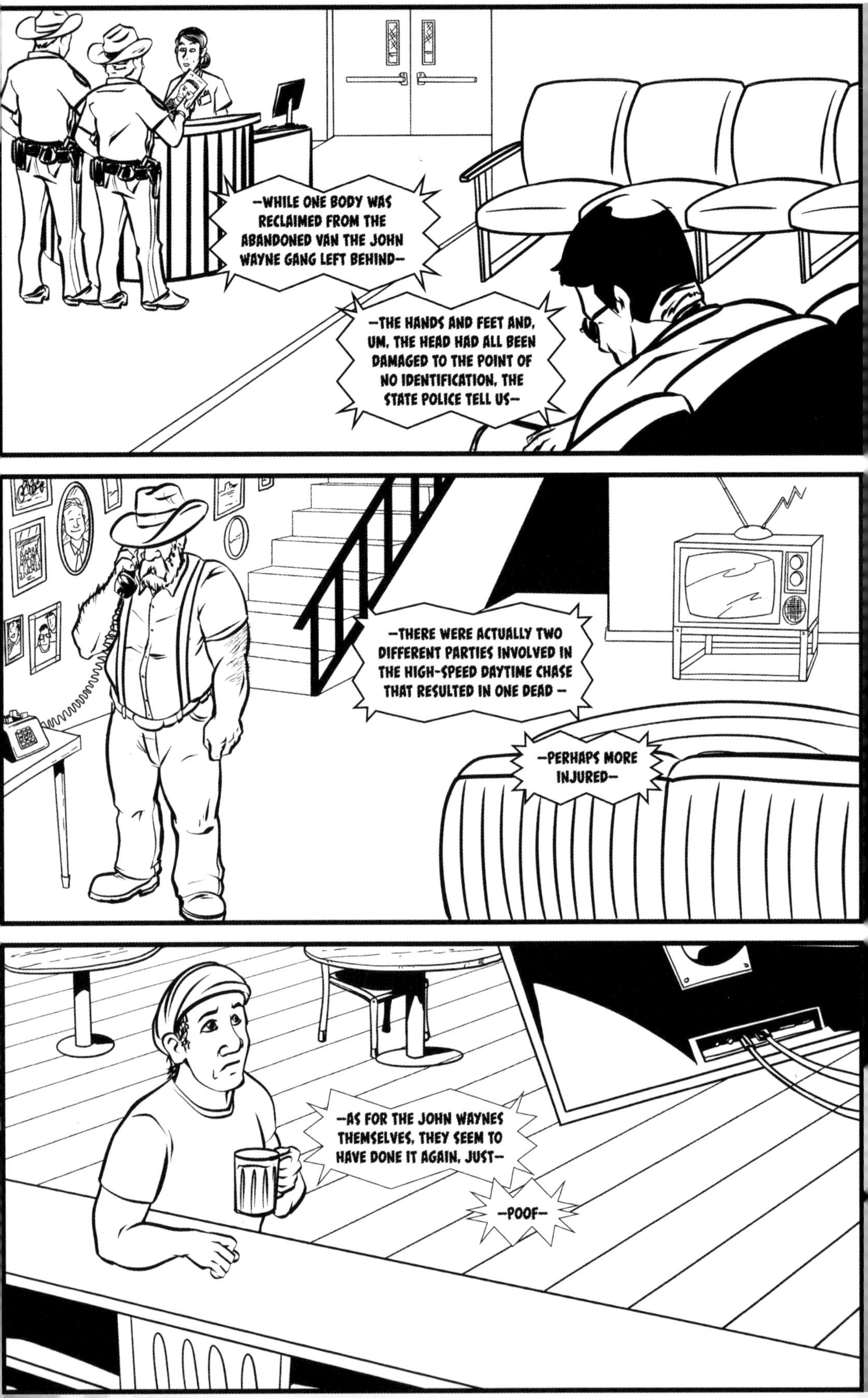
—WHILE ONE BODY WAS RECLAIMED FROM THE ABANDONED VAN THE JOHN WAYNE GANG LEFT BEHIND—
—THE HANDS AND FEET AND, UM, THE HEAD HAD ALL BEEN DAMAGED TO THE POINT OF NO IDENTIFICATION, THE STATE POLICE TELL US—
—THERE WERE ACTUALLY TWO DIFFERENT PARTIES INVOLVED IN THE HIGH-SPEED DAYTIME CHASE THAT RESULTED IN ONE DEAD —
—PERHAPS MORE INJURED—
—AS FOR THE JOHN WAYNES THEMSELVES, THEY SEEM TO HAVE DONE IT AGAIN, JUST—
—POOF—

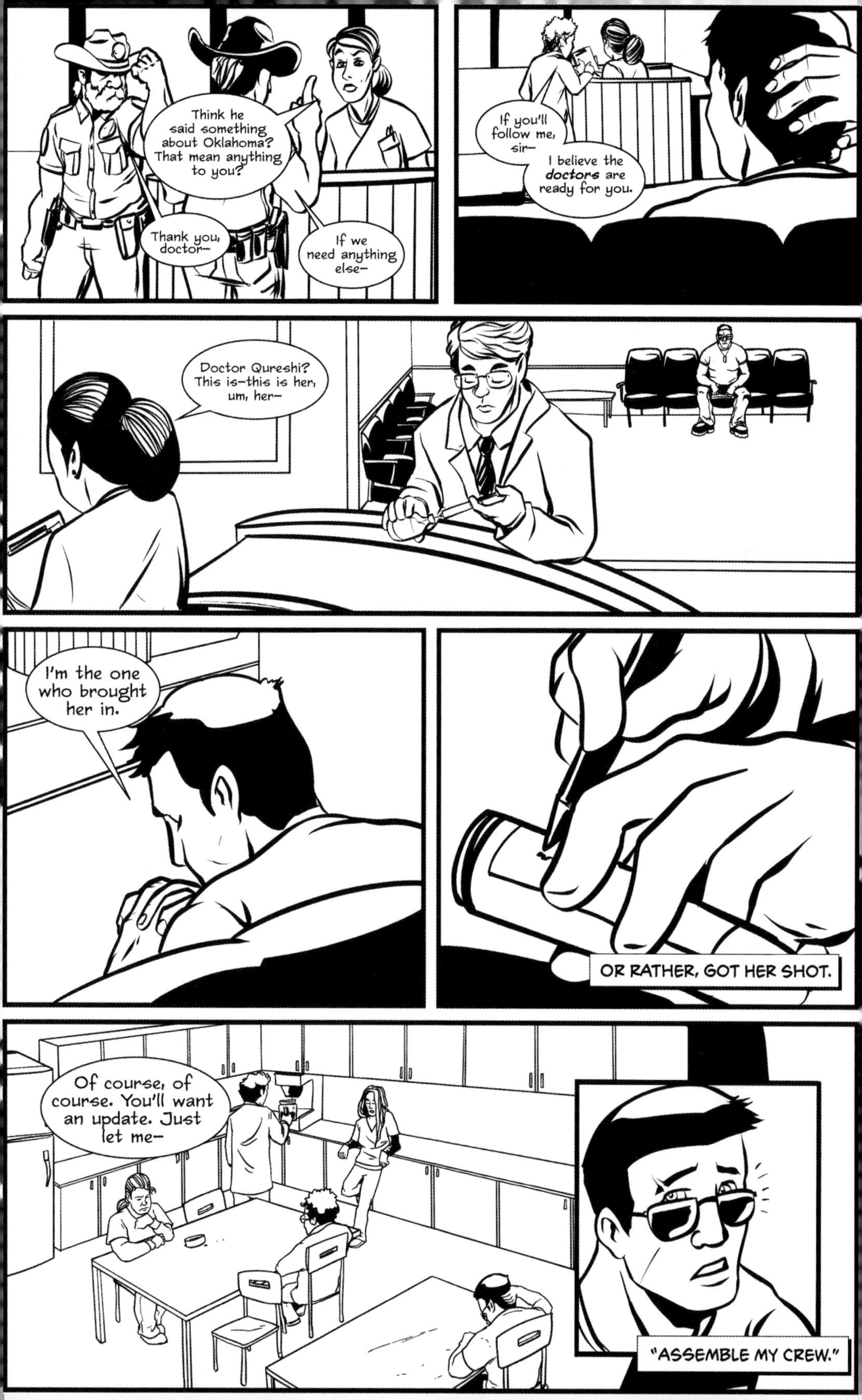
Think he said something about Oklahoma? That mean anything to you?
Thank you, doctor—
If we need anything else—
If you'll follow me, sir—
I believe the ***doctors*** are ready for you.
Doctor Qureshi? This is—this is her, um, her—
I'm the one who brought her in.
OR RATHER, GOT HER SHOT.
Of course, of course. You'll want an update. Just let me—
"ASSEMBLE MY CREW."

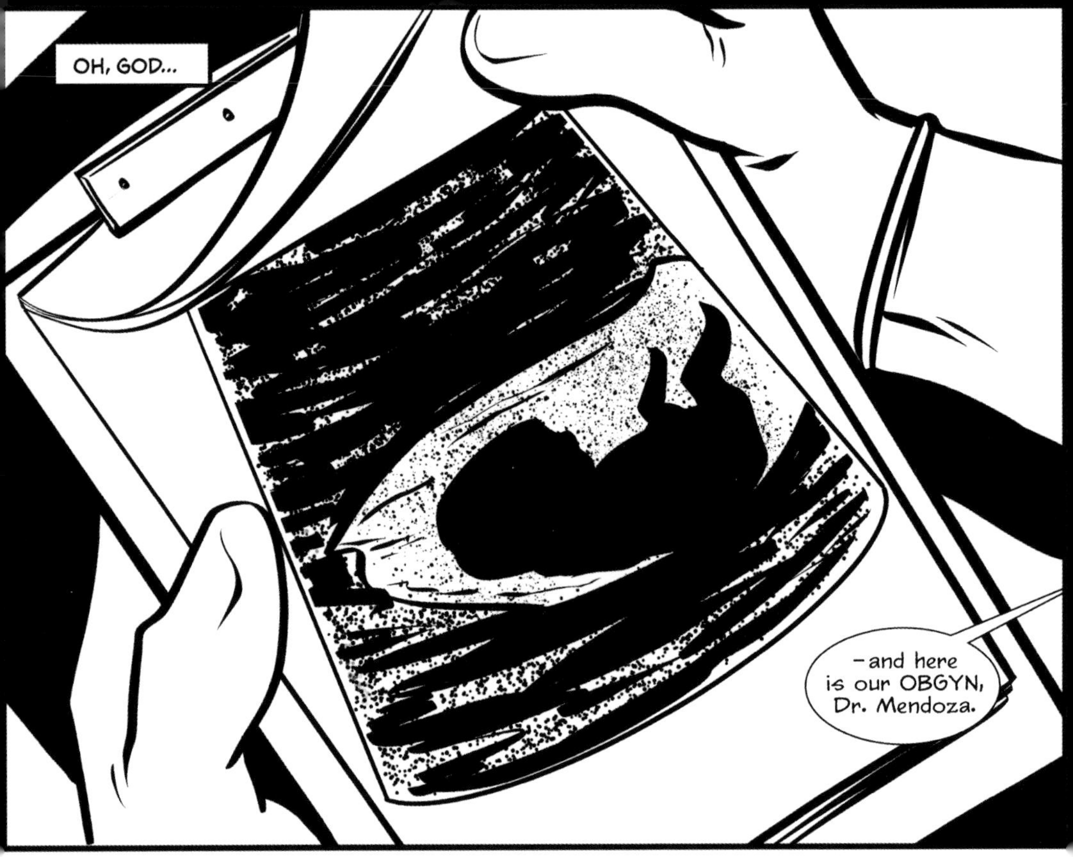
OH, GOD...
-and here is our OBGYN, Dr. Mendoza.

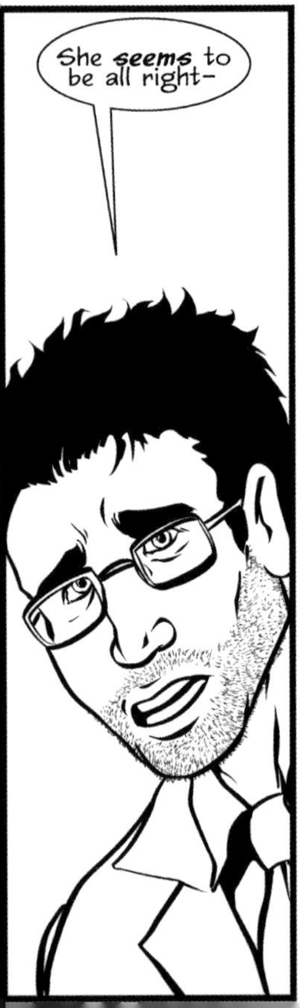
She *seems* to be all right-

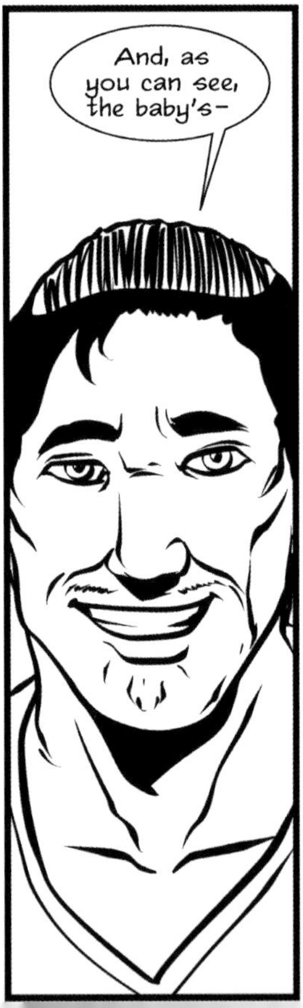
And, as you can see, the baby's-

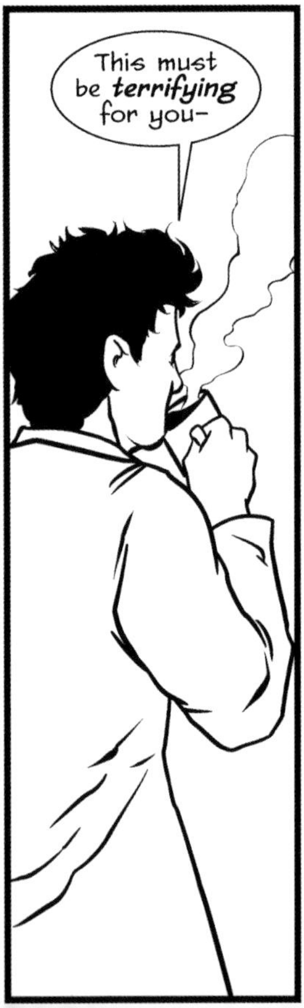
This must be *terrifying* for you-

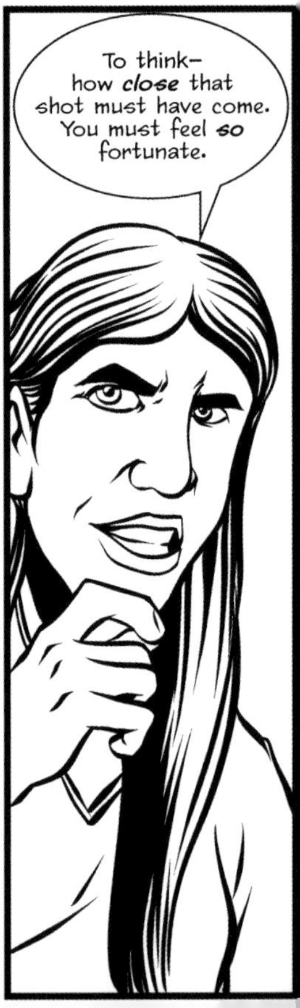
To think- how *close* that shot must have come. You must feel *so* fortunate.

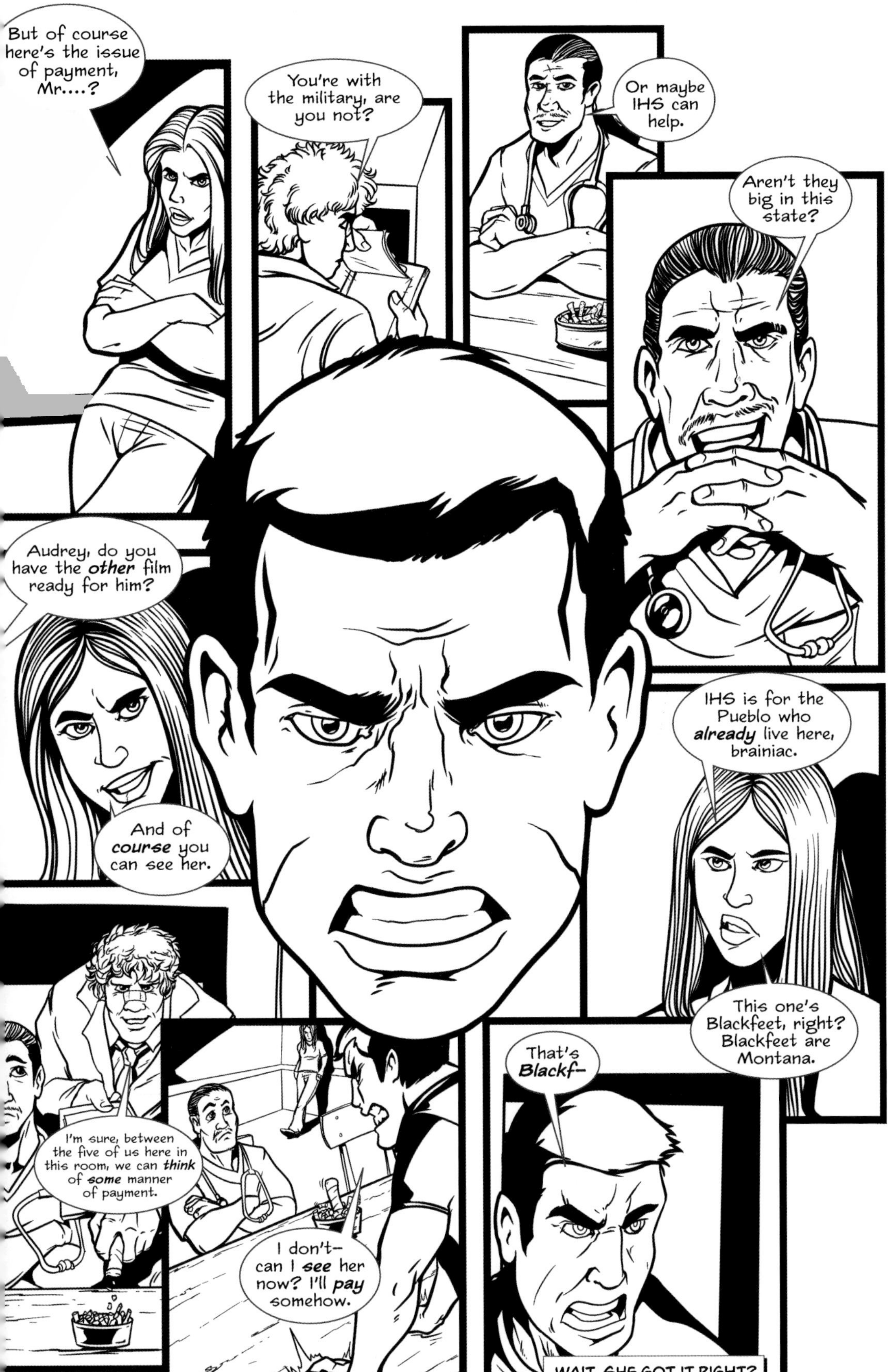

But of course here's the issue of payment, Mr....?
You're with the military, are you not?
Or maybe IHS can help.
Aren't they big in this state?
Audrey, do you have the *other* film ready for him?
And of *course* you can see her.
IHS is for the Pueblo who *already* live here, brainiac.
This one's Blackfeet, right? Blackfeet are Montana.
I'm sure, between the five of us here in this room, we can *think* of *some* manner of payment.
I don't— can I *see* her now? I'll *pay* somehow.
That's *Blackf—*
WAIT. SHE GOT IT RIGHT?

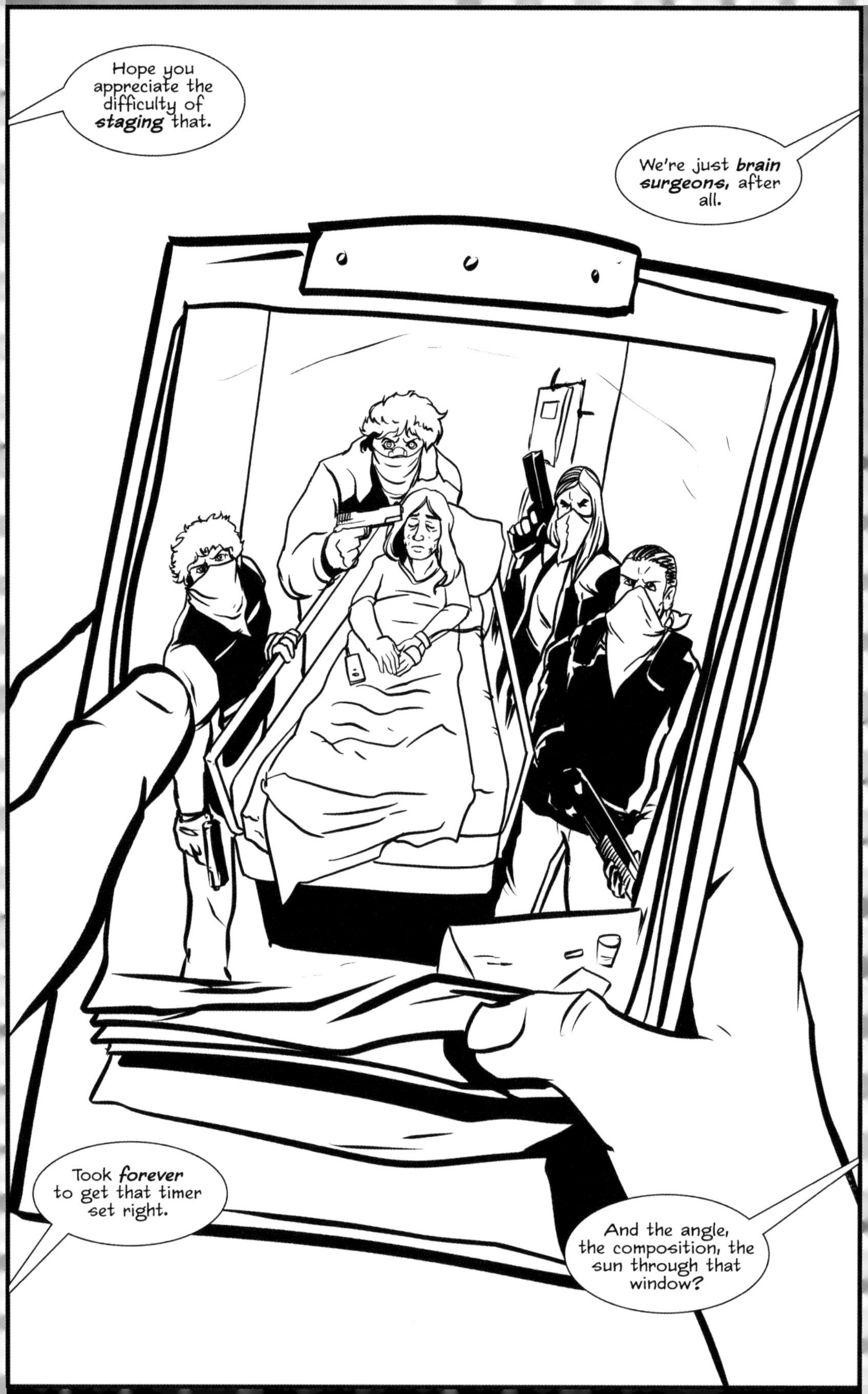
Hope you appreciate the difficulty of **staging** that.
We're just **brain surgeons,** after all.
Took **forever** to get that timer set right.
And the angle, the composition, the sun through that window?

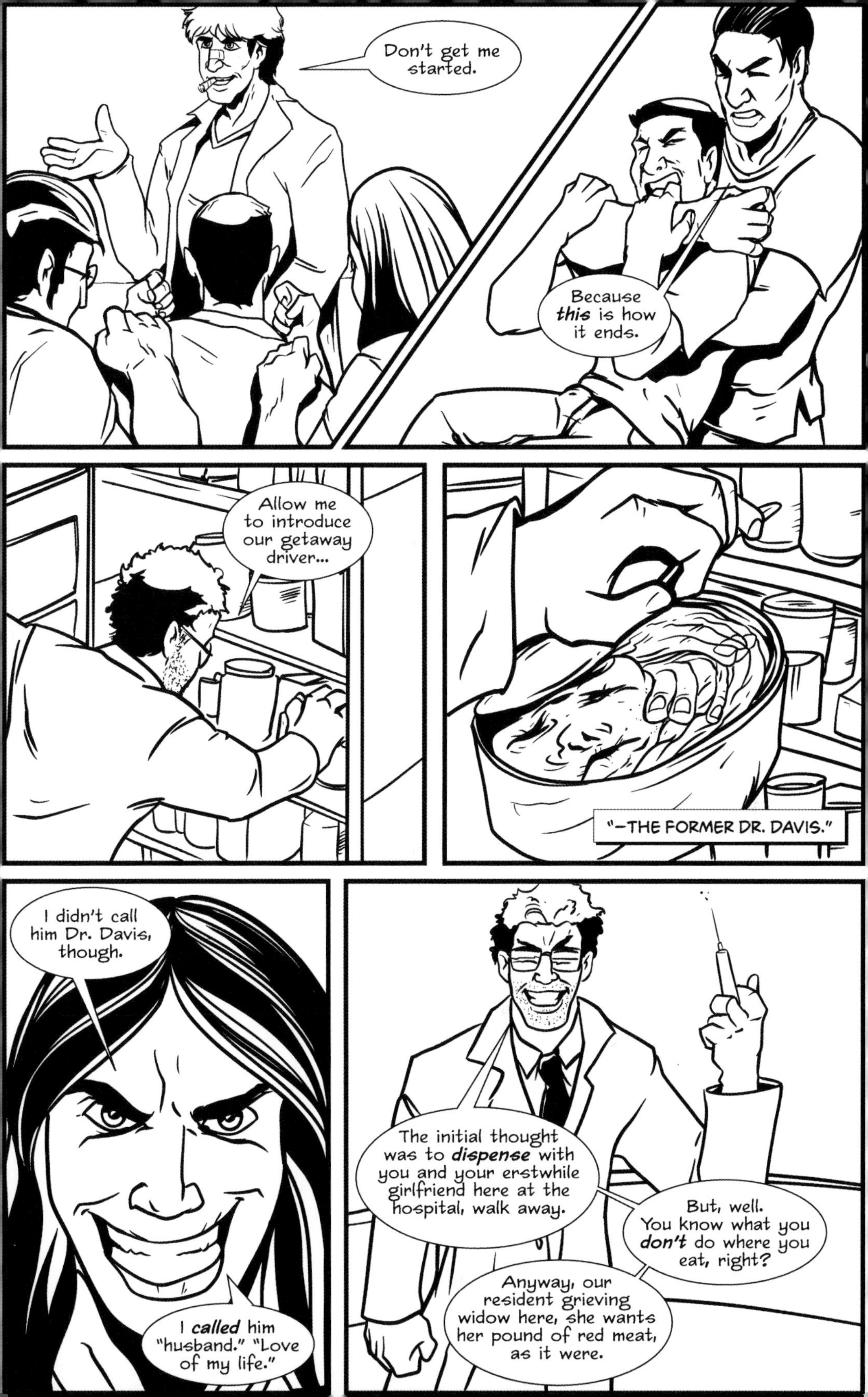

Don't get me started.
Because *this* is how it ends.
Allow me to introduce our getaway driver...
"—THE FORMER DR. DAVIS."
I didn't call him Dr. Davis, though.
I *called* him "husband." "Love of my life."
The initial thought was to *dispense* with you and your erstwhile girlfriend here at the hospital, walk away.
But, well. You know what you *don't* do where you eat, right?
Anyway, our resident grieving widow here, she wants her pound of red meat, as it were.

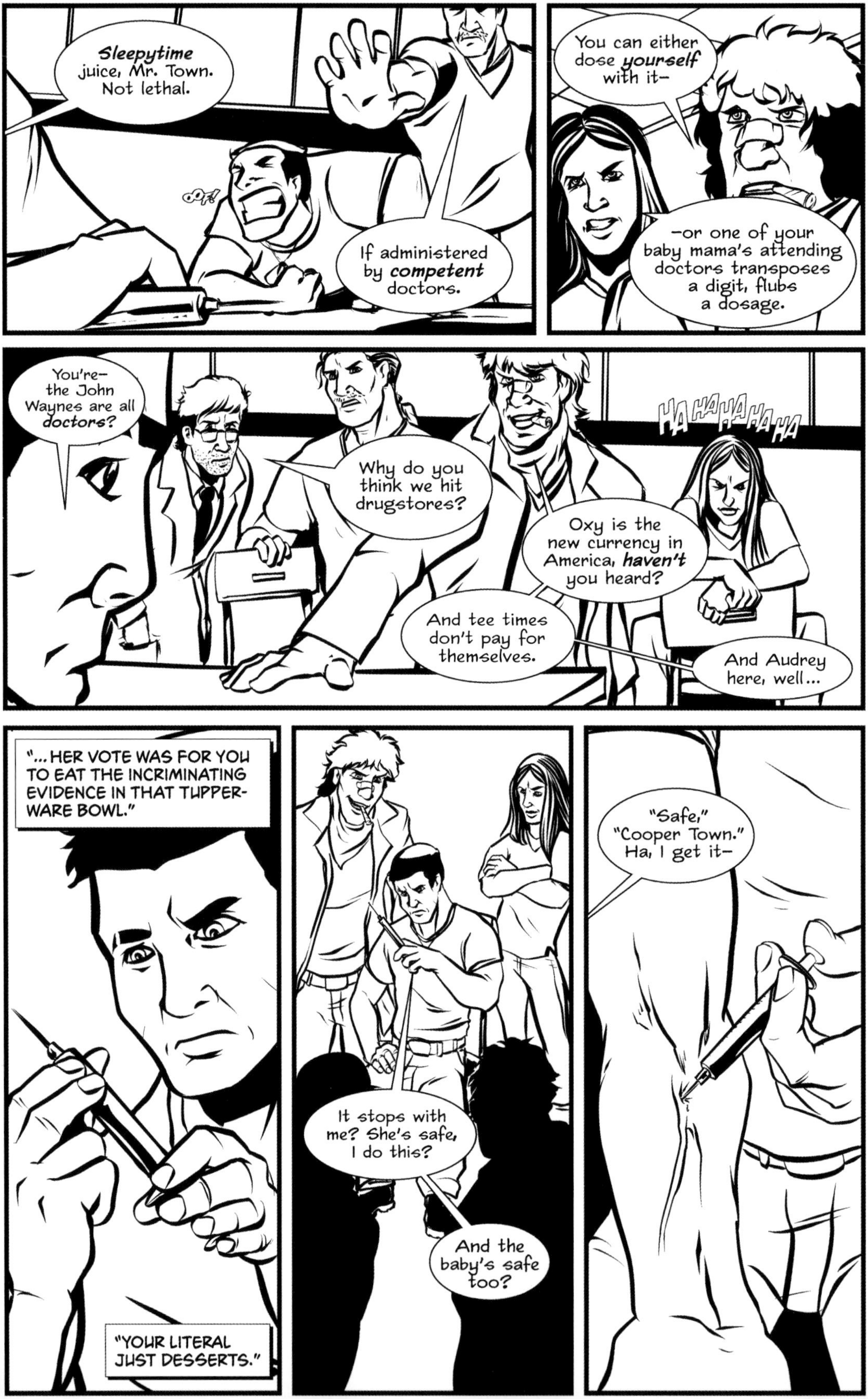
Sleepytime juice, Mr. Town. Not lethal.
OOF!
If administered by competent doctors.
You can either dose yourself with it–
–or one of your baby mama's attending doctors transposes a digit, flubs a dosage.
You're– the John Waynes are all doctors?
Why do you think we hit drugstores?
HA HA HA HA HA
Oxy is the new currency in America, haven't you heard?
And tee times don't pay for themselves.
And Audrey here, well...
"...HER VOTE WAS FOR YOU TO EAT THE INCRIMINATING EVIDENCE IN THAT TUPPERWARE BOWL."
"YOUR LITERAL JUST DESSERTS."
It stops with me? She's safe, I do this?
And the baby's safe too?
"Safe," "Cooper Town." Ha, I get it–

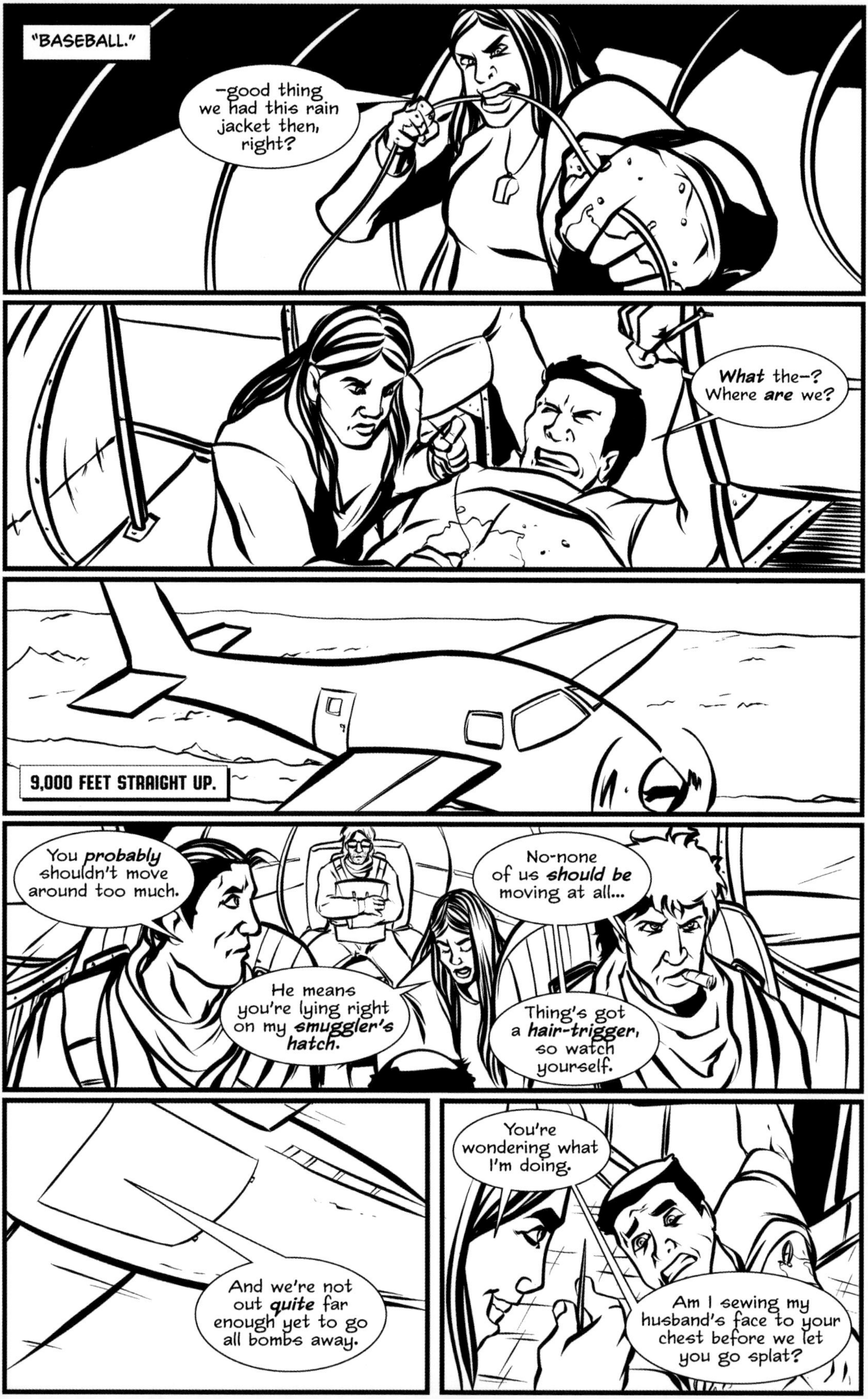
"BASEBALL."
–good thing we had this rain jacket then, right?
What the–? Where are we?
9,000 FEET STRAIGHT UP.
You probably shouldn't move around too much.
He means you're lying right on my smuggler's hatch.
No-none of us should be moving at all...
Thing's got a hair-trigger, so watch yourself.
And we're not out quite far enough yet to go all bombs away.
You're wondering what I'm doing.
Am I sewing my husband's face to your chest before we let you go splat?

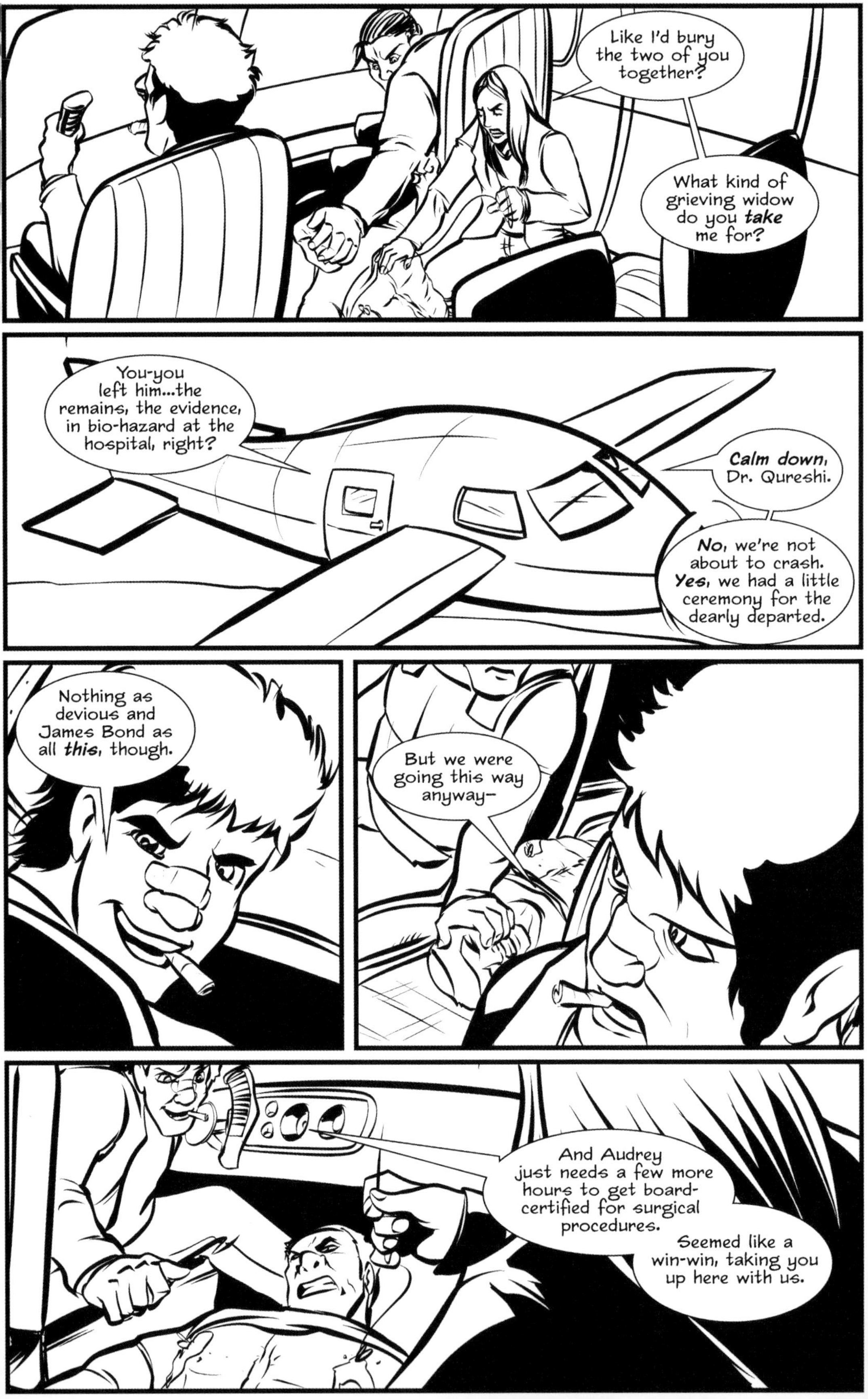

Like I'd bury the two of you together?
What kind of grieving widow do you *take* me for?
You-you left him...the remains, the evidence, in bio-hazard at the hospital, right?
Calm down, Dr. Qureshi.
No, we're not about to crash. *Yes*, we had a little ceremony for the dearly departed.
Nothing as devious and James Bond as all *this*, though.
But we were going this way anyway-
And Audrey just needs a few more hours to get board-certified for surgical procedures.
Seemed like a win-win, taking you up here with us.

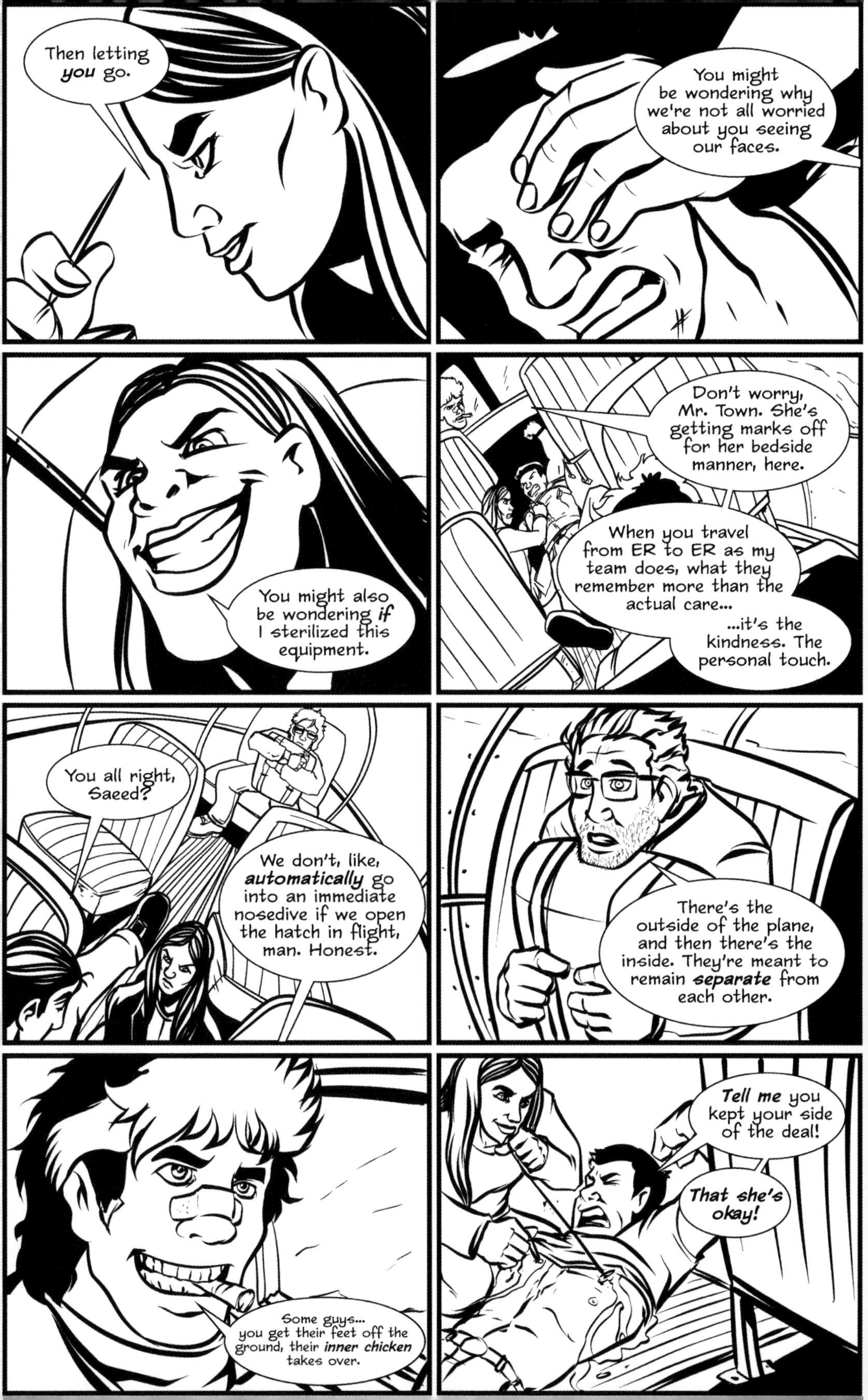
Then letting *you* go.
You might be wondering why we're not all worried about you seeing our faces.
You might also be wondering *if* I sterilized this equipment.
Don't worry, Mr. Town. She's getting marks off for her bedside manner, here.
When you travel from ER to ER as my team does, what they remember more than the actual care...
...it's the kindness. The personal touch.
You all right, Saeed?
We don't, like, ***automatically*** go into an immediate nosedive if we open the hatch in flight, man. Honest.
There's the outside of the plane, and then there's the inside. They're meant to remain ***separate*** from each other.
Some guys... you get their feet off the ground, their ***inner chicken*** takes over.
Tell me you kept your side of the deal!
That she's okay!

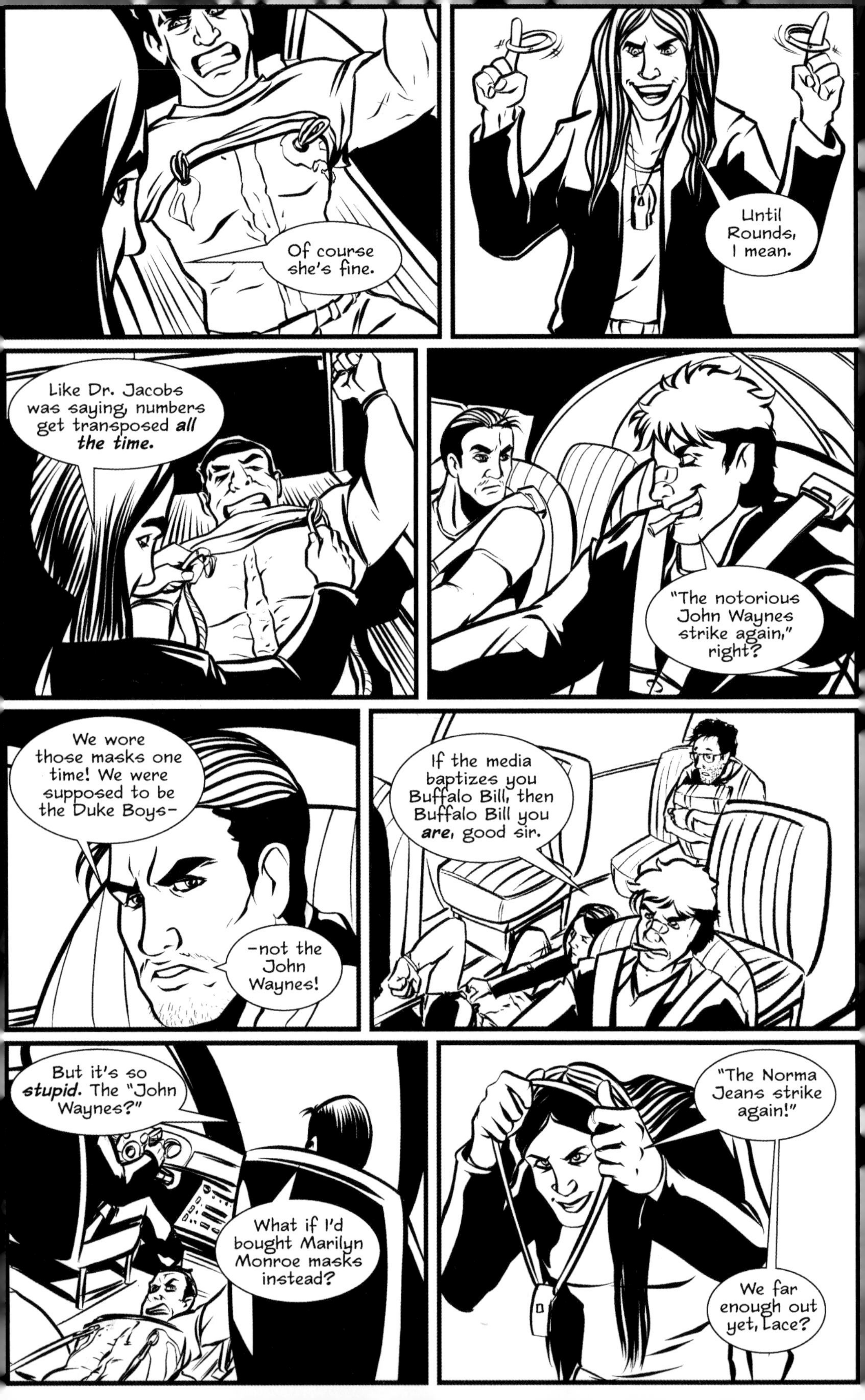
Of course she's fine.
Until Rounds, I mean.
Like Dr. Jacobs was saying, numbers get transposed ***all the time.***
"The notorious John Waynes strike again," right?
We wore those masks one time! We were supposed to be the Duke Boys-
-not the John Waynes!
If the media baptizes you Buffalo Bill, then Buffalo Bill you ***are***, good sir.
But it's so ***stupid***. The "John Waynes?"
What if I'd bought Marilyn Monroe masks instead?
"The Norma Jeans strike again!"
We far enough out yet, Lace?

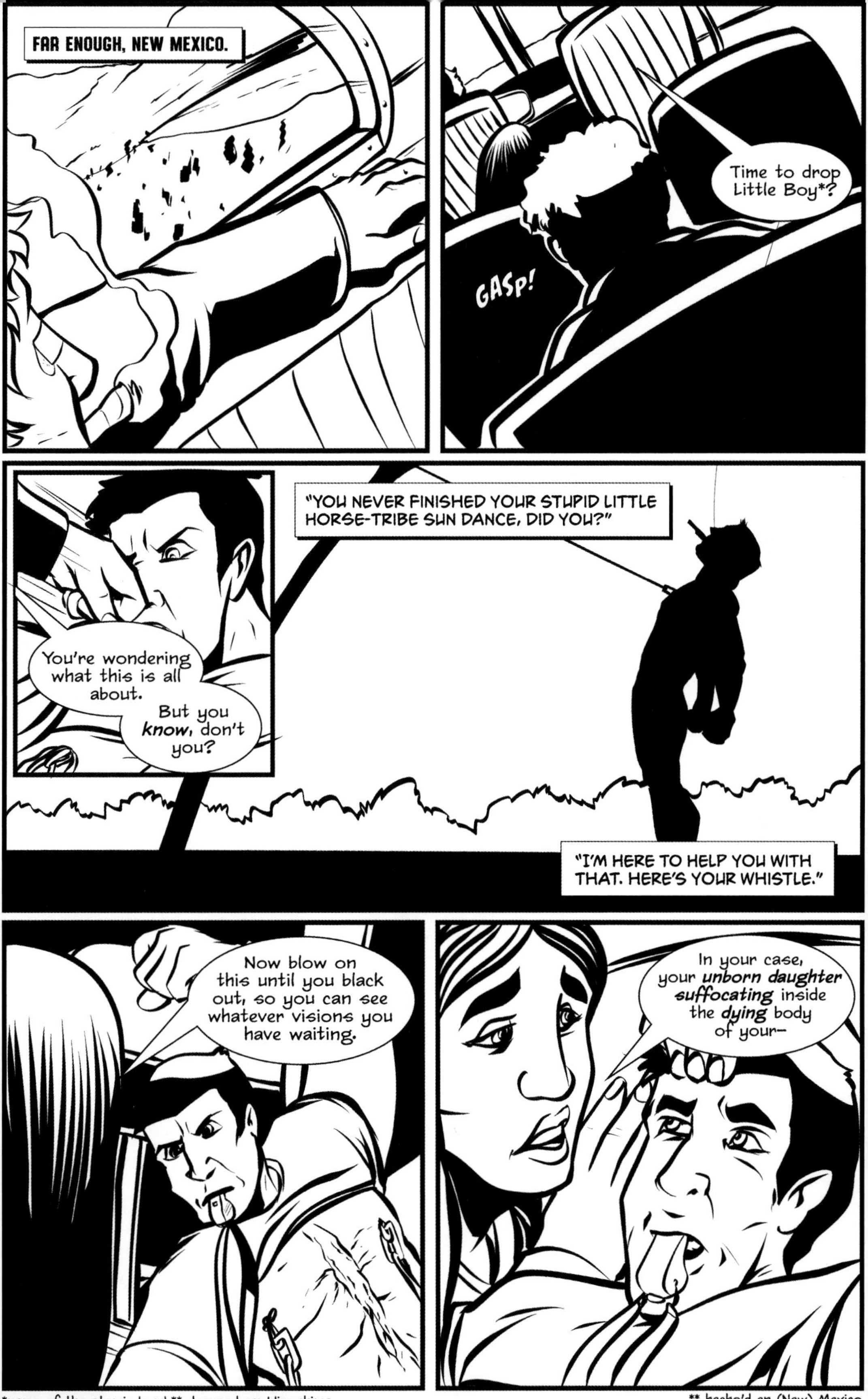
FAR ENOUGH, NEW MEXICO.
Time to drop Little Boy*?
GASP!
"YOU NEVER FINISHED YOUR STUPID LITTLE HORSE-TRIBE SUN DANCE, DID YOU?"
You're wondering what this is all about.
But you *know*, don't you?
"I'M HERE TO HELP YOU WITH THAT. HERE'S YOUR WHISTLE."
Now blow on this until you black out, so you can see whatever visions you have waiting.
In your case, your ***unborn daughter suffocating*** inside the ***dying*** body of your–

*name of the atomic bomb** dropped on Hiroshima

** hecho'd en (New) Mexico

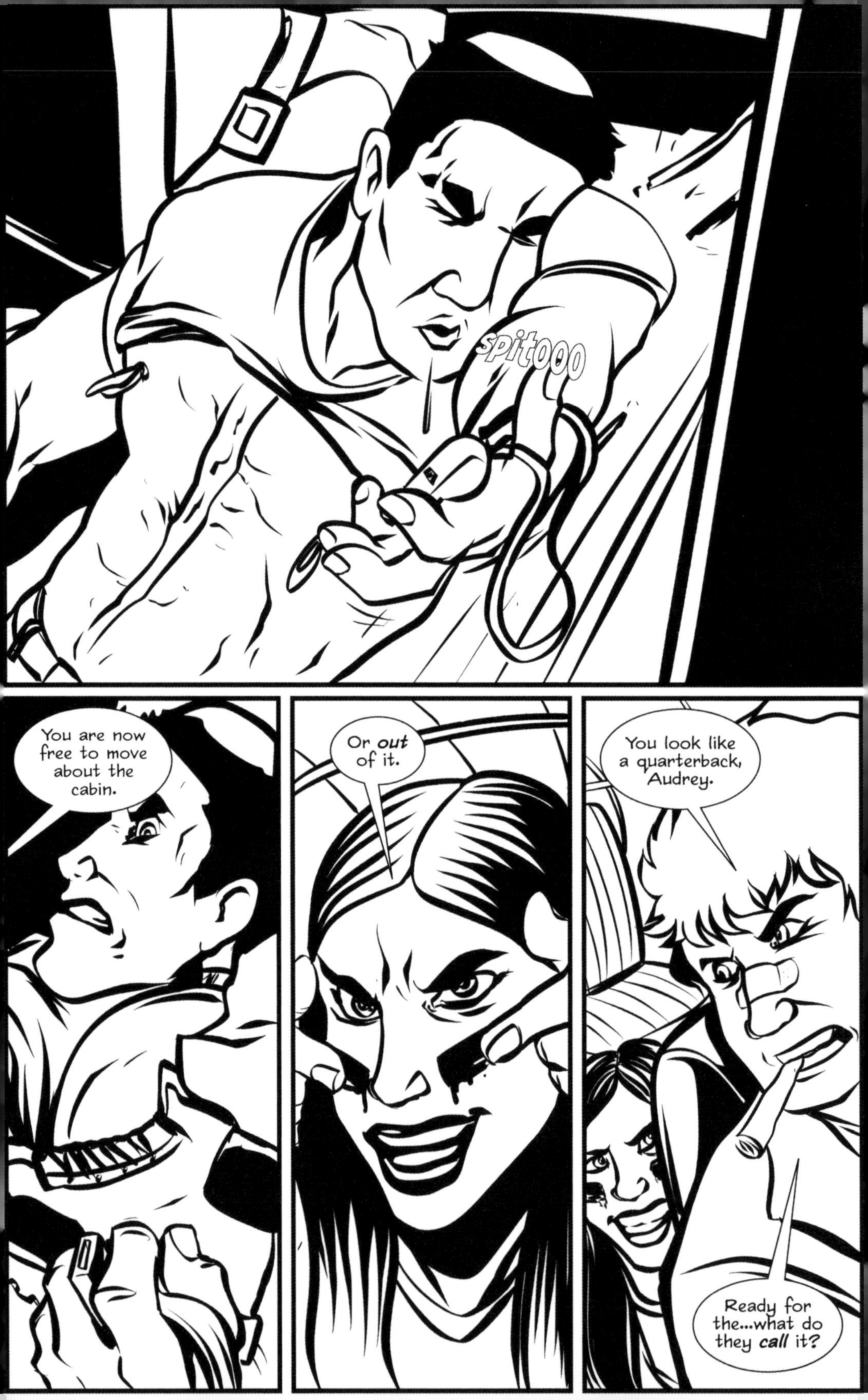
spitooo
You are now free to move about the cabin.
Or **out** of it.
You look like a quarterback, Audrey.
Ready for the...what do they **call** it?

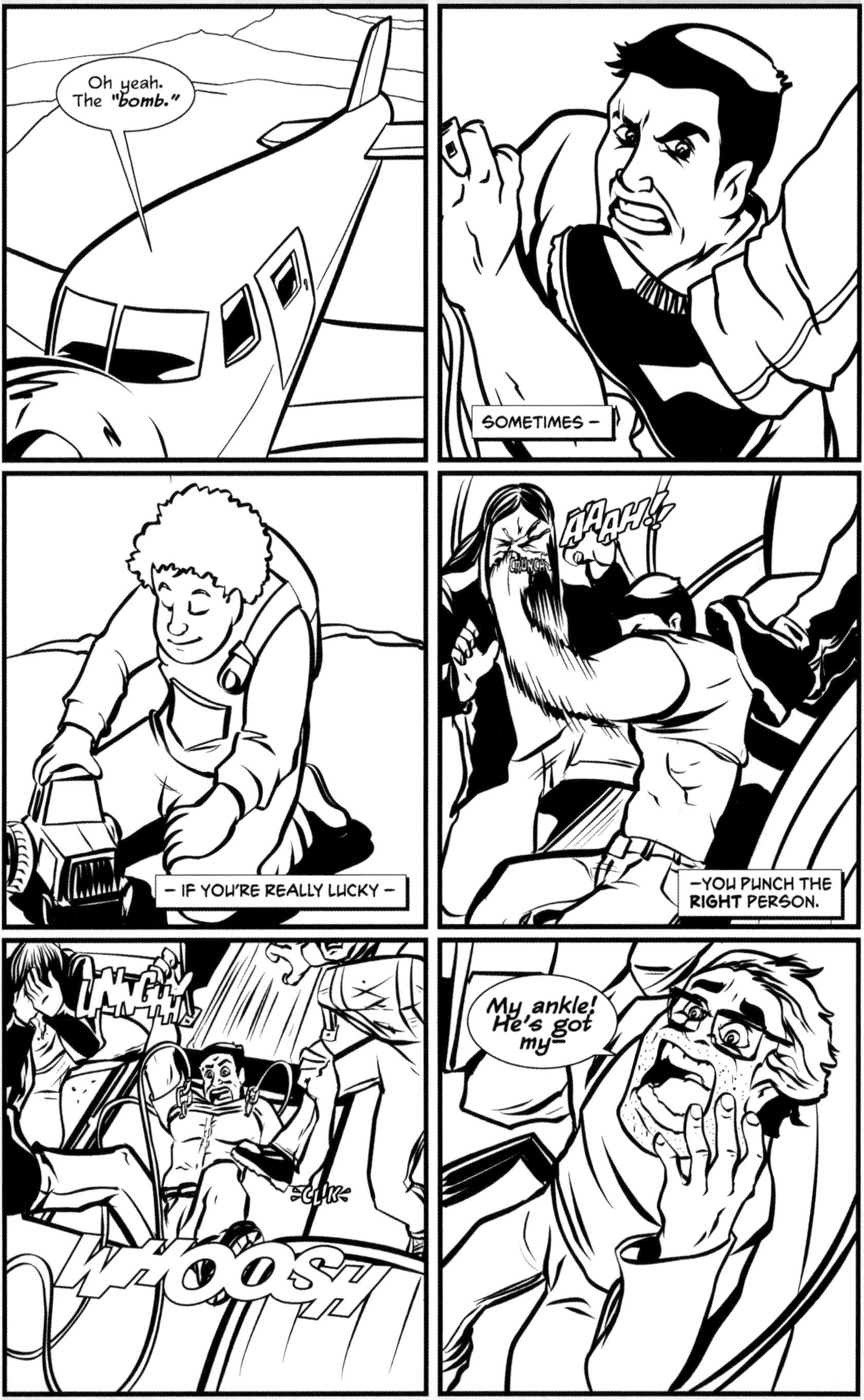

Oh yeah. The "*bomb.*"
SOMETIMES –
– IF YOU'RE REALLY LUCKY –
AAAH!!
CRUNCH
—YOU PUNCH THE **RIGHT** PERSON.
UNNGH!
CLIK
WHOOSH
My ankle! He's got my—

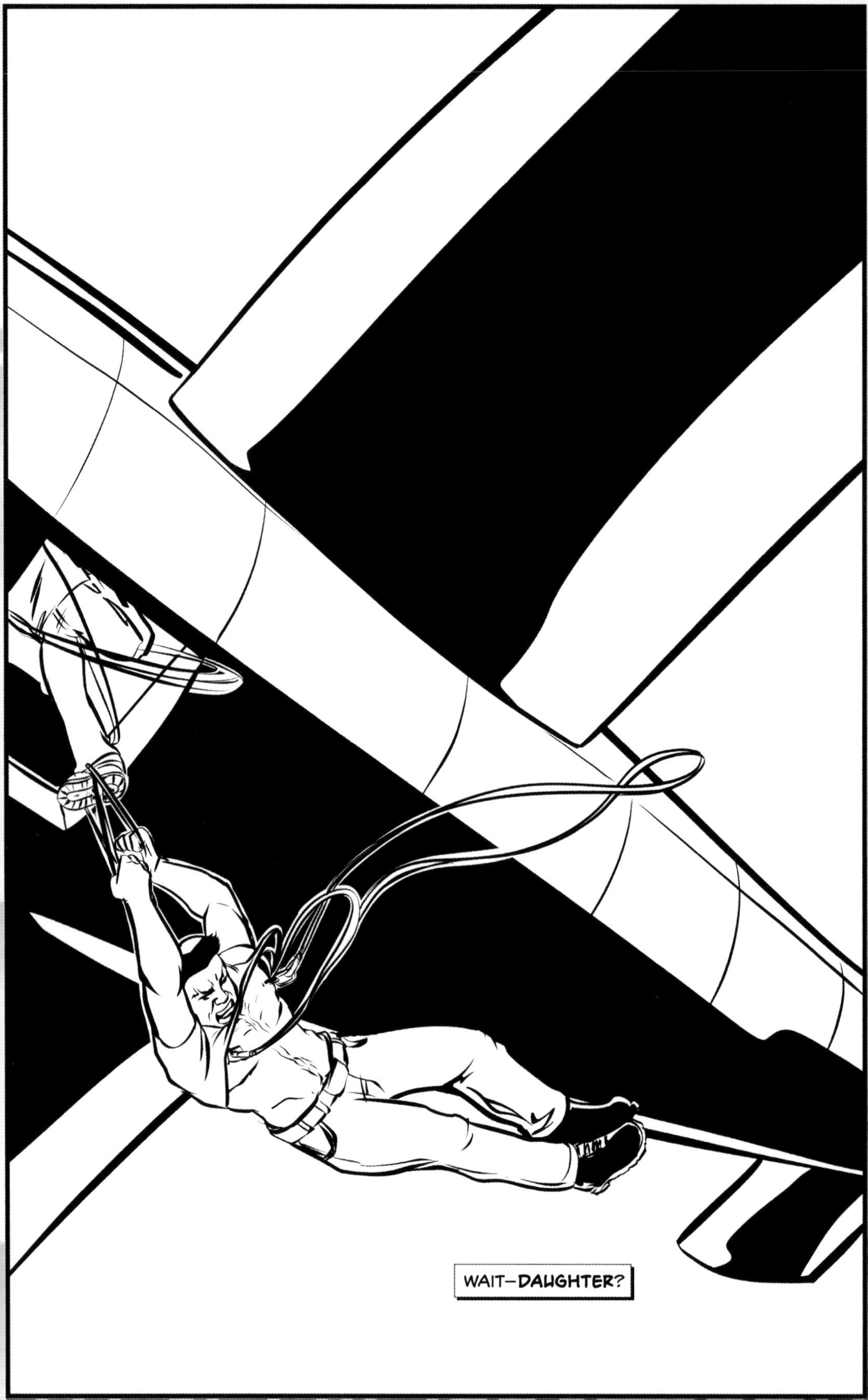
WAIT—DAUGHTER?

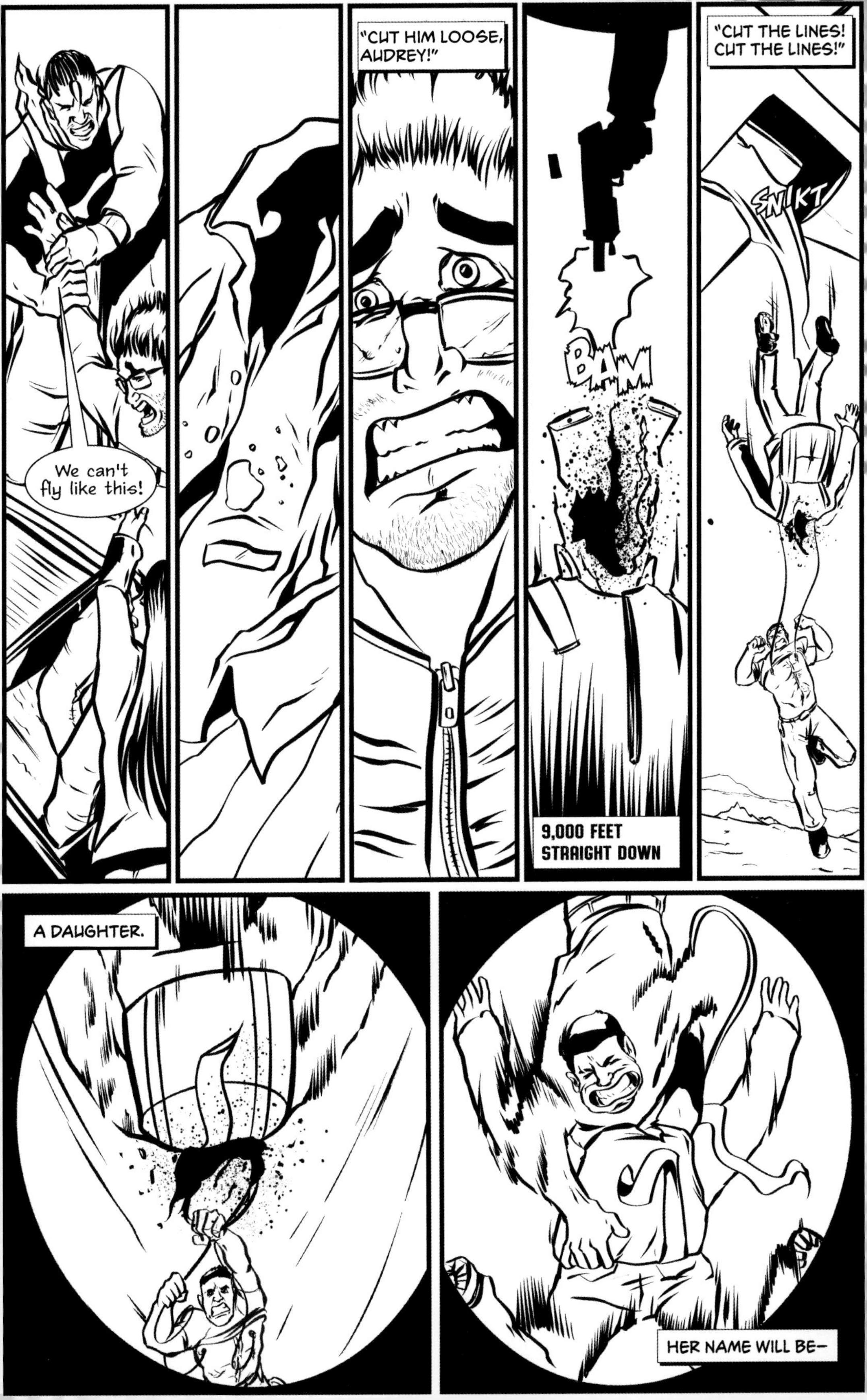
We can't fly like this!
"CUT HIM LOOSE, AUDREY!"
BAM
9,000 FEET STRAIGHT DOWN
"CUT THE LINES! CUT THE LINES!"
SNIKT
A DAUGHTER.
HER NAME WILL BE–

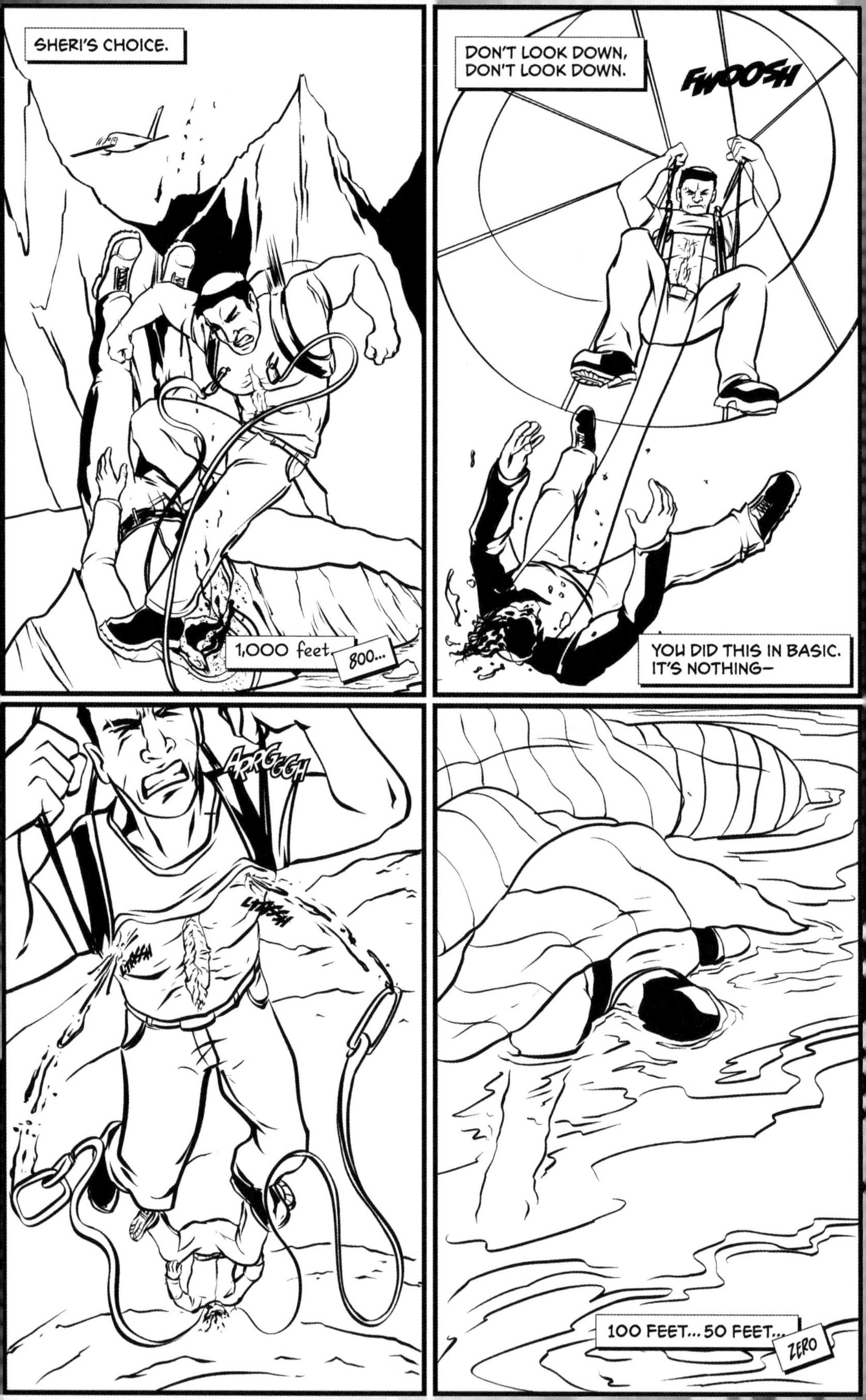
SHERI'S CHOICE.
1,000 feet
800...
DON'T LOOK DOWN, DON'T LOOK DOWN.
FWOOSH
YOU DID THIS IN BASIC. IT'S NOTHING—
ARRGGGH
100 FEET... 50 FEET...
ZERO

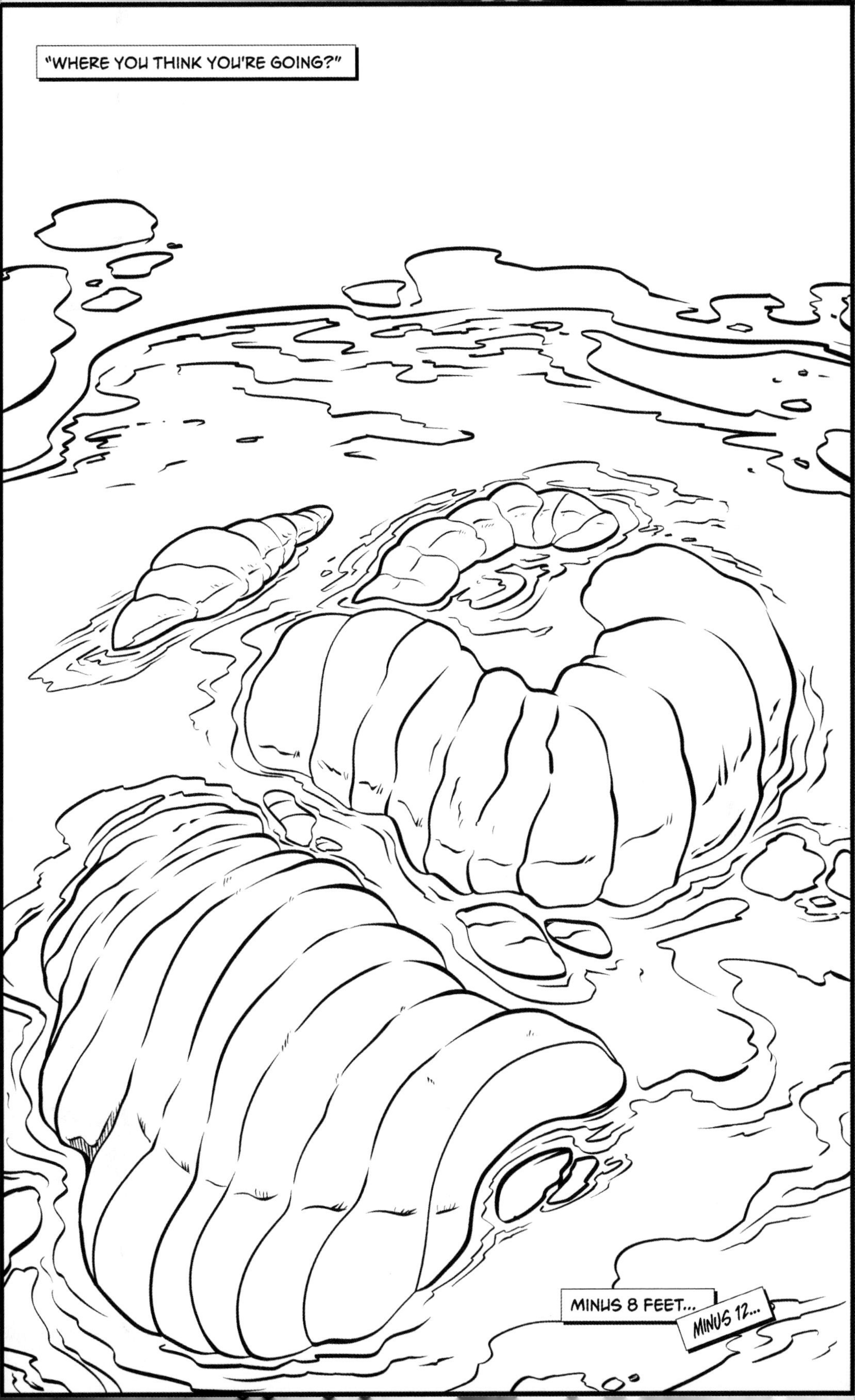
"WHERE YOU THINK YOU'RE GOING?"
MINUS 8 FEET...
MINUS 12...

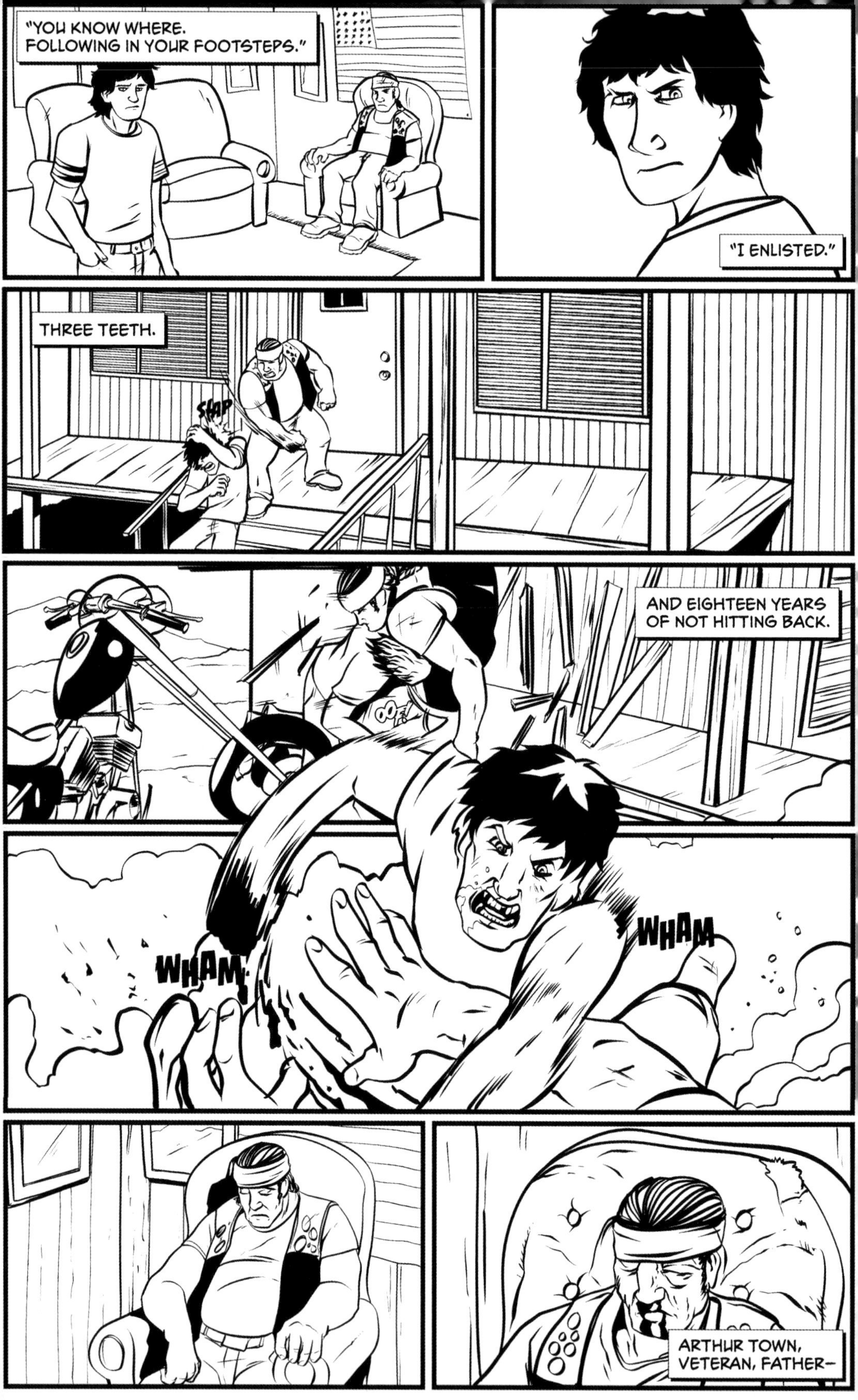
"YOU KNOW WHERE.
FOLLOWING IN YOUR FOOTSTEPS."
"I ENLISTED."
THREE TEETH.
SLAP
AND EIGHTEEN YEARS
OF NOT HITTING BACK.
WHAM
WHAM
ARTHUR TOWN,
VETERAN, FATHER—

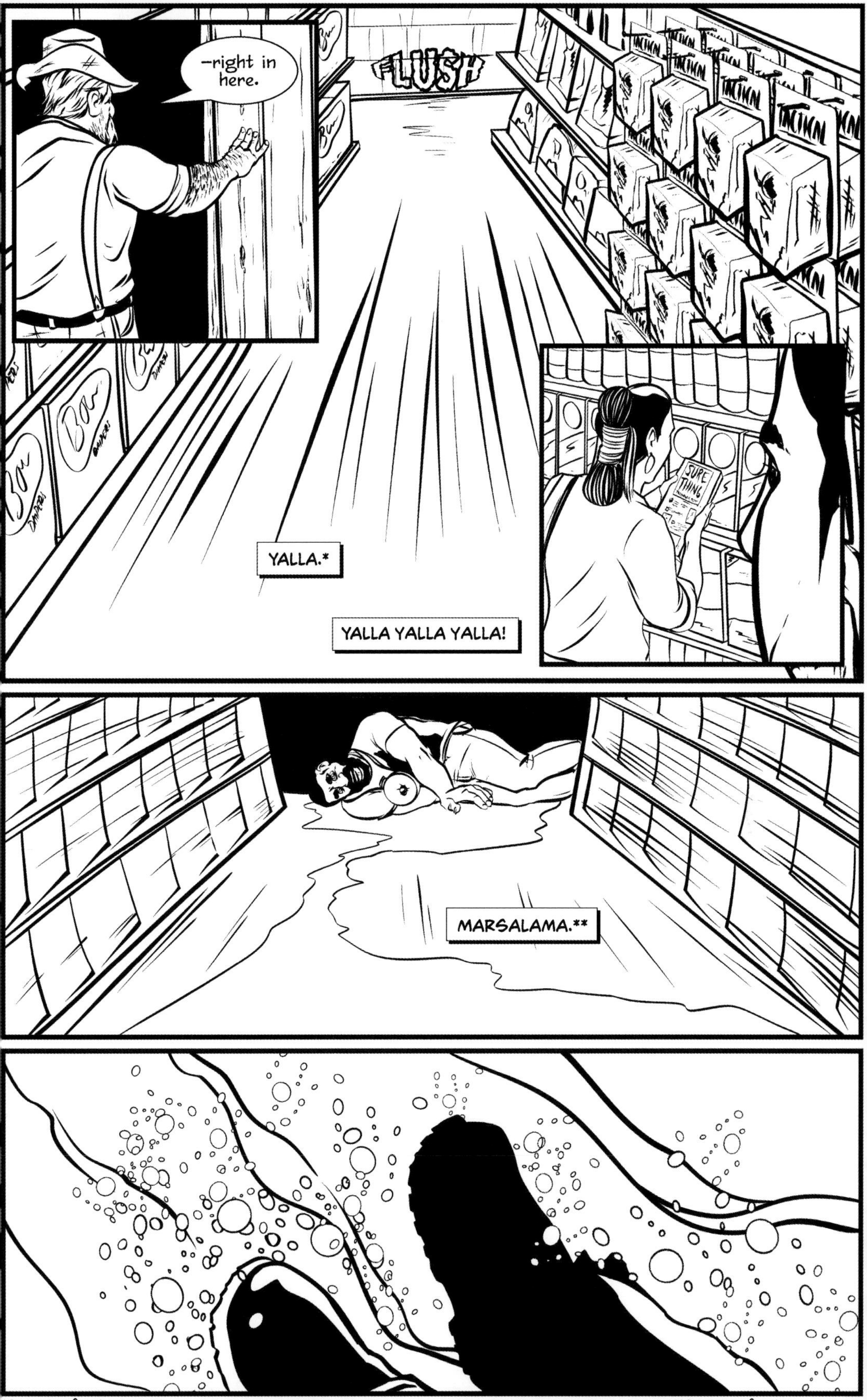
–right in here.
FLUSH
SURE THING
YALLA.*
YALLA YALLA YALLA!
MARSALAMA.**

*GI-Arabic for "run, now"

**GI-Arabic for "go in peace"

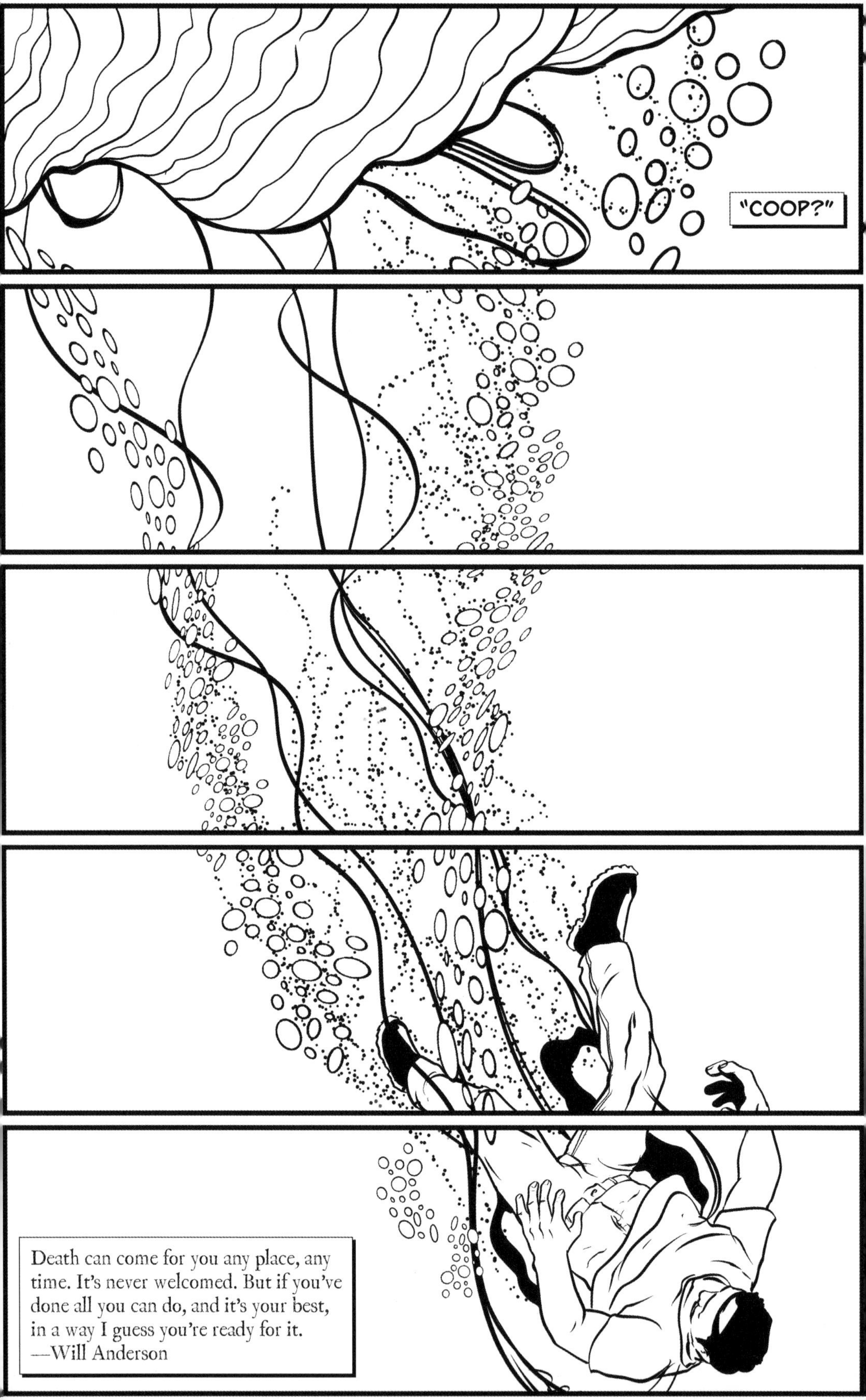
"COOP?"
Death can come for you any place, any time. It's never welcomed. But if you've done all you can do, and it's your best, in a way I guess you're ready for it.
—Will Anderson

PART FOUR

JOHN WAYNE MUST DIE.

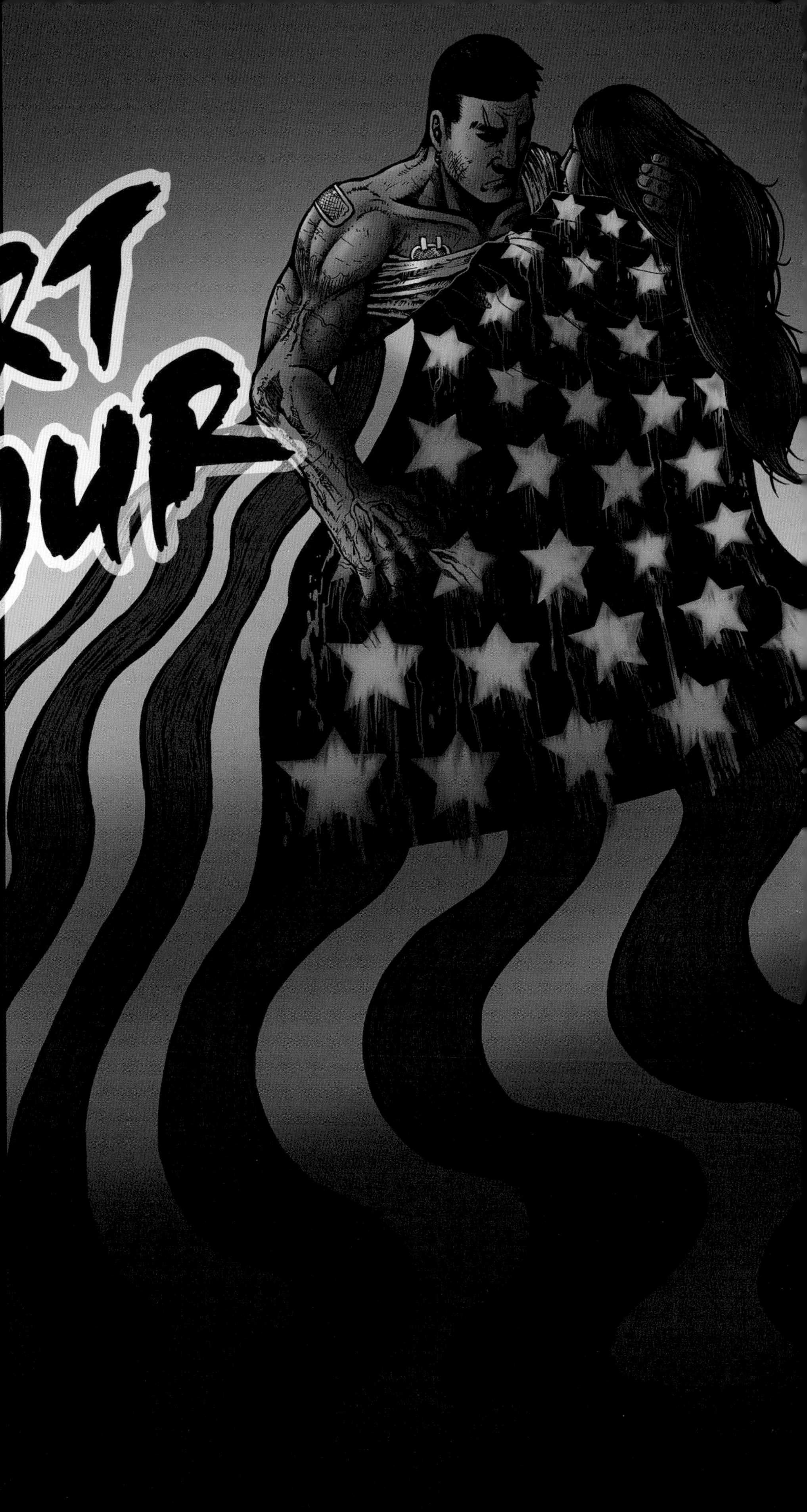

HOME FROM THE WAR FOR HIS ESTRANGED FATHER'S FUNERAL, COOPER TOWN AND HIS GIRLFRIEND SHERI MUN STUMBLED INTO A DRUGSTORE HEIST AND ENDED UP IN A RUNNING GUNNING BATTLE WITH THE DREADED JOHN WAYNES GANG, WHO TURNED OUT TO BE EMERGENCY ROOM DOCTORS – SPECIFICALLY, ONES WITH PLANES, ONES WHO LIKE TO TAKE INDIANS UP INTO THE SKY TO SEE IF THEY CAN FLY...

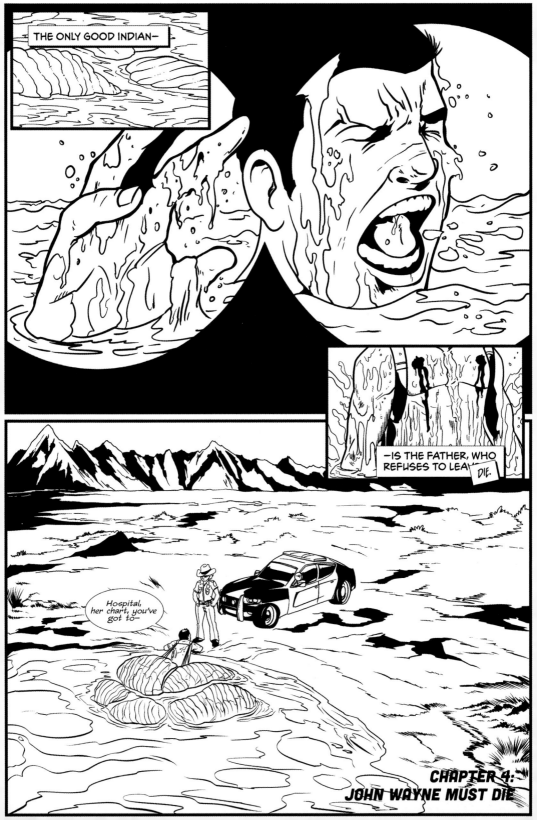

THE ONLY GOOD INDIAN—

—IS THE FATHER, WHO REFUSES TO LEAVE. DIE.

Hospital, her chart, you've got to—

CHAPTER 4:
JOHN WAYNE MUST DIE

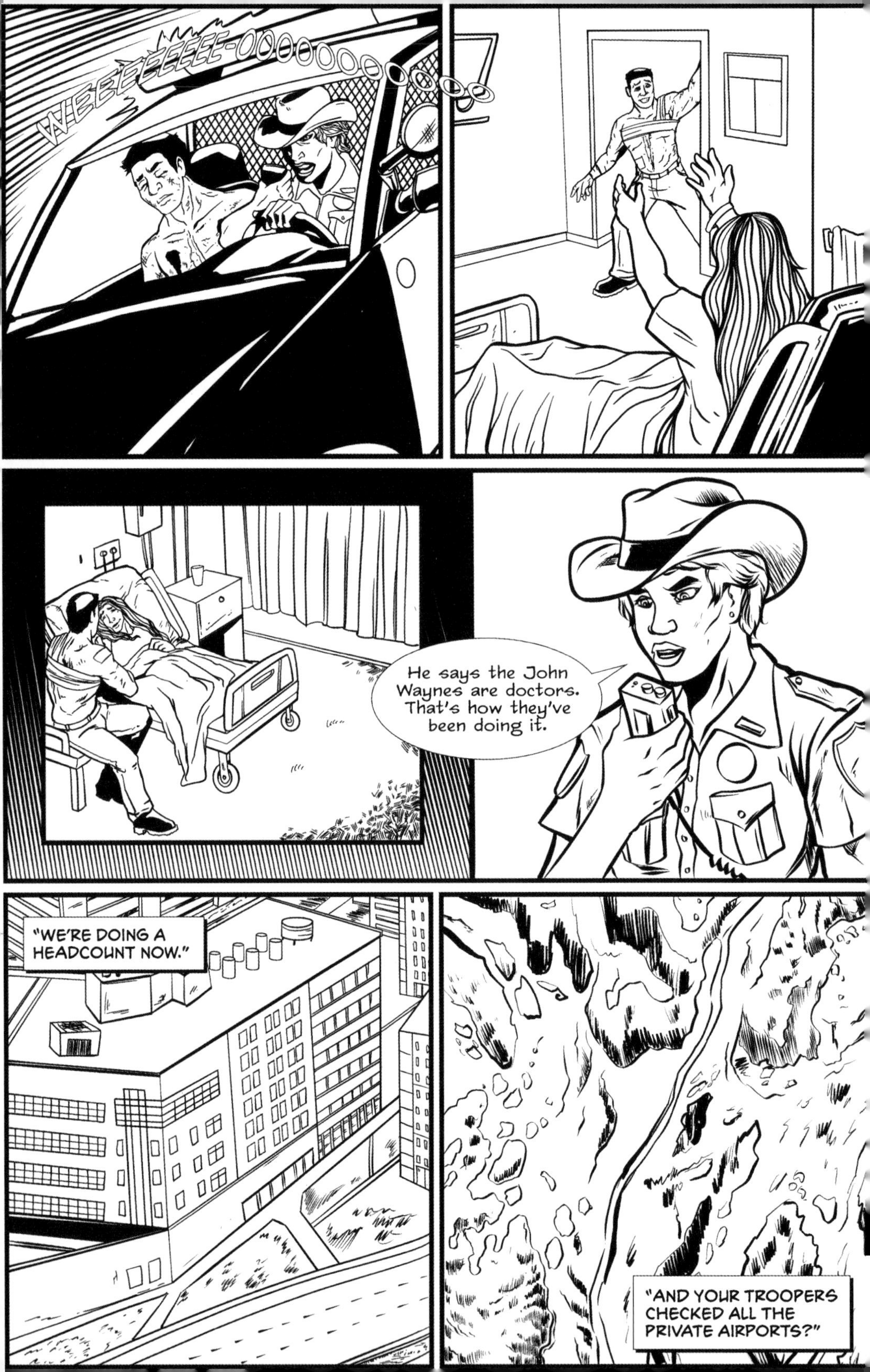
WEEEEEEEEE-OOOOOOOOOOO
He says the John Waynes are doctors. That's how they've been doing it.
"WE'RE DOING A HEADCOUNT NOW."
"AND YOUR TROOPERS CHECKED ALL THE PRIVATE AIRPORTS?"

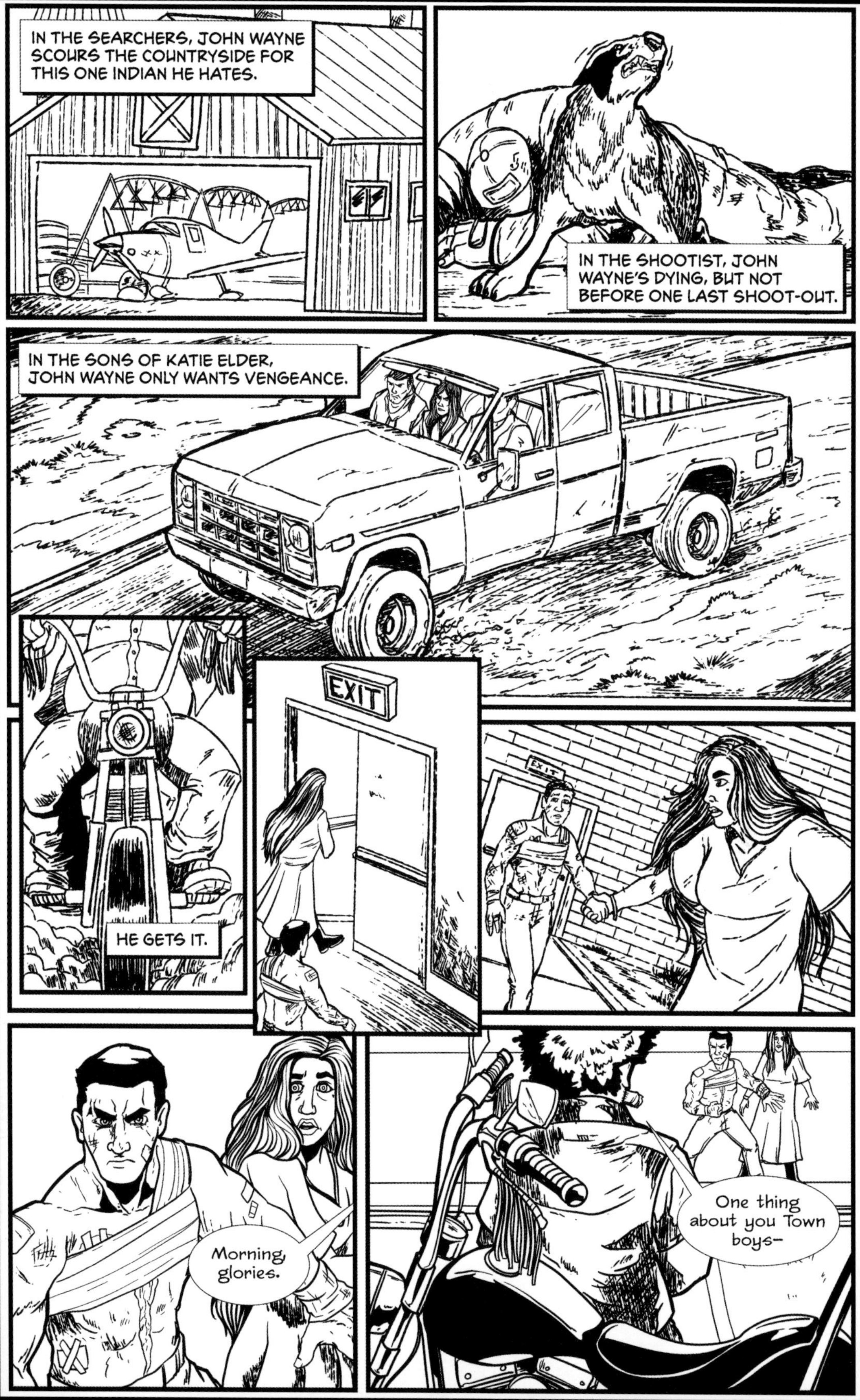
IN THE SEARCHERS, JOHN WAYNE SCOURS THE COUNTRYSIDE FOR THIS ONE INDIAN HE HATES.
IN THE SHOOTIST, JOHN WAYNE'S DYING, BUT NOT BEFORE ONE LAST SHOOT-OUT.
IN THE SONS OF KATIE ELDER, JOHN WAYNE ONLY WANTS VENGEANCE.
HE GETS IT.
EXIT
EXIT
Morning, glories.
One thing about you Town boys–

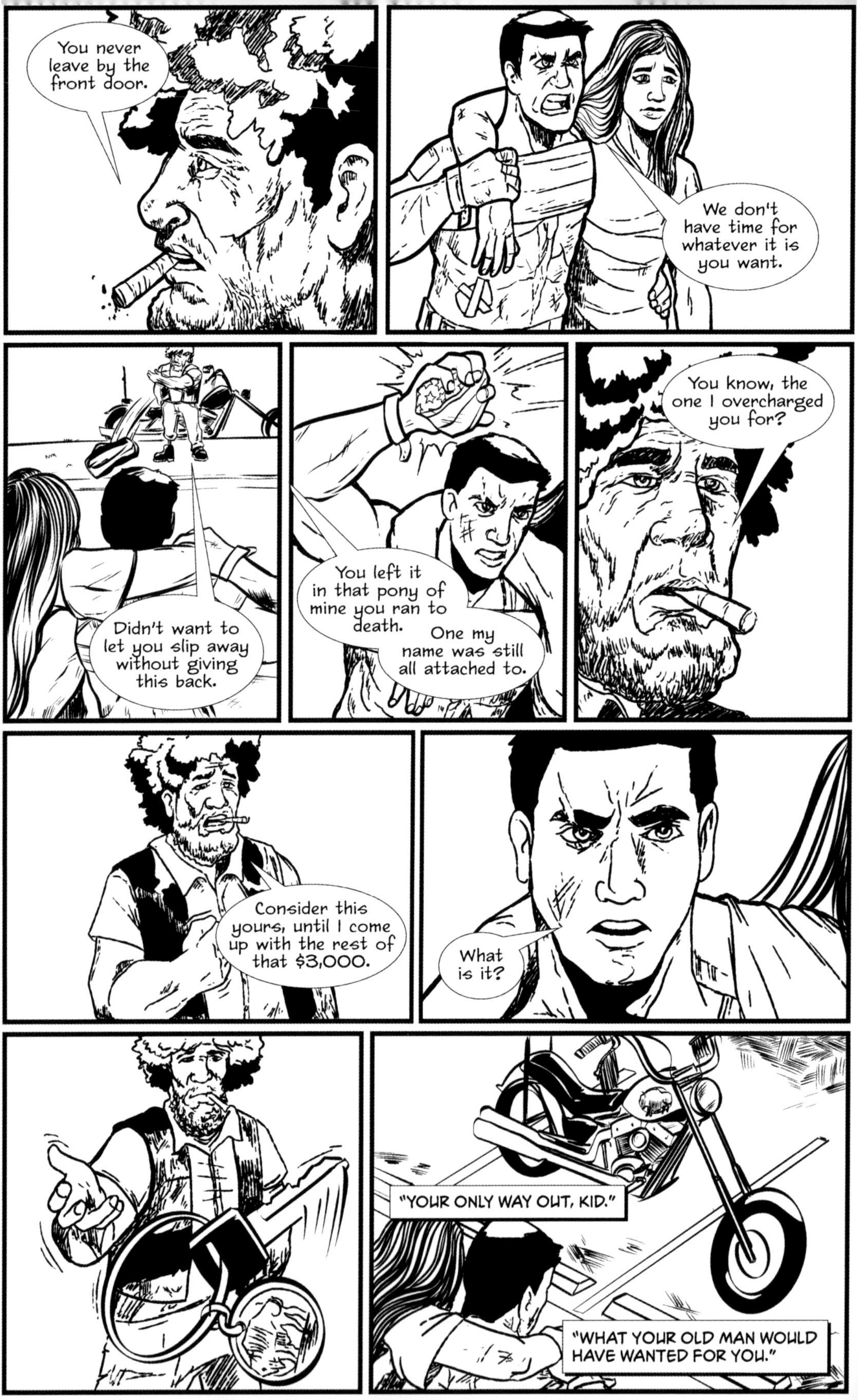
You never leave by the front door.
We don't have time for whatever it is you want.
Didn't want to let you slip away without giving this back.
You left it in that pony of mine you ran to death.
One my name was still all attached to.
You know, the one I overcharged you for?
Consider this yours, until I come up with the rest of that $3,000.
What is it?
"YOUR ONLY WAY OUT, KID."
"WHAT YOUR OLD MAN WOULD HAVE WANTED FOR YOU."

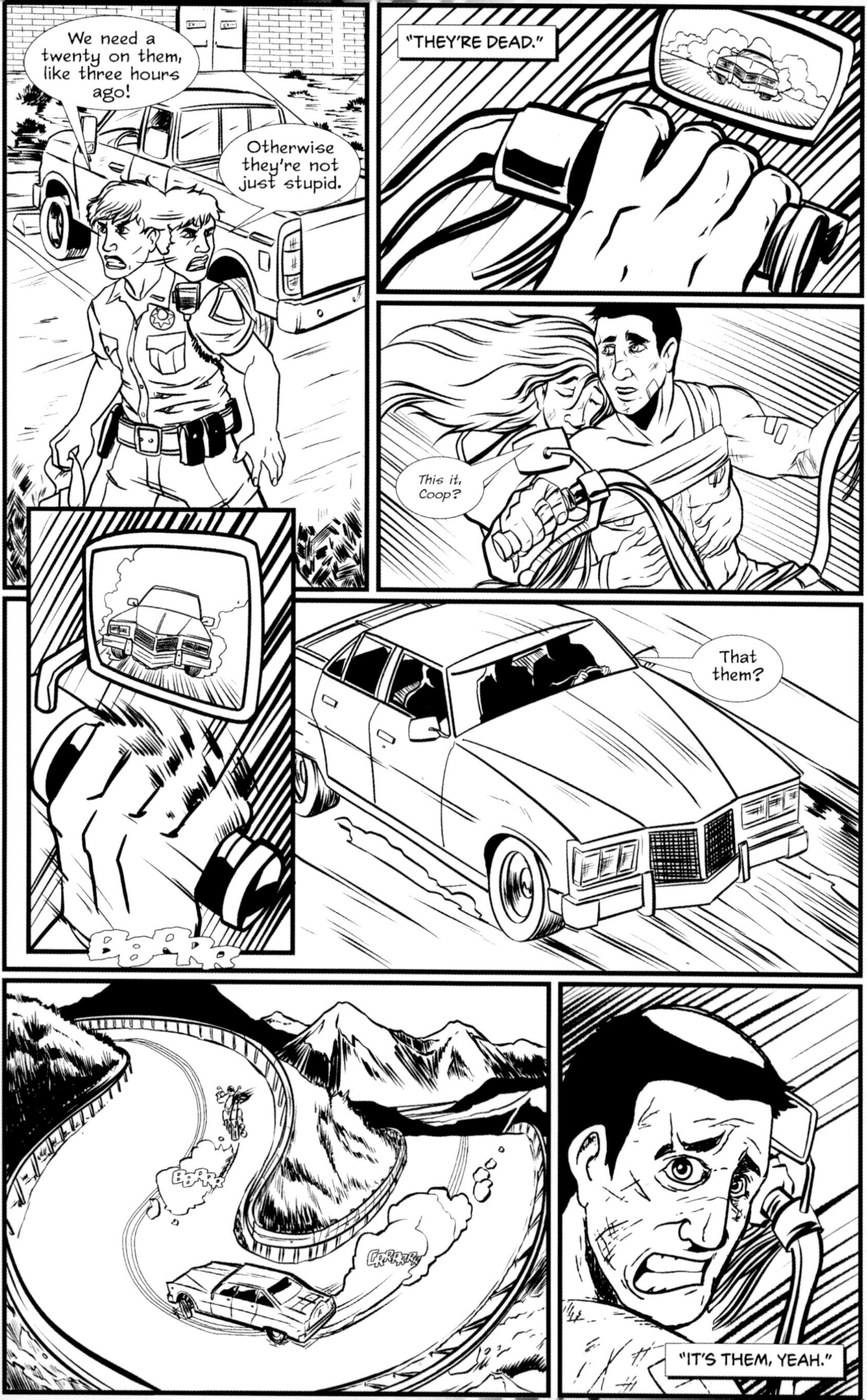
We need a twenty on them, like three hours ago!
Otherwise they're not just stupid.
"THEY'RE DEAD."
This it, Coop?
That them?
BOORR
BOORR
CRRRRR
"IT'S THEM, YEAH."

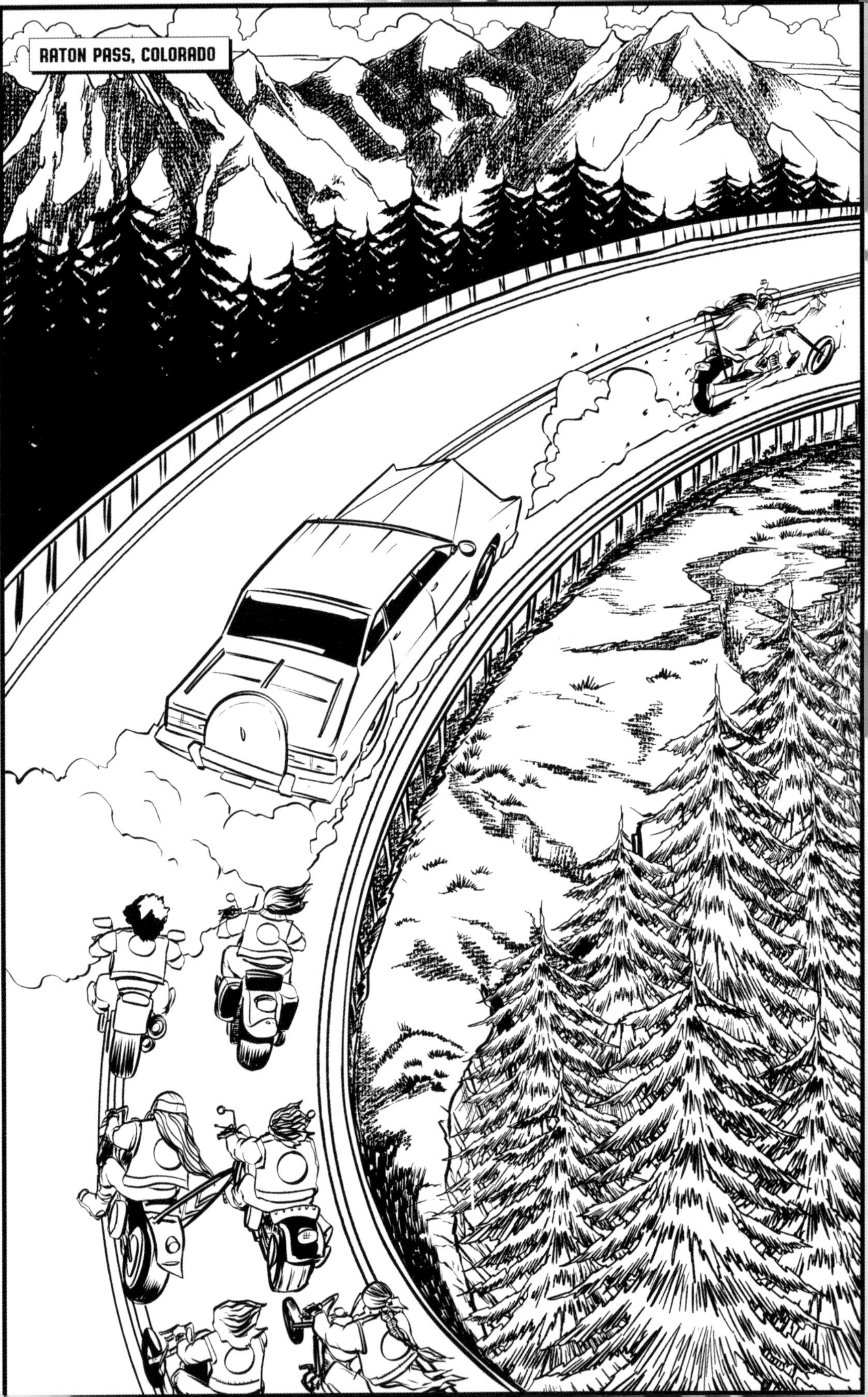
RATON PASS, COLORADO

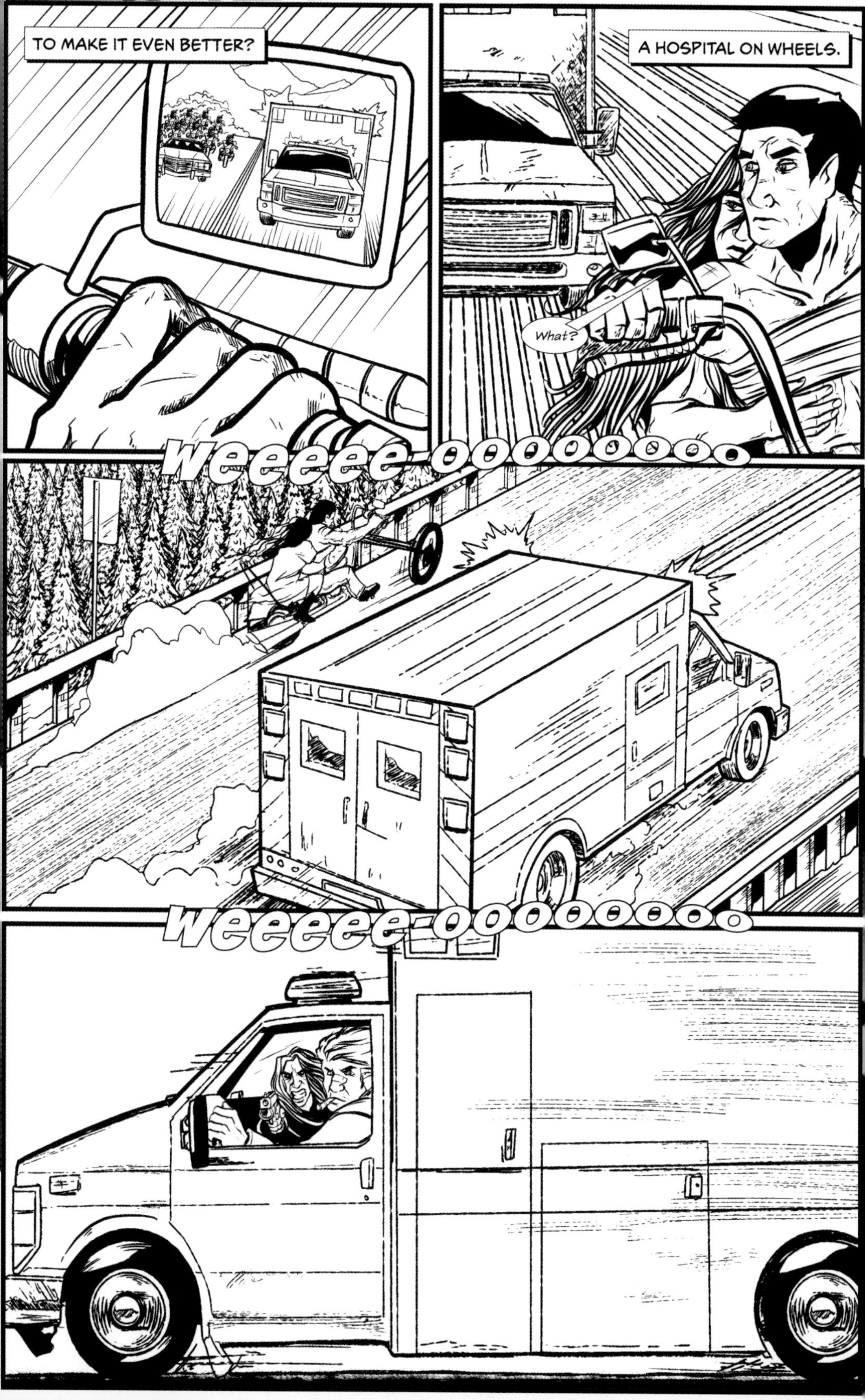
TO MAKE IT EVEN BETTER?
A HOSPITAL ON WHEELS.
What?
weeeee-oooooooo
weeeee-oooooooo

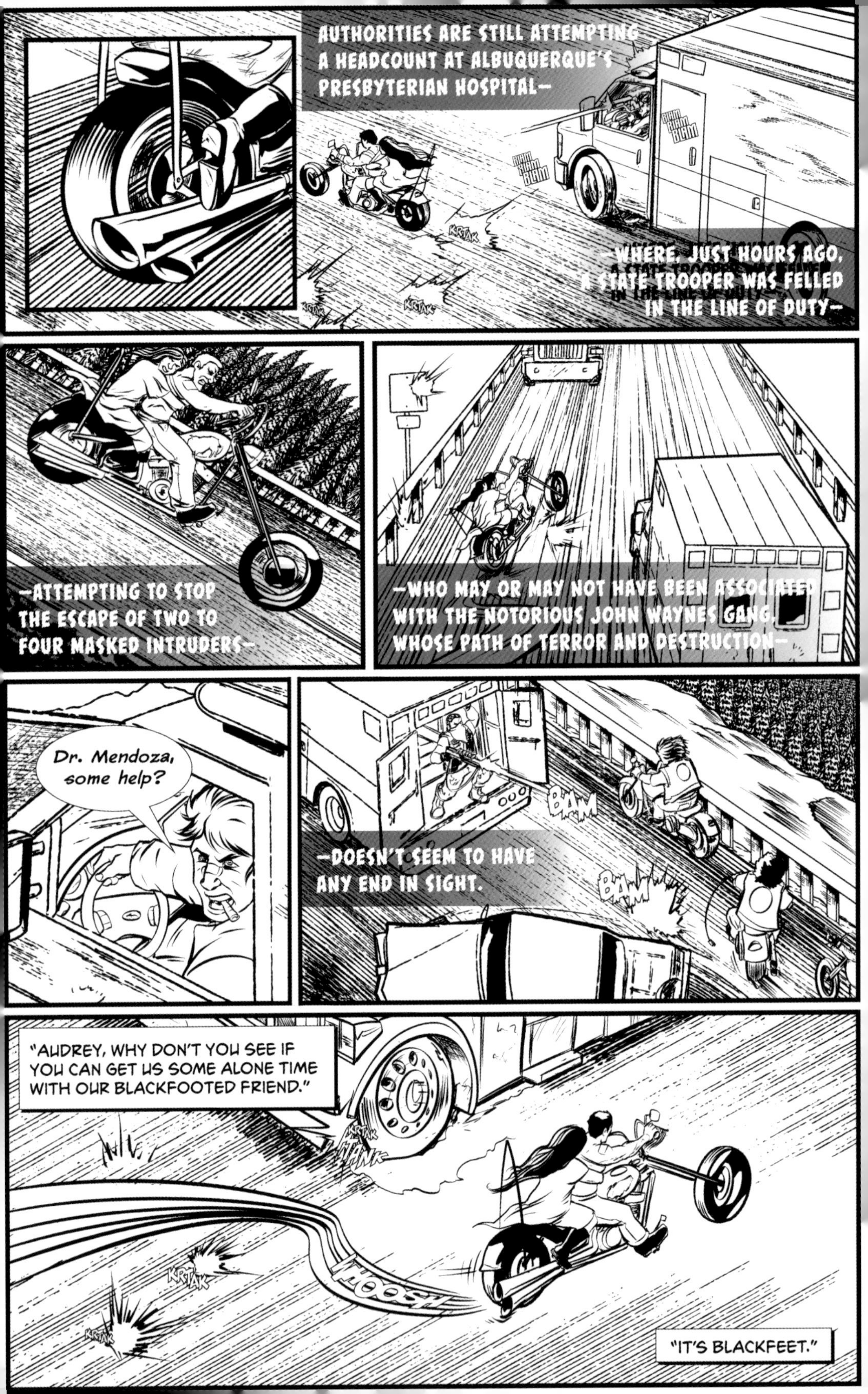
AUTHORITIES ARE STILL ATTEMPTING A HEADCOUNT AT ALBUQUERQUE'S PRESBYTERIAN HOSPITAL—
BLAM BLAM BLAM
BLAM BLAM BLAM
KRTAK
—WHERE, JUST HOURS AGO, A STATE TROOPER WAS FELLED IN THE LINE OF DUTY—
KRTAK
KRTAK
—ATTEMPTING TO STOP THE ESCAPE OF TWO TO FOUR MASKED INTRUDERS—
—WHO MAY OR MAY NOT HAVE BEEN ASSOCIATED WITH THE NOTORIOUS JOHN WAYNES GANG, WHOSE PATH OF TERROR AND DESTRUCTION—
Dr. Mendoza, some help?
BAM
—DOESN'T SEEM TO HAVE ANY END IN SIGHT.
BAM
"AUDREY, WHY DON'T YOU SEE IF YOU CAN GET US SOME ALONE TIME WITH OUR BLACKFOOTED FRIEND."
KRTAK
KLANK
WHOOSH
KRTAK
KRTAK
"IT'S BLACKFEET."

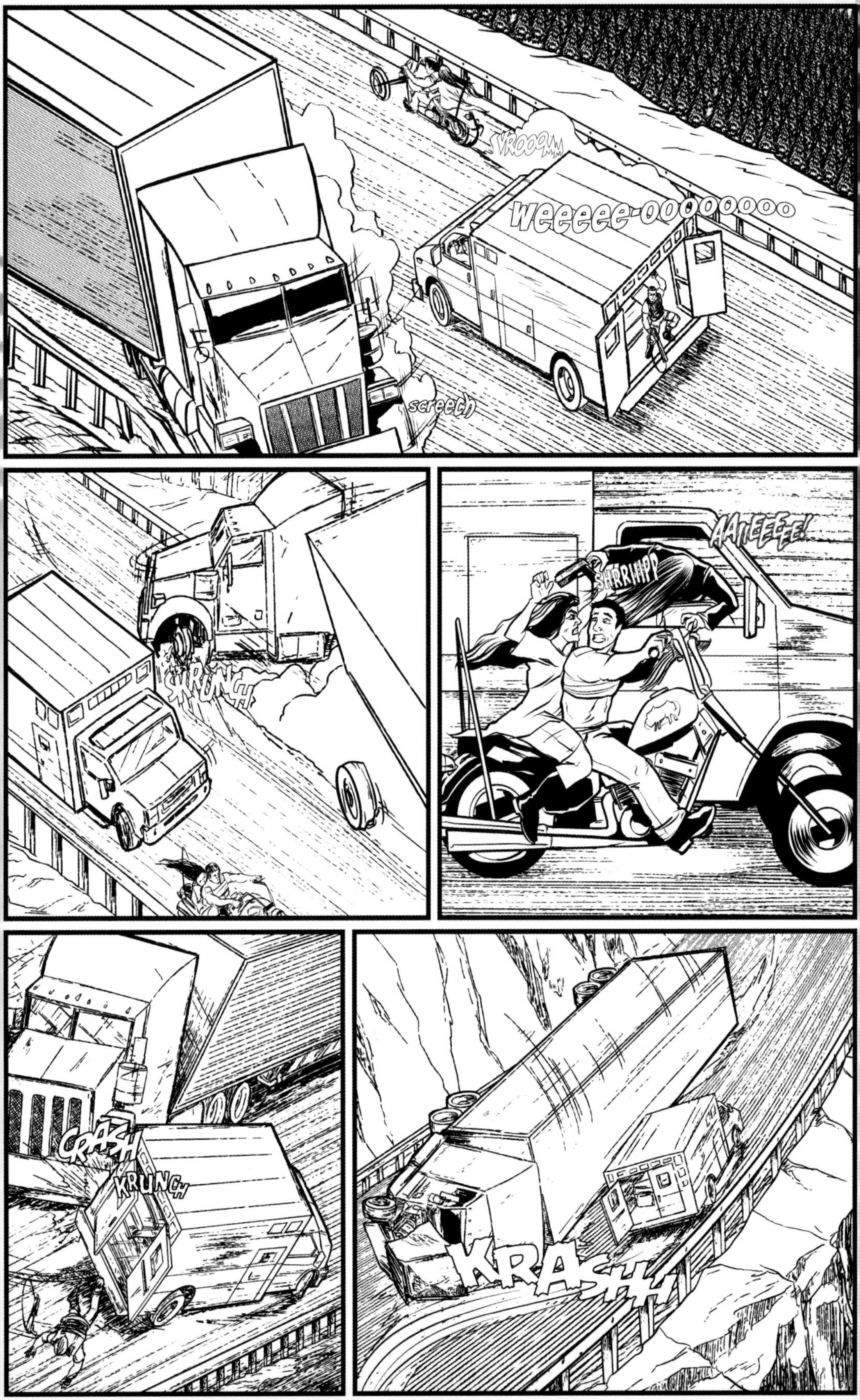
VROOOMMM
weeeee-ooooooooo
screech
SHRUNCH
AAIIEEEEE!
SHRRIIPPP
CRASH
KRUNCH
KRASHH

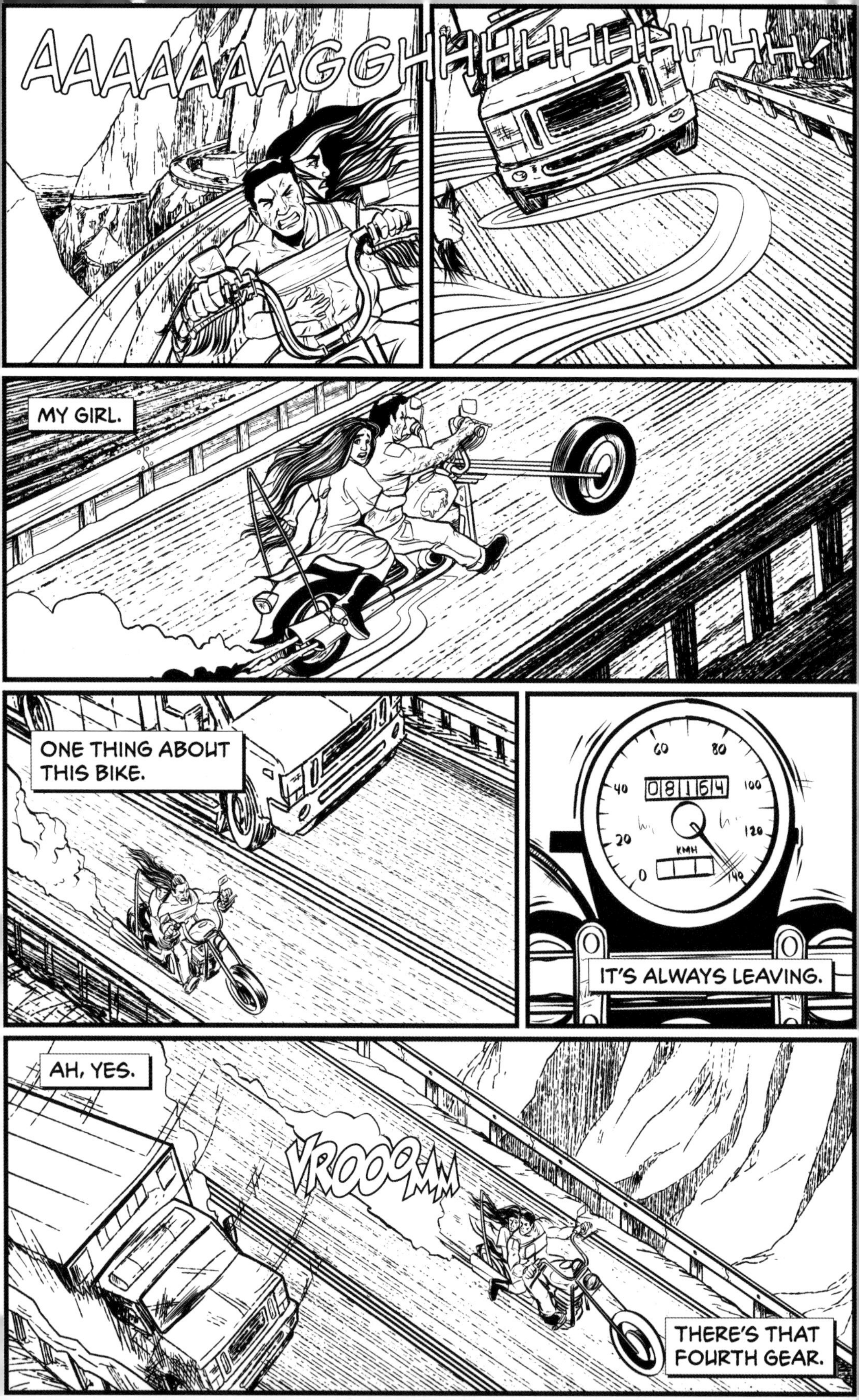
AAAAAAAAGGHHHHHHHHHHH!
MY GIRL.
ONE THING ABOUT THIS BIKE.
IT'S ALWAYS LEAVING.
AH, YES.
VROOOMMM
THERE'S THAT FOURTH GEAR.

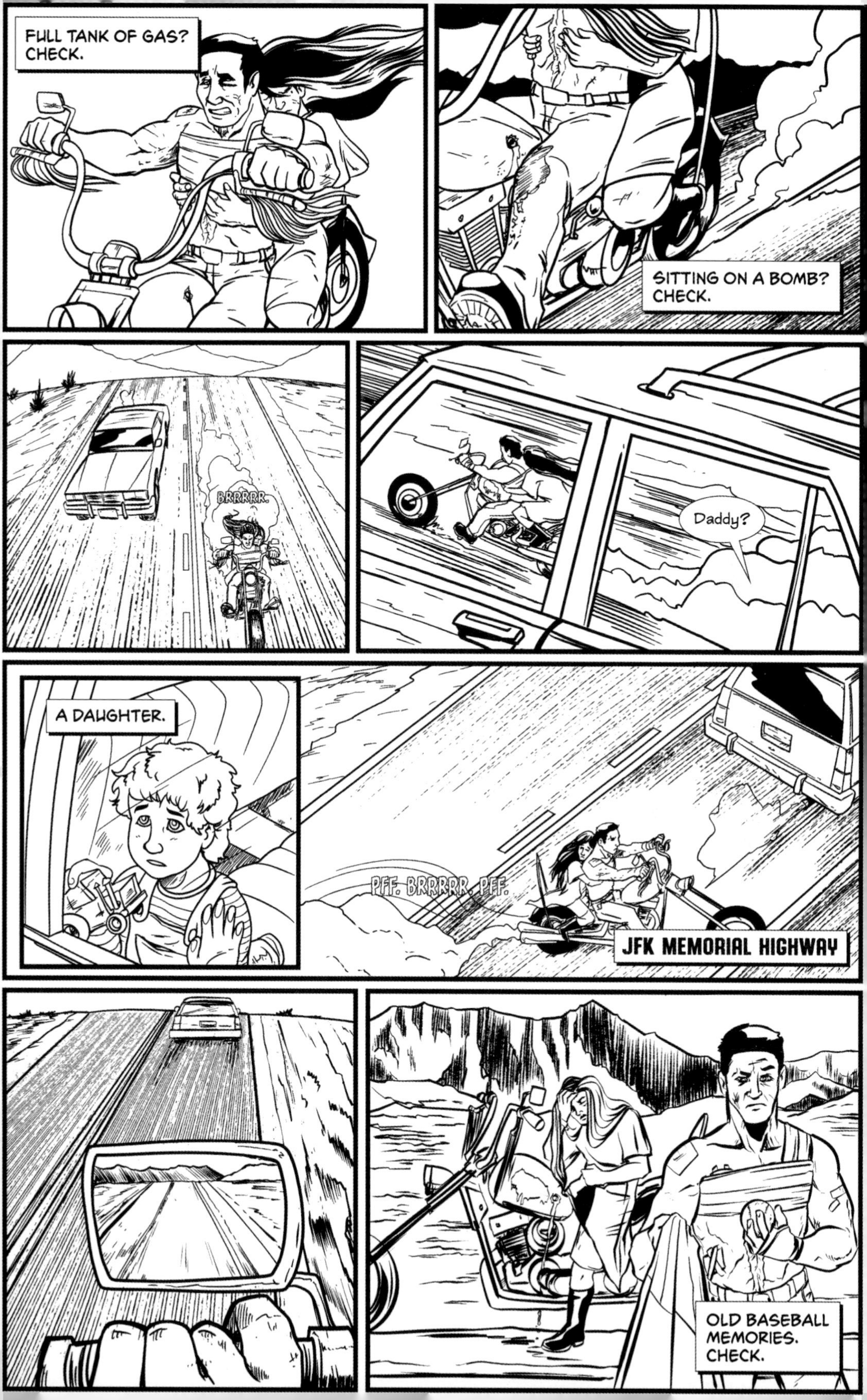
FULL TANK OF GAS? CHECK.
SITTING ON A BOMB? CHECK.
BRRRRR.
Daddy?
A DAUGHTER.
PFF. BRRRRR. PFF.
JFK MEMORIAL HIGHWAY
OLD BASEBALL MEMORIES. CHECK.

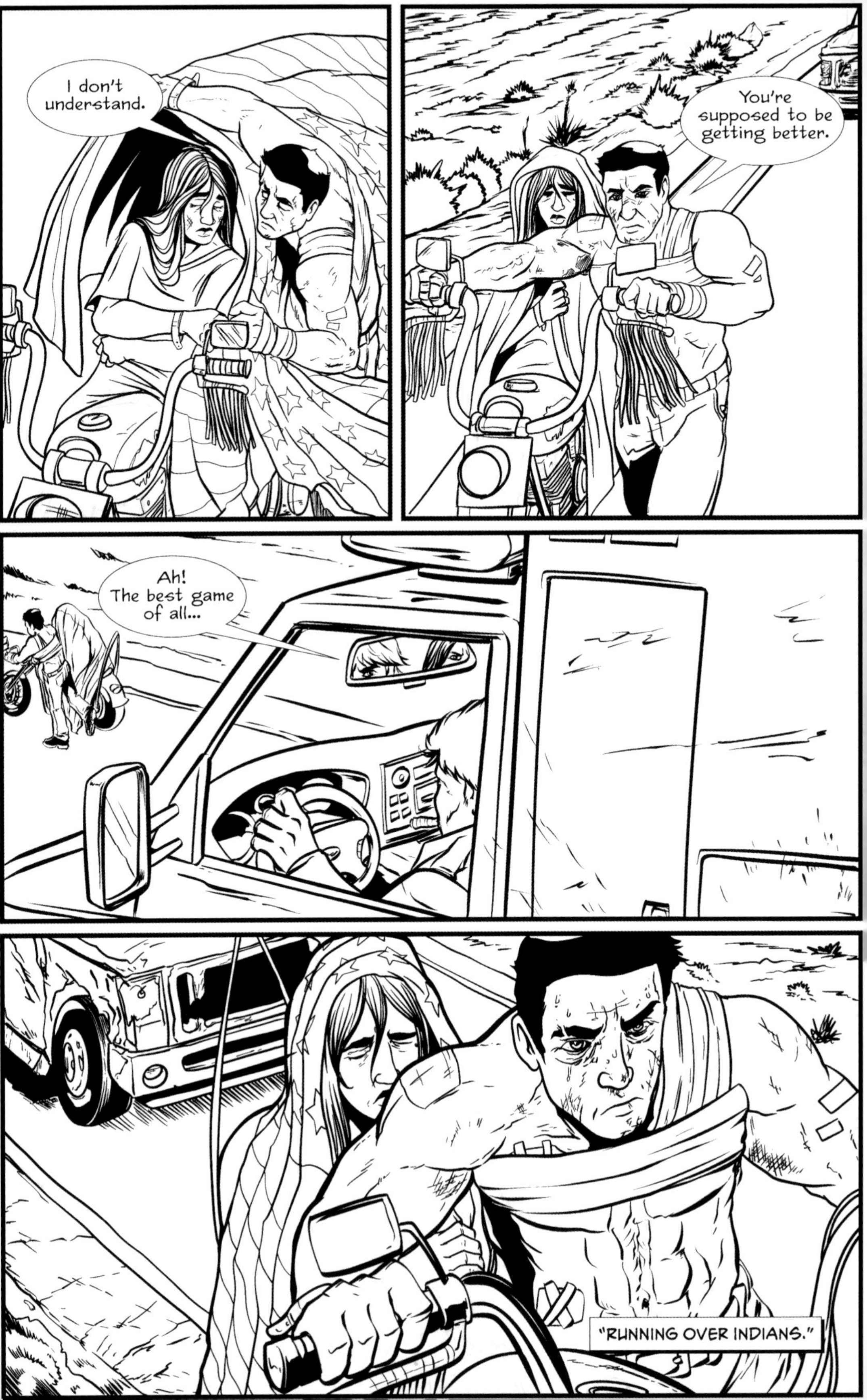
I don't understand.
You're supposed to be getting better.
Ah! The best game of all...
"RUNNING OVER INDIANS."

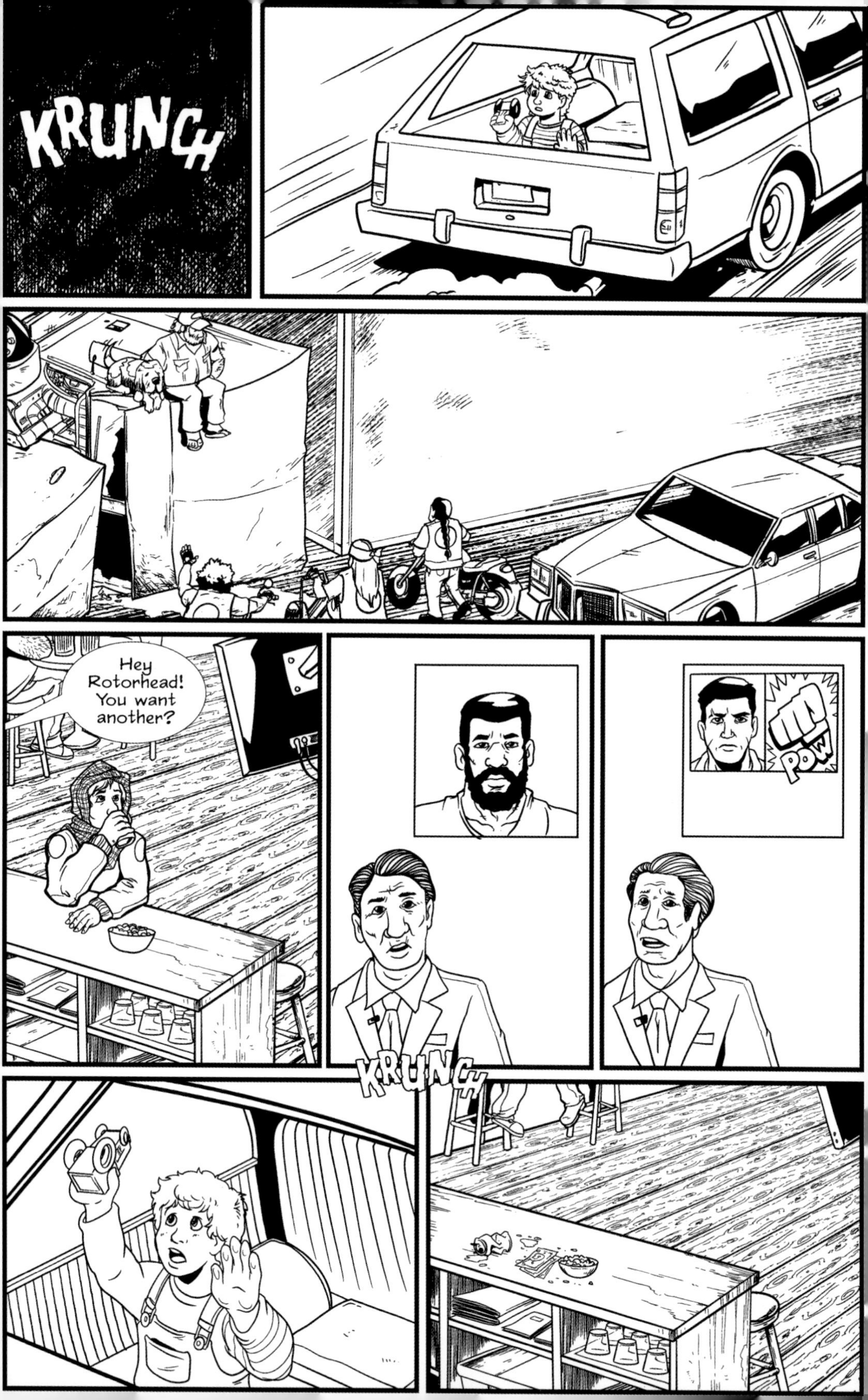
KRUNCH
Hey Rotorhead! You want another?
POW
KRUNCH

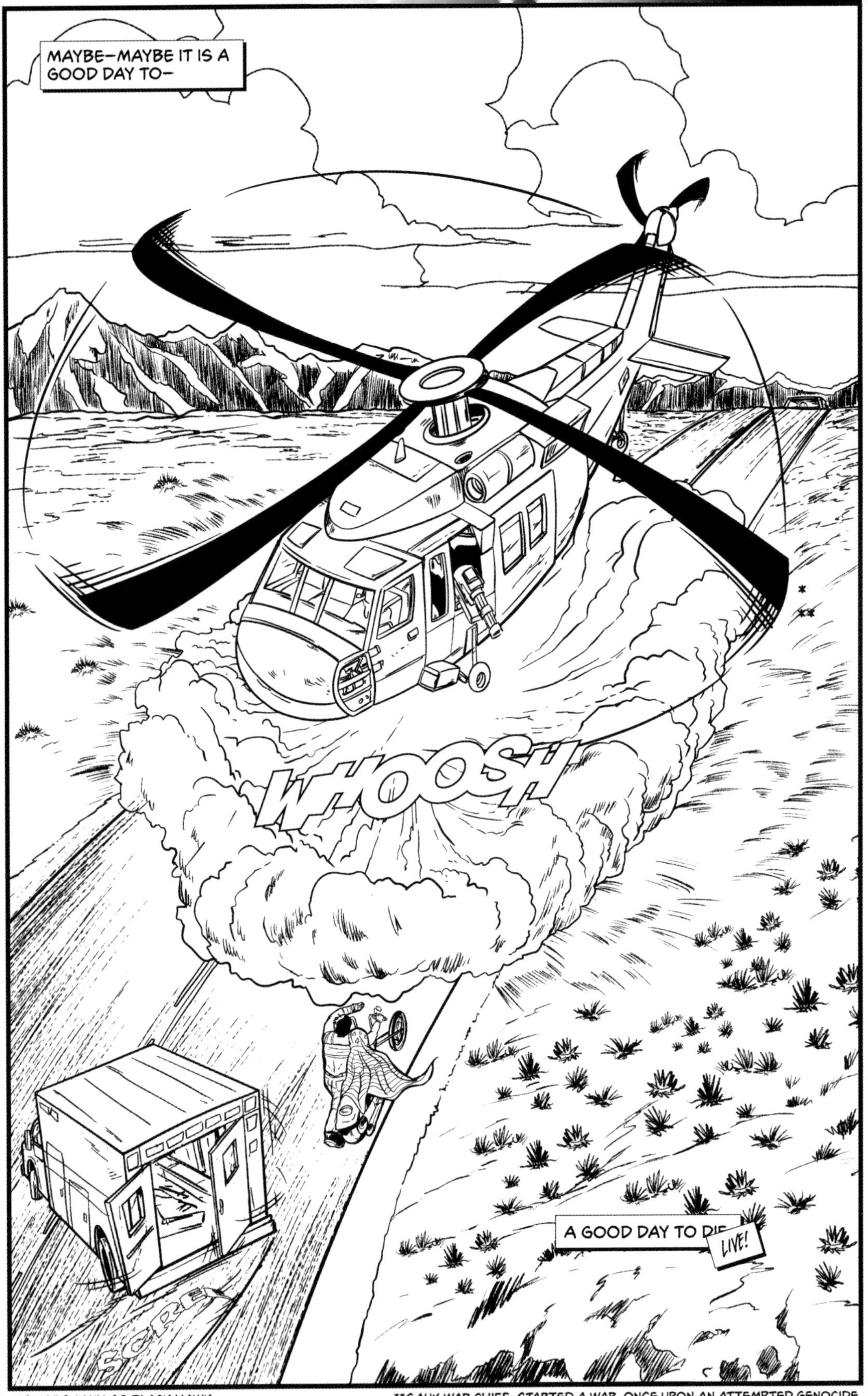
MAYBE—MAYBE IT IS A GOOD DAY TO—
*
**
WHOOSH
A GOOD DAY TO DI
LIVE!
SCRE

*SIKORSKY UH-60 BLACK HAWK

**SAUK WAR CHIEF, STARTED A WAR, ONCE UPON AN ATTEMPTED GENOCIDE.

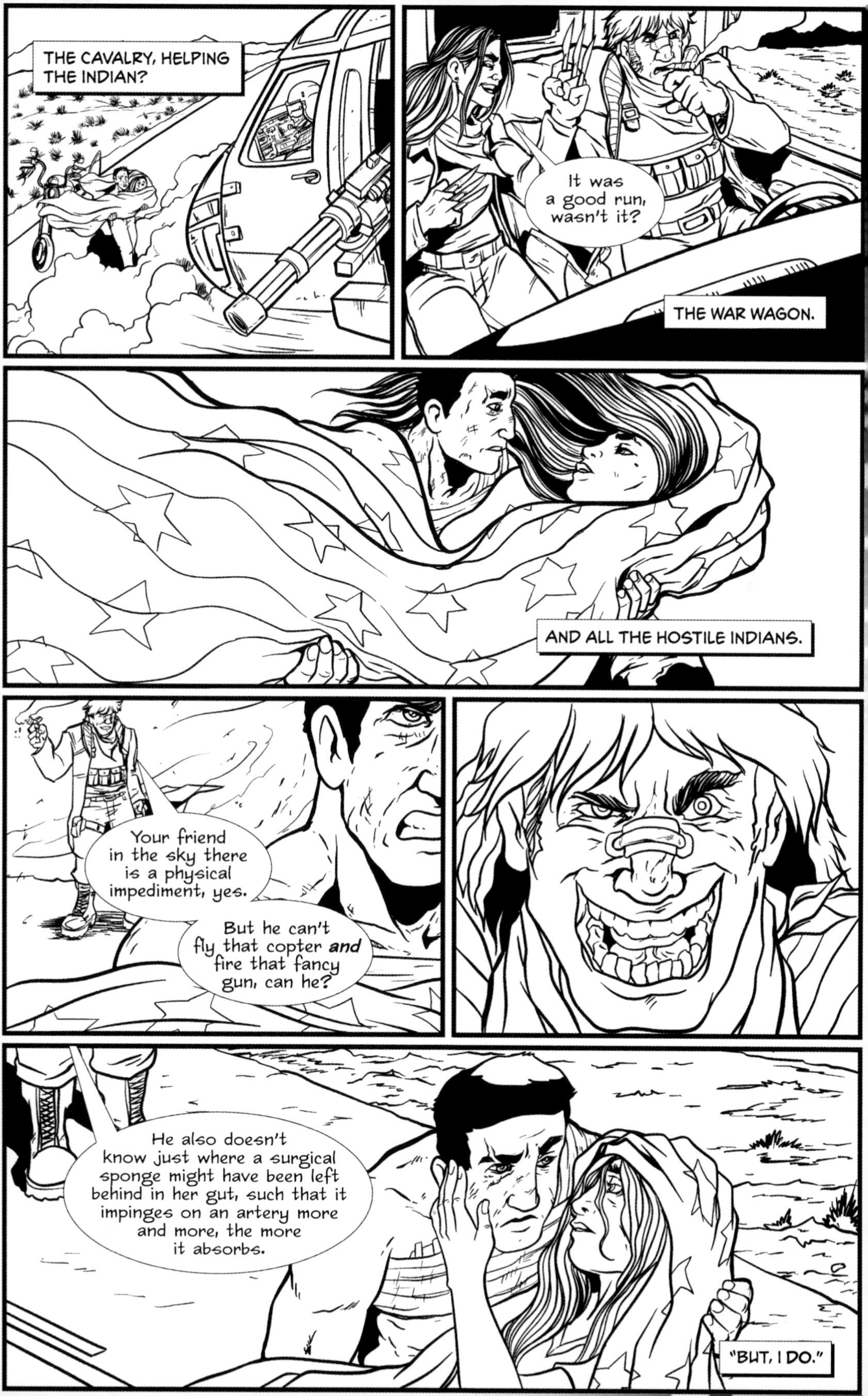
THE CAVALRY, HELPING THE INDIAN?
It was a good run, wasn't it?
THE WAR WAGON.
AND ALL THE HOSTILE INDIANS.
Your friend in the sky there is a physical impediment, yes.
But he can't fly that copter **and** fire that fancy gun, can he?
He also doesn't know just where a surgical sponge might have been left behind in her gut, such that it impinges on an artery more and more, the more it absorbs.
"BUT, I DO."

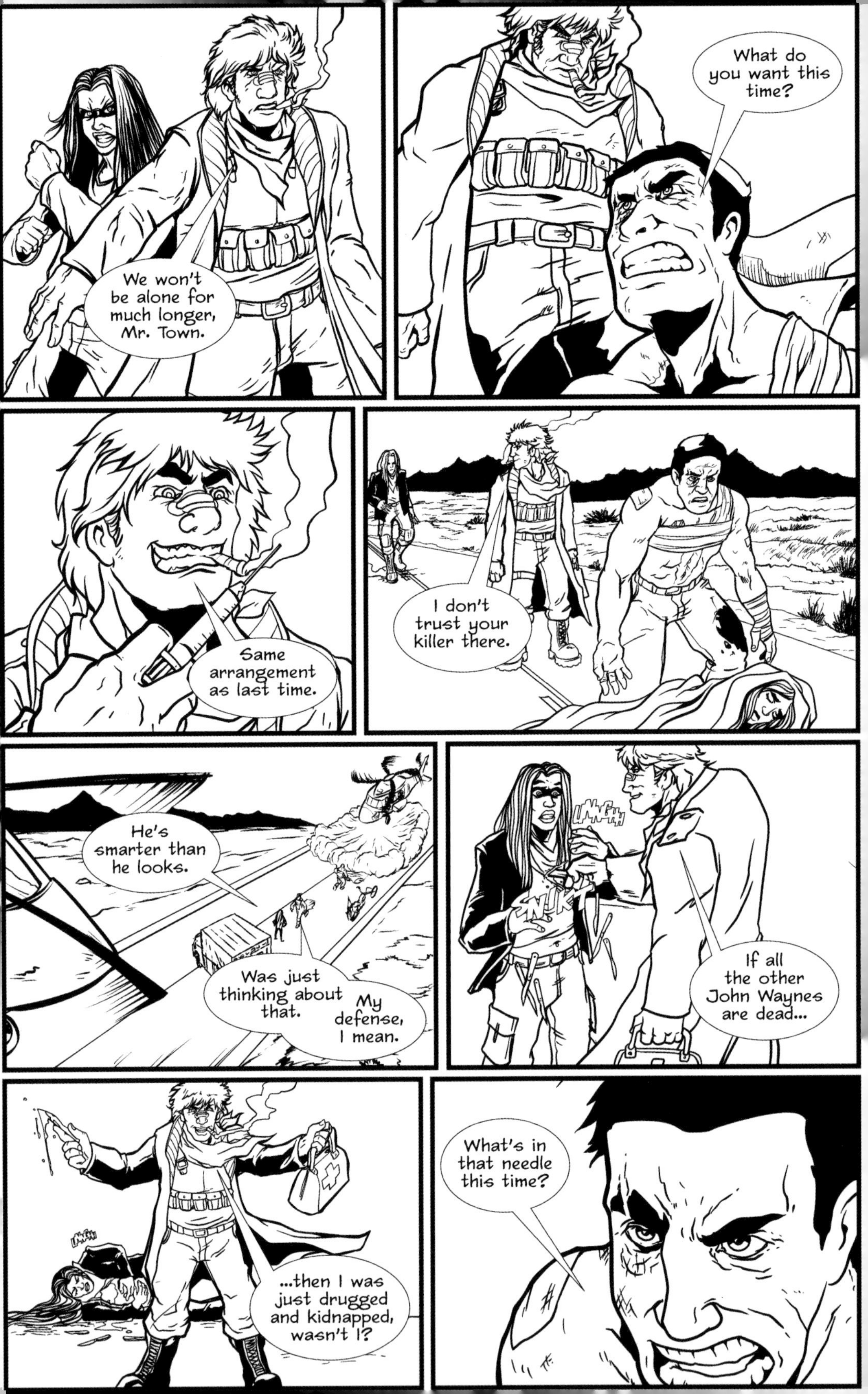
We won't be alone for much longer, Mr. Town.
What do you want this time?
Same arrangement as last time.
I don't trust your killer there.
He's smarter than he looks.
Was just thinking about that.
My defense, I mean.
If all the other John Waynes are dead...
...then I was just drugged and kidnapped, wasn't I?
What's in that needle this time?

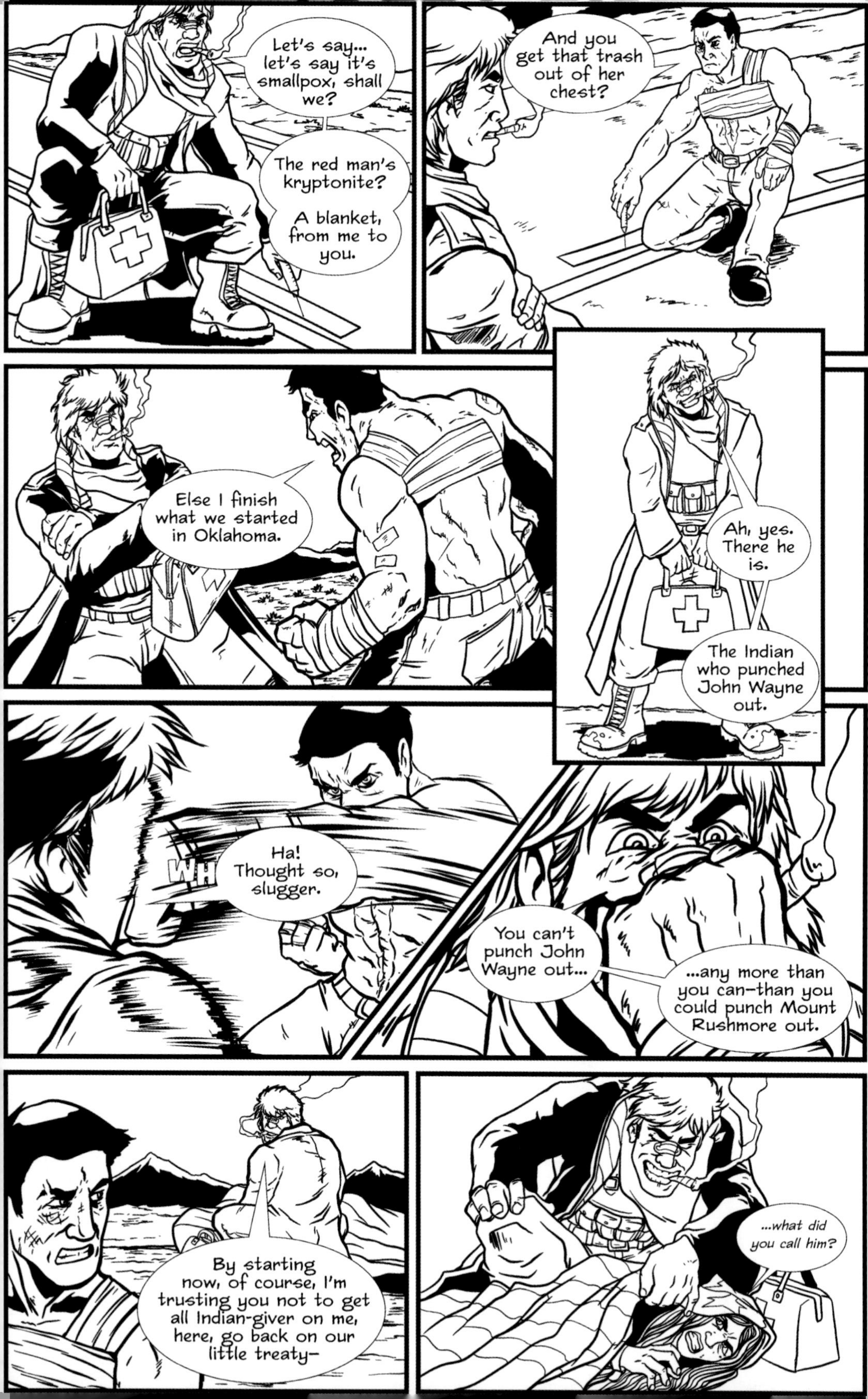
Let's say... let's say it's smallpox, shall we?
The red man's kryptonite?
A blanket, from me to you.
And you get that trash out of her chest?
Else I finish what we started in Oklahoma.
Ah, yes. There he is.
The Indian who punched John Wayne out.
WH
Ha! Thought so, slugger.
You can't punch John Wayne out...
...any more than you can–than you could punch Mount Rushmore out.
By starting now, of course, I'm trusting you not to get all Indian-giver on me, here, go back on our little treaty–
...what did you call him?

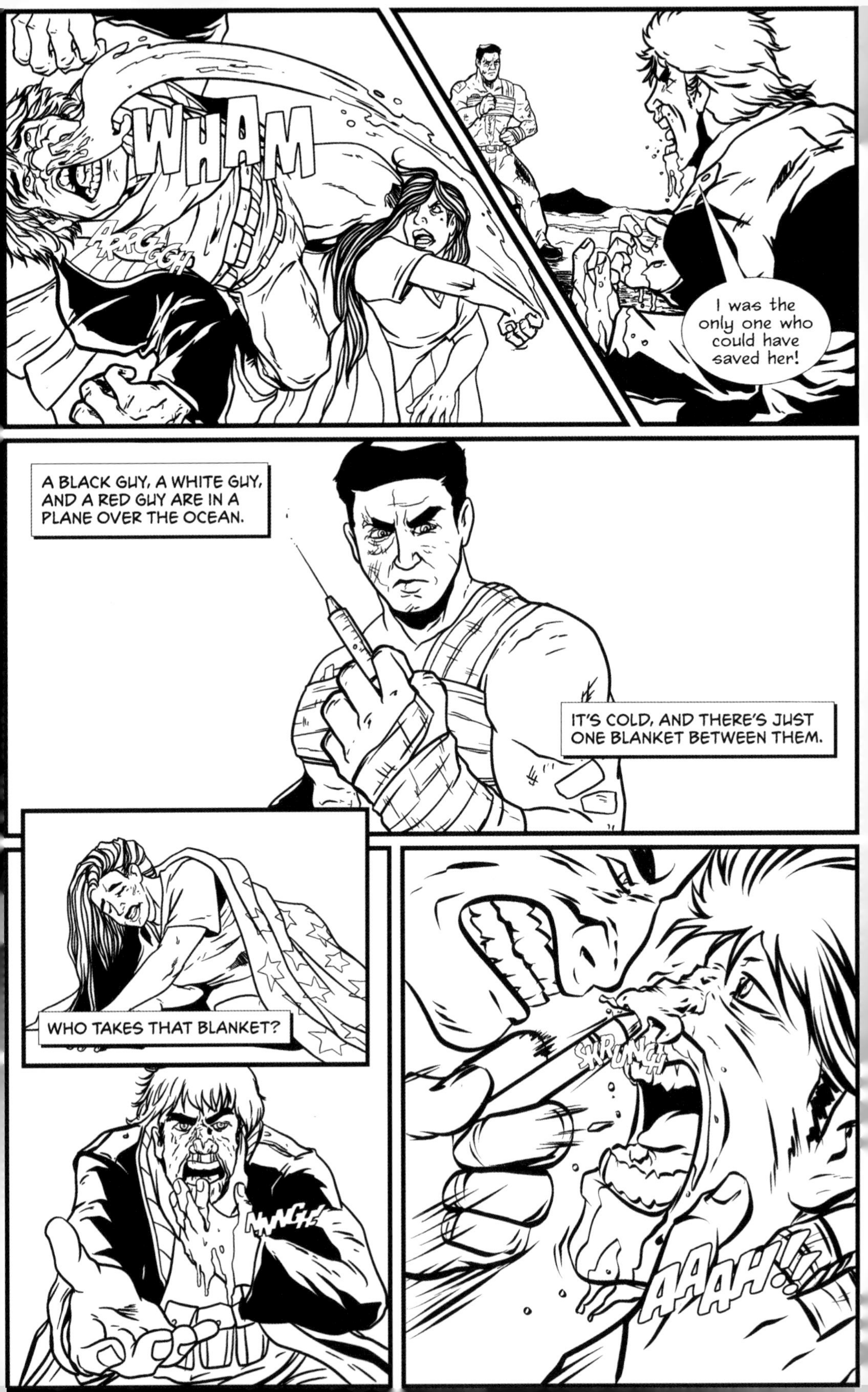
WHAM
ARRGGH!
I was the only one who could have saved her!
A BLACK GUY, A WHITE GUY, AND A RED GUY ARE IN A PLANE OVER THE OCEAN.
IT'S COLD, AND THERE'S JUST ONE BLANKET BETWEEN THEM.
WHO TAKES THAT BLANKET?
NNNGH!
SKRUNCH
AAAH!!

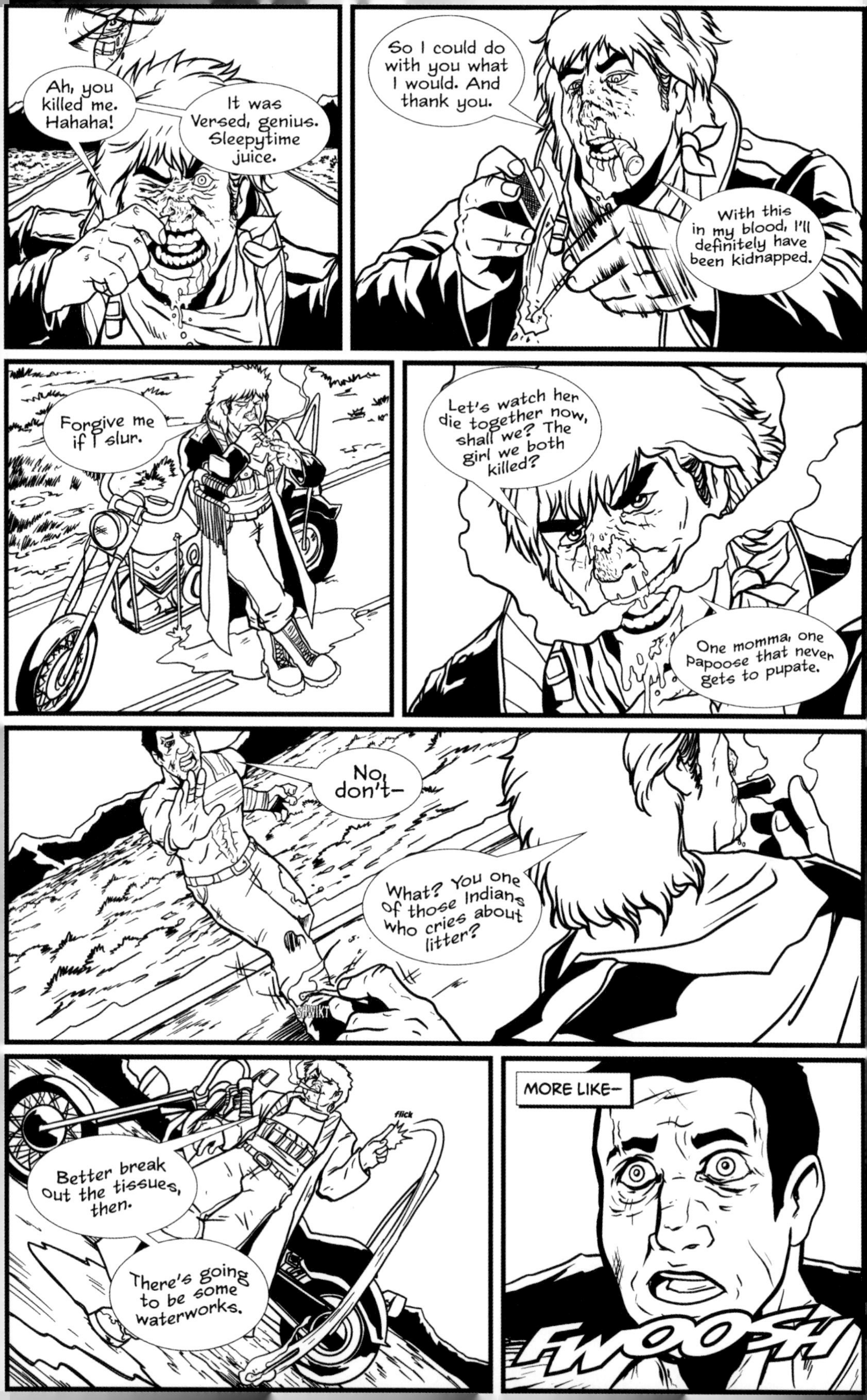
Ah, you killed me. Hahaha!
It was Versed, genius. Sleepytime juice.
So I could do with you what I would. And thank you.
With this in my blood, I'll definitely have been kidnapped.
Forgive me if I slur.
Let's watch her die together now, shall we? The girl we both killed?
One momma, one papoose that never gets to pupate.
No, don't–
What? You one of those Indians who cries about litter?
SHWIKT
flick
Better break out the tissues, then.
There's going to be some waterworks.
MORE LIKE–
FWOOSH

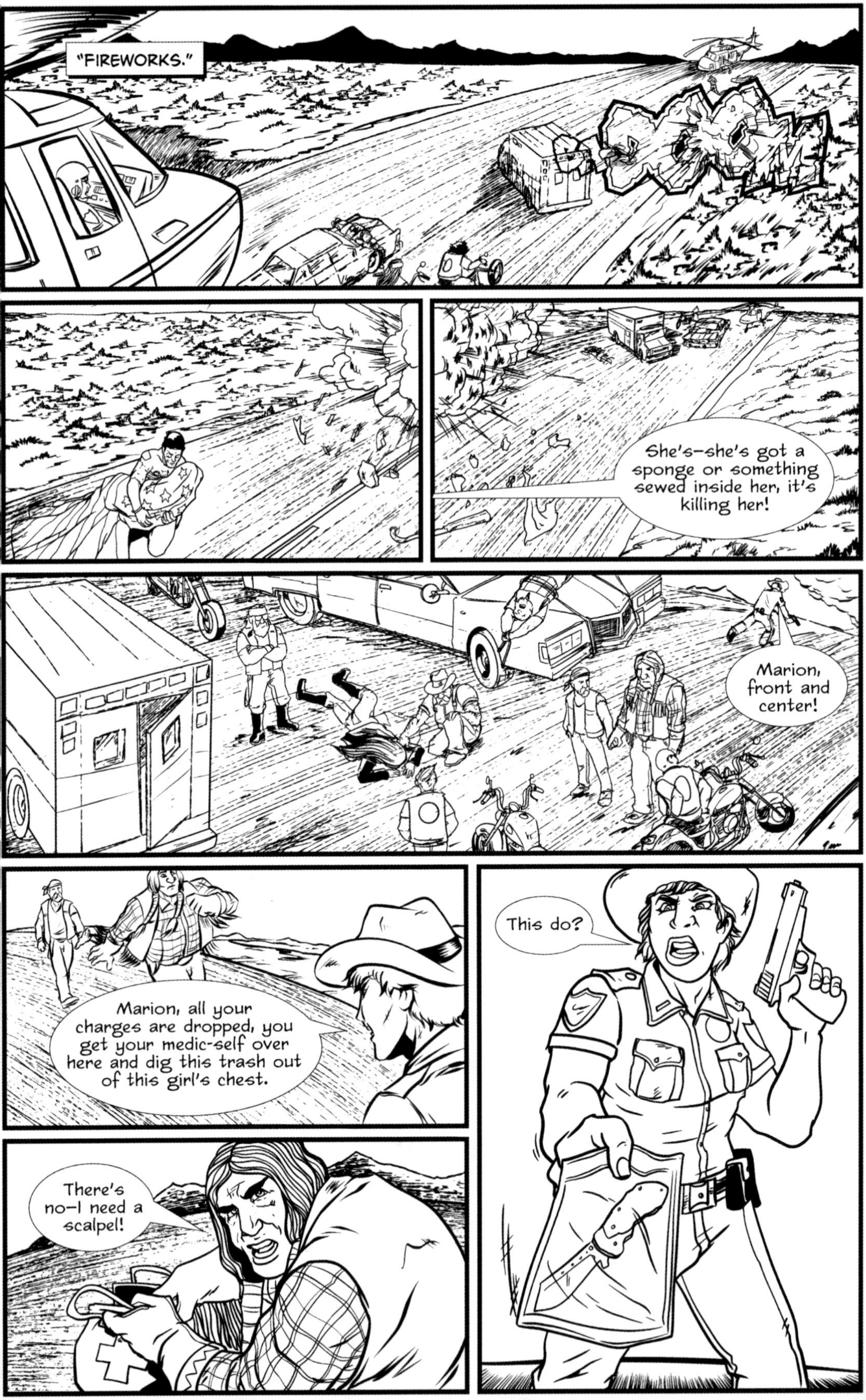
"FIREWORKS."
She's—she's got a sponge or something sewed inside her, it's killing her!
Marion, front and center!
Marion, all your charges are dropped, you get your medic-self over here and dig this trash out of this girl's chest.
There's no—I need a scalpel!
This do?

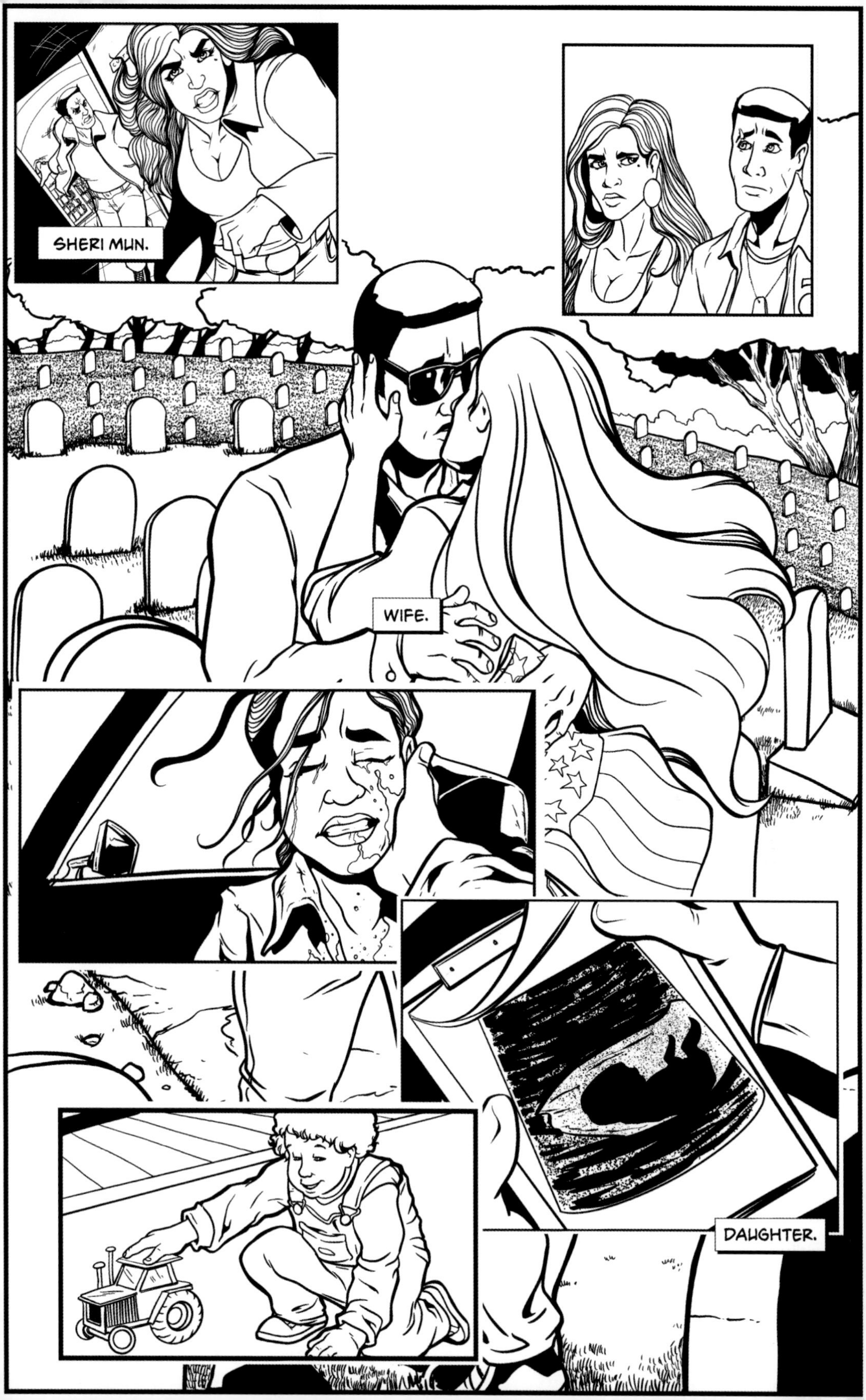
SHERI MUN.
WIFE.
DAUGHTER.

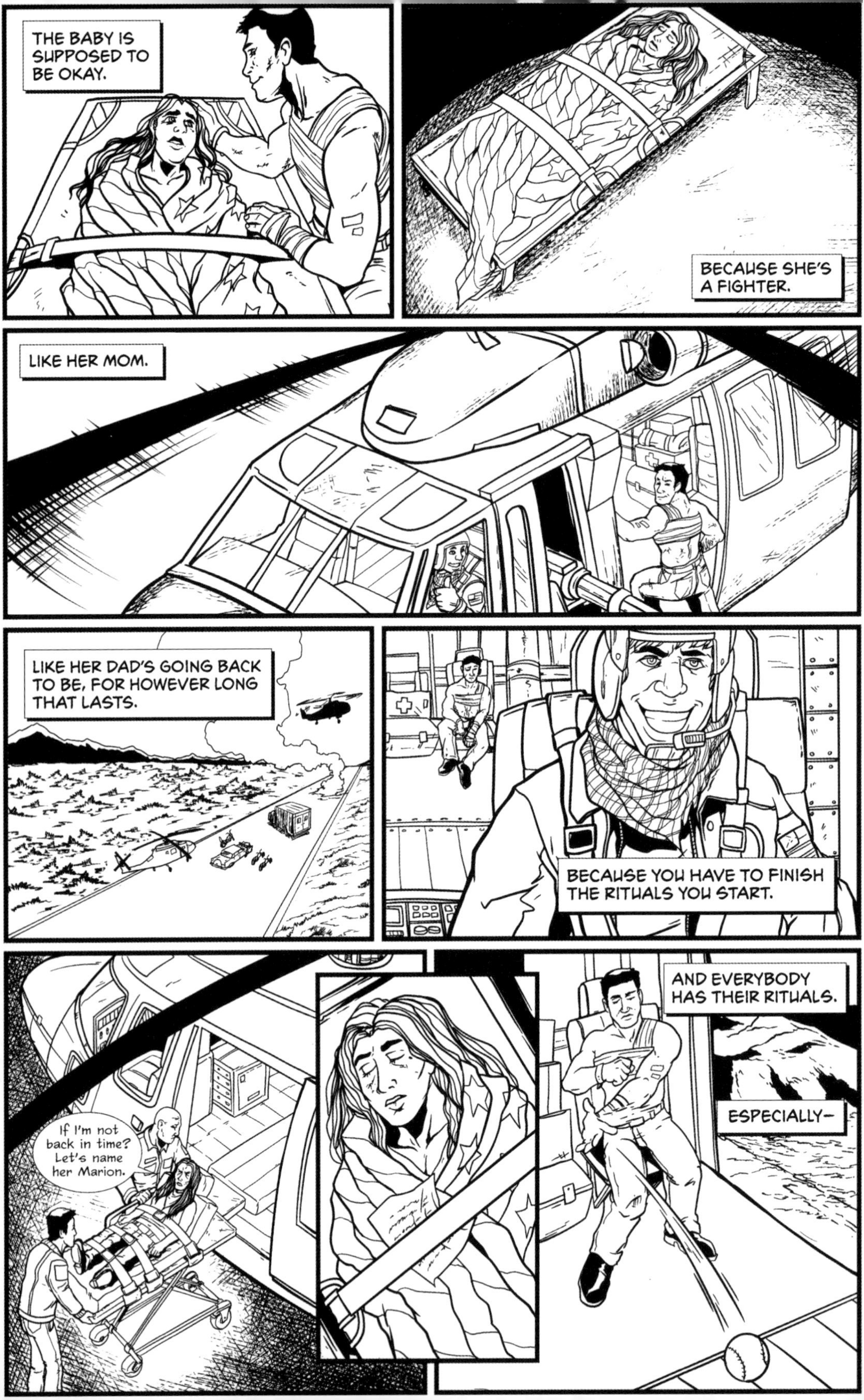
THE BABY IS SUPPOSED TO BE OKAY.
BECAUSE SHE'S A FIGHTER.
LIKE HER MOM.
LIKE HER DAD'S GOING BACK TO BE, FOR HOWEVER LONG THAT LASTS.
BECAUSE YOU HAVE TO FINISH THE RITUALS YOU START.
If I'm not back in time? Let's name her Marion.
AND EVERYBODY HAS THEIR RITUALS.
ESPECIALLY—

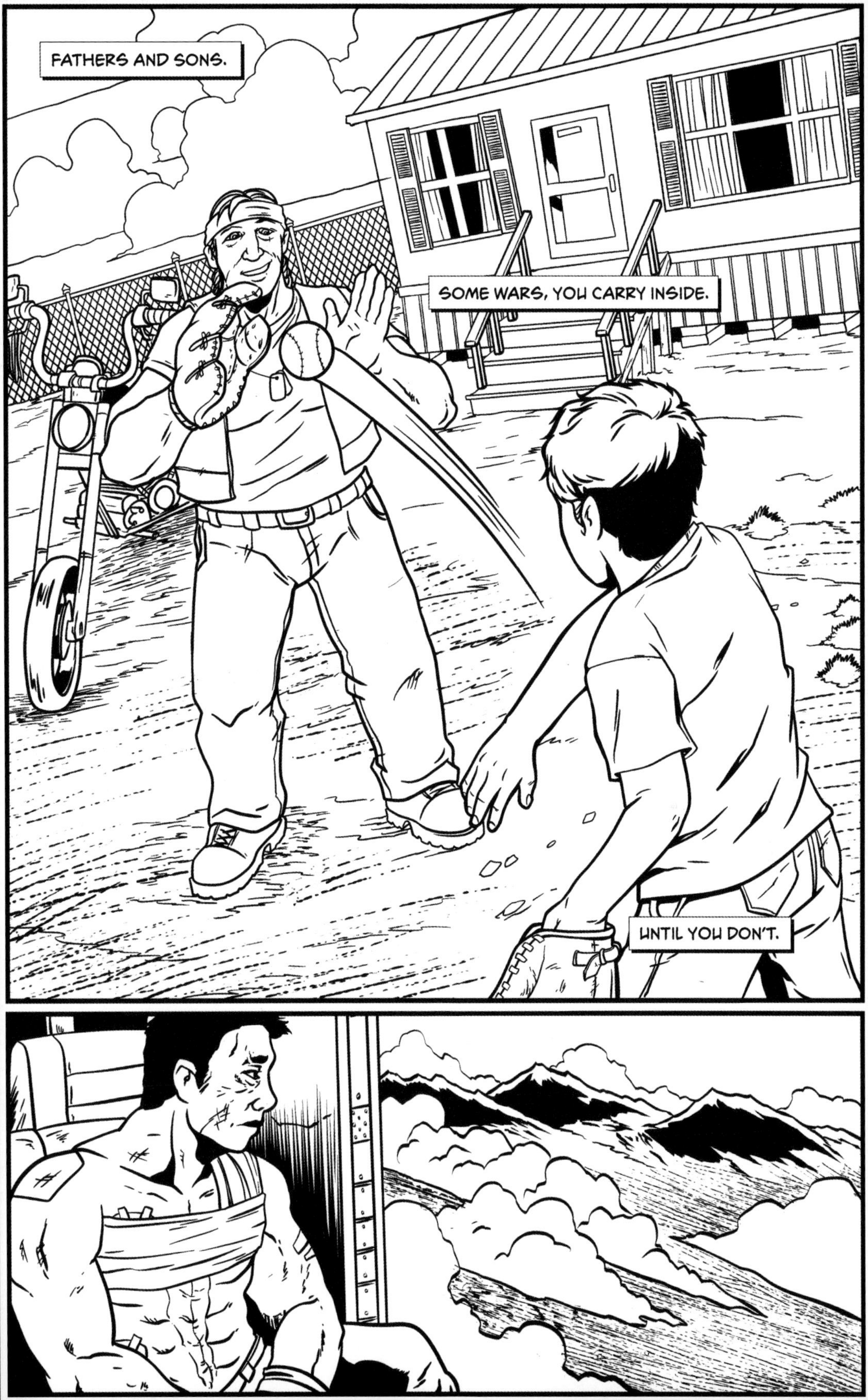
FATHERS AND SONS.
SOME WARS, YOU CARRY INSIDE.
UNTIL YOU DON'T.

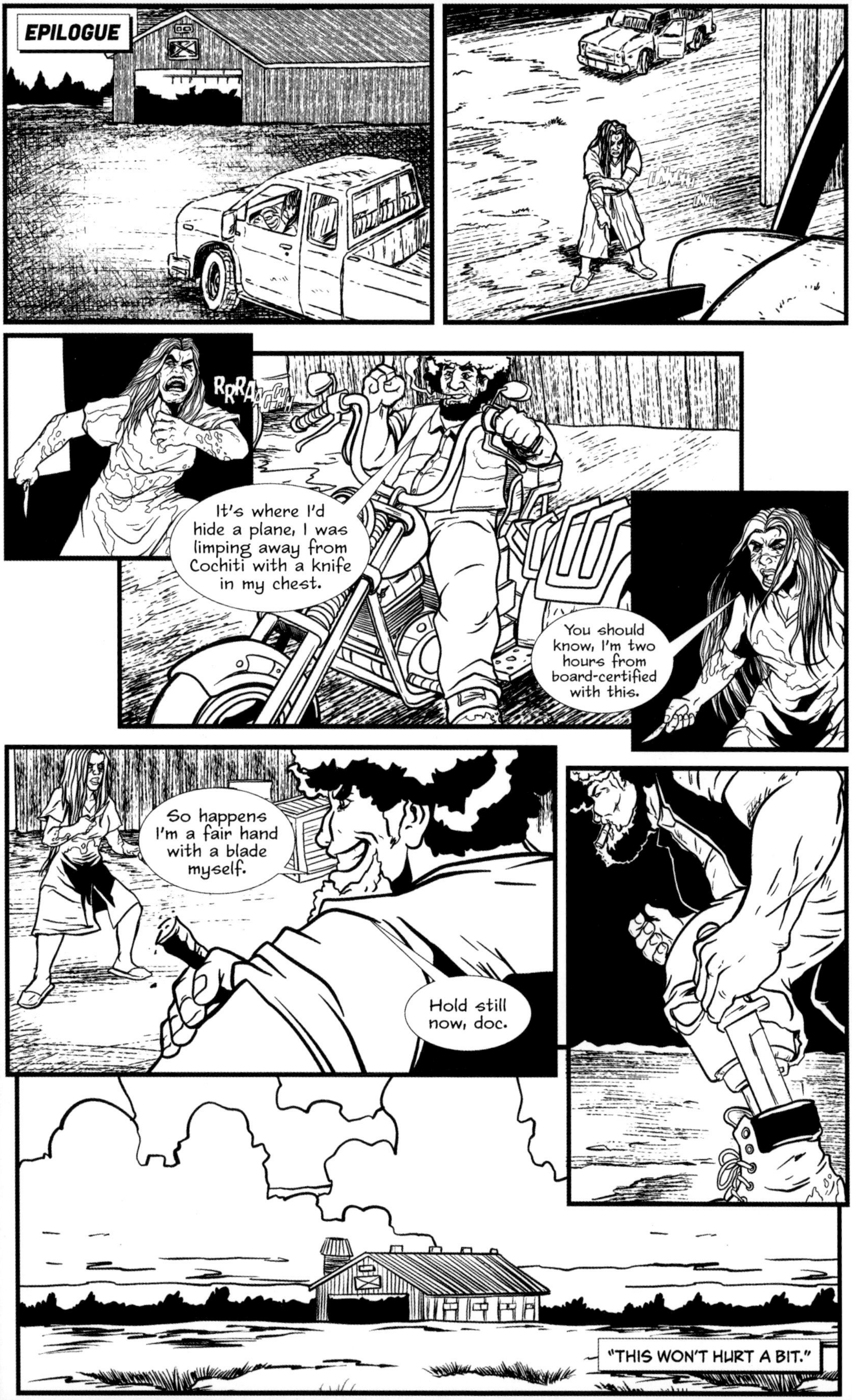

EPILOGUE
UNNGH
UNGH
RRRAAGHH
It's where I'd hide a plane, I was limping away from Cochiti with a knife in my chest.
You should know, I'm two hours from board-certified with this.
So happens I'm a fair hand with a blade myself.
Hold still now, doc.
"THIS WON'T HURT A BIT."